The Legend of Dave the Villager

BOOKS 1–5

by Dave Villager

Third Print Edition (June 2021)

Website: davethevillager.com
Email: davevillagerauthor@gmail.com

CONTENTS

BOOK 1

The Adventure Begins

Dave the Villager

CHAPTER ONE
The Secret Stronghold

DAVE

STEVE

BAM BAM BAM!

Dave awoke with a start. Someone was punching a hole in his bedroom wall.

He rubbed the sleep from his eyes and saw that most of his room was gone. His parents smiled back at him from what was left of the lounge. The morning light shone down from holes in the roof.

"What happened to the house?" he asked.

"Steve has blessed us!" said his mom happily. "He's using blocks from our house to build one of his masterpieces!"

A fist punched through his wall—BAM BAM BAM!

The wall disappeared to reveal a man in a light blue t-shirt and jeans.

"It's Steve!" said Dave's dad, clambering over the remains of the kitchen to get into Dave's bedroom. He ran up to the blue-t-shirted figure and knelt down before him.

"Thank you Steve, for blessing our home, thank you, thank you."

Dave's mom came over and knelt next to her husband.

"It's an honor Steve," she said. "Thank you so much."

Dave got out of bed, frowning.

"Steve, you've destroyed our house!"

"Have I destroyed it, bro?" said Steve, grinning at him, "Or have I *improved* it!"

"No," said Dave, "you've definitely destroyed it."

"Just come and see!" said Steve, and ran off. Dave and his parents followed him outside.

The village was a mess. All the houses had bits missing, and there were huge holes in the ground too. The villagers were all gathered outside, looking on in awe as Steve finished building a huge structure where the town hall used to be.

"It's so beautiful, Steve!" said one villager.

"Great work, Steve!" said another.

Dave looked up at the structure as Steve put the finishing touches to it. At first he couldn't work out what it was supposed to be, but then he realized—it was a huge wooden statue... of Steve.

"You destroyed our village to make a statue of yourself?!" Dave said, angrily. Steve jumped down from the top of the statue's head and landed in front of him.

"Cool, isn't it?"

Before Dave could speak, the other villagers all flocked round Steve, shaking his hand and congratulating him.

"Amazing work, Steve!"

"Another masterpiece!"

Dave sighed. It was always the same. Dave was a villager—and villagers were all meant to love Steve.

Steve went on adventures, killed monsters and built huge, pointless things, but villagers did none of that.

"Remember Dave," his mother told him once, when he was still a baby villager, "a villager has two purposes in life: to stand around all day doing nothing, and to trade emeralds with Steve."

"What about Grandma?" he asked. "She's a witch. Can't I be a witch?"

"We don't talk about Grandma," she said.

But Dave had never bought into all that. Why couldn't he go on an adventure? Why couldn't he kill monsters and build things?

Steve pushed away from the crowd of admiring villagers.

"Thank you, you're all too kind."

He walked over to a switch stuck to the side of the statue's leg.

"And now, for the grand finale, I'm going to blow the statue up!"

Everyone clapped and cheered.

"Wait, what?" said Dave.

Steve put a hand on Dave's shoulder.

"I've filled the statue with TNT blocks, and now I'm going to blow it up! How awesome is that going to be!"

"But Steve... the statue's in the middle of our village."

"I know," grinned Steve, "how lucky are you—you all get front row seats for the explosion!"

Dave turned to the other villagers.

"You're ok with him destroying our village?"

"It will be an honor to have our village destroyed by a great hero like Steve," said the Mayor, sticking his chest out proudly.

"But we're all going to be blown to bits," said Dave.

"It will be an honor to be blown to bits by a great hero like Steve," said the Mayor.

Dave rolled his eyes.

"You're all crazy," he said.

"Don't worry," said Steve, "I'm going to give you all plenty of warning—no-one's going to get hurt." He flipped the switch. "Ok, everyone run!"

Steve ran off as fast as his legs could carry him. With terrified yelling and screaming, the villagers ran off after him.

KABOOM!!!

Thankfully everyone made it out in time, but Dave was horrified to see his village—the place he'd lived his entire life—in ruins. All that was left was a blocky, gray pit.

The villagers—seemingly forgetting that a moment ago they'd been running for their lives—all cheered.

"Top job, Steve old chap!" said the Mayor. "That was an amazing explosion!"

"Thanks bro," said Steve, "but you guys are the real heroes. Actually, who am I kidding—I'm the real hero. Obviously."

"Look," someone shouted from the edge of the pit, "there's something down there!"

The explosion had revealed some sort of ancient underground building. There were stone brick walls and pits of lava.

Old Man Johnson, the oldest villager, waddled over with his walking stick.

"Well, I'll be—it's a stronghold! I remember hearing legends about these when I was a boy. I never dreamed there was one underneath our village all this time!"

"That's why you wanted to blow up our village, Steve, isn't that right?" said Dave's mum. "You knew there was a stronghold underneath!"

"Er, yeah," said Steve, "that was why. It definitely wasn't just because I thought it would be funny."

They all made their way carefully down the crater where the village used be. Steve built some wooden steps so they could all go through the hole in the ceiling and down into the stronghold.

Over a pit of lava there was a square frame made up of single blocks, half of which were gone. Most of the blocks had weird green things in them that looked like eyes.

"It's an end portal," said Old Man Johnson, "the Ancients

built them long ago to travel to the End."

"What's the End?" asked Dave.

"I've heard of the End!" said Steve. "It's where the ender dragon lives! Get that portal fired up, old timer—I've got a dragon to slay!"

"I'm afraid I can't," said Old Man Johnson. "It seems that some of the blocks of the frame were destroyed in the explosion. The portal is broken."

Steve was disappointed, but soon took his mind off it by checking the stronghold for treasure.

Dave had a look round too, and found a small underground library. Most of the books had been destroyed by old age or by the explosion, but one caught his eye. The title on the cover was *How to get to the End.*

Most of the pages crumbled to dust when he tried to read them, but there was one passage that had an image that looked familiar: a picture of a scary-looking green eye. Underneath the picture was a caption: *An eye of ender.*

Dave read the passage. The language was old and difficult to understand, but after a few reads he realized what it was telling him to do.

Most of the villagers were still gathered in the portal room as Dave returned, the book under his arm.

"I guess we should find somewhere to build ourselves a new village," Dave overheard one of them say.

"Maybe we could build it in a mushroom biome," another villager replied, "I always fancied myself as a mooshroom farmer."

Dave walked up the stone steps that led to the end portal.

"Dave, what are you doing?" his mother said, running up to him. "Be careful of the lava!"

"Don't worry Mum," Dave replied, "I know what I'm doing."

There were only seven of the end portal frame blocks left. Dave could see from the design that there were meant to be twelve—five had been destroyed or lost.

Six of the remaining seven had *ender eyes* inside them—the strange eye objects that Dave had seen the picture of in the book.

He reached down and pulled one of the ender eyes out. It was a round disk with a thin black pupil in the middle. If Dave hadn't known better, he would have sworn the eye was looking at him—it was creepy.

Dave carefully made his way around the lava pit, removing the other ender eyes until he had all six. Then he walked up the wooden stairs to the edge of the crater that had been his village. After being underground so long, his eyes stung from the bright sunlight. The other villagers followed behind him, curious about what he was going to do.

Dave climbed to the top of the crater and stood on the grass. The other villagers stood around him.

"What's going on, bro?" said Steve. "Hey, those little eye things are cool. Can I have one? I'll give you one emerald for the lot."

These are ender eyes," Dave said. "If what I read is correct, they should reveal the location of the nearest working end portal. And this time, I'm going to be the one who finds it—I'll find the end portal, slay the ender dragon, and be a hero!"

"Er, villagers can't be heroes, bro," said Steve. "Only Steves can be heroes. And I'm the only Steve."

"Well, maybe villagers can be heroes too," said Dave, "it's just that they've never tried before."

Dave threw an ender eye into the air. It hovered there for a moment, then zoomed off towards the horizon.

"It worked!" said Dave, laughing, "It actually worked! It went north, so all I have to do is head north and I'll eventually get to another stronghold!"

Suddenly, Steve grabbed the other five ender eyes out of Dave's hands.

"Hey!" said Dave. "Give those back!"

"I'm sorry, little buddy," Steve replied, "but as a hero it would be irresponsible for me to let you go off and search for dragons. I know my life must seem really cool, but it's too dangerous for someone like you. You're a villager—you should be doing villager things. Like, I dunno, growing wheat?"

Steve whistled and a horse came running over. He jumped on its back.

"Sorry fans, I've got to split. I've got a dragon to kill!"

And with that, he rode off.

"That's not fair!" said Dave. "Those were my ender eyes!"

Dave's mum and dad came over. Dave's dad put a hand on his shoulder.

"It's for the best son," he said. "Adventuring is for Steves, not villagers."

The villagers started to walk away. Eventually Dave was standing all by himself. Sadly, he took another look at the book.

Old Man Johnson came hobbling over.

"Don't listen to them, Dave. When I was your age I wanted to go on adventures too—and everyone always told me not to go. I wish I'd never listened to them. It's too late for me, but perhaps not for you."

He handed Dave an old book.

OLD MAN JOHNSON

BOOK

"*A beginners guide to crafting,*" Dave said, reading the cover.
"Now you can craft, just like Steve!"

"This is amazing, thank you!" Dave said, flicking through the
pages. Then he saw something that made his heart leap.

"They have how to make ender eyes in here!" said Dave
happily. "Wait, what's blaze powder?"

"The recipe for that is in there too," said Old Man Johnson.
"That book won't have every crafting recipe ever, but it should get
you started at least."

"I don't know what to say."

"Just promise me you'll defeat the ender dragon before Steve
does, and prove once and for all that villagers can be heroes."

"I promise!"

Dave's parents weren't happy when he told them he was going
on an adventure, but in the end they had to accept it.

"Just be careful," his mum told him as they said their goodbyes. "Watch out for creepers and if you see an enderman, stare at it to keep it away. Or was that *don't* stare at it? I never can remember…"

"Goodbye, Dave," said his dad. "I got you this—I hope it helps."

He handed Dave an iron sword.

"The blacksmith made it. He says he normally only makes them for Steve, but he made an exception."

"Thanks, Dad."

And after a big hug with both his parents, Dave was off on his adventure.

CHAPTER TWO
Dave on the Road

The sun was shining and the birds were singing as Dave set out. He'd never been very far from the village before, and was enjoying the walk. The hills around him were green and blocky, and cows and sheep watched him as he walked past.

By midday he was feeling hungry, so he found a pig and hit it with his sword until it turned into porkchops.

He tried to eat the chops raw, but the taste was horrible. Back home his father had done all of the cooking, so Dave turned to the book the old man had given him for advice.

"How to build a furnace..." he said, starting to read. "Eight cobblestone blocks needed. Where do I get cobblestone from?"

Crafting, it seemed, was more complicated than Dave had thought it would be. To get cobblestone, you needed to dig up stone. To dig up stone you needed a pickaxe. To craft a pickaxe you needed a crafting table. To make a crafting table you needed wood.

It made Dave's brain hurt.

So it all started with wood. Dave went up to a tree. There were hundreds of them about, all made of wood. But how was he supposed to get the wood from them? He'd seen a crafting recipe for an axe in the book, but to make an axe you needed wood.

He tapped the tree lightly with his hand. The smallest of cracks appeared in the grain for a split second, but then it was gone. He tapped it again and the crack reappeared; then again, and more cracks appeared. He started to punch it, the cracks spreading across the wood. Finally the tree block broke, leaving a gap in the middle of the tree's trunk.

On the ground was a tiny block—a miniature version of the wood block that had been part of the tree's trunk. Dave picked it up, looking at it in amazement. He wanted to take another look at his book, to remind him of how to craft a pickaxe, but when he placed the wood block on the floor, something amazing happened—it turned back into a full-sized wooden block.

He tried to pick it up again, but the block was stuck to the floor. He punched it and it broke again—turning back into a miniature block.

"Weird," he thought. He placed the tiny block in his backpack. Thankfully it didn't turn back into a full-sized block this time.

He knew he might need quite a lot of wood for building, so he went back to the tree, breaking the remaining blocks until the tree's trunk was no more, and the leaves above faded into nothing.

Following the instructions in the book, he placed one of the tiny wood blocks in the palm of his hand and waited. He didn't have to wait long: in less than a couple of seconds there was a *POP*, and the wooden block had turned into four tiny blocks of wooden planks.

He made a few plank blocks, then put four of them together in his hand, where they merged into a tiny crafting table.

He slammed the crafting table into the ground and, as if by magic, it grew into a full-sized crafting table.

"That is so cool," said Dave, grinning to himself. The table had a nine-square grid carved onto its surface. Each of the nine squares was the same size as the tiny blocks.

Dave took another look at his book. To make a wooden pickaxe he needed wooden planks and sticks. He had the planks, but no sticks—so he looked up the recipe. He placed two tiny wooden plank blocks on the crafting table, and they transformed into a bunch of sticks.

Next he placed three wooden plank blocks along the top three squares of the crafting table, and two sticks underneath. There was a *POP* and suddenly a pickaxe appeared. His very first tool.

"Awesome!" said Dave. He immediately started to dig at the soil, but his pickaxe barely did any damage to it. With a *SNAP* the pickaxe broke.

Dave went back to the book and saw that for mud and sand a shovel worked better. So he made one, as well as a new wooden pickaxe.

The book also explained how you could use tools to dig up

materials to make better tools. A wooden pickaxe could dig up cobblestone to make a stone pickaxe, a stone pickaxe could dig up iron to make an iron pickaxe (with a bit of help from some smelting to turn the iron ore into ingots) and so on. The best tools, according to the book, were made of diamond, but diamond was very rare.

"One day I'll have all diamond tools and weapons," Dave thought, looking through the book. The book said you could even make armor for horses out of diamond. "I'd be invincible," Dave said to himself, "wearing diamond armor and riding a diamond-armored horse!"

On the page about tools there was a message written in the margin in red ink—it looked like the old man had written it on the page himself.

NEVER DIG STRAIGHT DOWN!

Dave took his shovel and started to dig. Following the old man's advice he dug down in a diagonal direction. He dug through a few dirt blocks, then reached stone—so he changed to his pickaxe.

It was slow going. Every stone block he broke turned into cobblestone. Just like the wood, the cobblestone blocks were tiny, and he was able to fit them in his backpack.

Eventually he realized that he wouldn't be able to go any further without torches.

He made his way back up the stone corridor he'd dug, making his way back up towards the light. His rucksack was full of cobblestone, making the going slow.

When he got back outside the sun was beginning to set. He looked in his rucksack and was pleased to see that he had found some coal. It had been so dark in the tunnel that he'd thought it had all been cobblestone.

He used the crafting table to make a furnace: eight cobblestone blocks with a gap in the middle. Then he placed the furnace next to the crafting table.

The book said that wood or coal (or quite a few other things) could be used as fuel for the furnace, but Dave decided to use wood, as he wanted to save the coal for making torches (a piece of coal on top of a stick, according to the book).

He lit the furnace and sat in front of it, enjoying the warmth as his porkchop cooked.

When it was done he gobbled it up in seconds, he was so hungry. Then he started cooking a second.

After eating his third porkchop he sat down and enjoyed the cool evening air. The sun had almost set now, and it was getting properly dark.

"Maybe I could sleep out in the open tonight," he thought. The weather was warm and the idea of looking up at the stars all night appealed to him.

Then he heard a noise that chilled his soul.

"BURRRRRR!!!"

Something was walking towards him through the darkness. He quickly crafted a torch and placed it down in front of him.

"Er, hello?" Dave said. "Who's there?"

A figure stepped into the torchlight. For a moment Dave thought it was Steve, but then he saw its rotted green skin and black eyes—it was a zombie!

Another zombie appeared out of the darkness, then another, until a whole crowd of them were surrounding Dave.

"Get back!" he yelled, shaking his sword at them.

He was surrounded, with no way out. There were zombies on every side.

"What am I going to do?" he thought. Was this how it was going to end for him—eaten by zombies on the very first night of his big adventure?

A zombie started to waddle closer. Dave swung his sword, hitting the zombie on the head. The zombie groaned and stepped backwards. Dave swung his sword again, as a warning, but his pickaxe fell off his belt, clattering on the grass.

ZOMBIES!

And that gave Dave an idea.

NEVER DIG STRAIGHT DOWN the old man's note in the book had warned. But down was the only safe way for Dave to go. He grabbed his pickaxe and started to dig.

His pickaxe cut through block after block, and the small square of night sky above got smaller and smaller. The zombies were looking down at him, groaning with frustration at having missed out on their dinner.

"I'll just go a bit further down," he thought, "then I'll wait until daylight and dig my way to the surface again."

Then he cut through a block and suddenly there was nothing below his feet.

"So that's why you don't dig straight down," he thought, as he fell through the roof of a cavern towards a huge lake of lava.

CHAPTER THREE
Porkins

"Waaaaaaaa!!!"

Dave fell towards the lava, flailing his arms like a crazy person.

He closed his eyes, then landed on something hard.

"Is this heaven?" he wondered.

He opened his eyes and saw that he wasn't in heaven: he was lying on a tiny block of stone, which lay in the middle of the lava lake.

For a moment he was overjoyed at being alive—then he realized that he was trapped. There was lava on every side, and no way out.

What was he going to do? He tried to think what Steve would do. Steve liked to build things, kill things and blow things up. He had no TNT, so blowing stuff up was out of the question, there was nothing to kill... so maybe he could build his way out?

Suddenly his little stone platform lit up. He looked up and saw light shining down from the tiny square hole far above him. It was day time again.

"I can build my way up!" Dave yelled happily. He pulled out a tiny cobblestone block from his backpack, jumped up and placed it below his feet—where it turned into a full-sized block. He did this again and again, until he was standing on a tall tower, far above the lava.

He reached into his backpack to grab some more cobblestone, but accidentally dropped the bag—its contents spilling out and falling into the lava below!

Thankfully Dave managed to keep hold of the bag, and his two books didn't fall out, but most of his blocks were gone. He had nowhere near enough to build his way up to the surface.

He was in a worse predicament than before now—stuck on a tower in the middle of a lake of lava.

"Help!" Dave yelled desperately. "Someone help me!"

He sighed and sat down. He was all alone, there was no-one here to save him. He should have listened to his parents and Steve—villagers weren't meant to go on adventures. This had all been a big mistake.

"Ahoy there!"

Dave jumped so much he nearly fell off of his tower. He looked around to try and see where the voice had come from.

"I say, down here!"

Dave looked down and saw a pig standing by the edge of the lava lake. Wait, he thought, pigs can't stand... but this one was definitely standing; standing on two legs.

"Hello there!" said the standing pig.

"Er, hello," said Dave.

"Need a hand?" asked the pig.

"Yes please."

The pig started throwing blocks of sand into the lava. The sand soaked up the lava and sunk to the bottom of it. Soon the pig had built a sand bridge all the way across the lava lake to Dave's tower.

Dave dug his way down, destroying each block of his tower until he was just above the lake. Then he jumped down onto the pig's sand bridge.

"This way," said the pig, leading Dave across the bridge to the side of the lake. When he got back to solid ground, Dave breathed a big sigh of relief.

"Thank you!" he said to the pig. "I thought my bacon was cooked! Uh, no offense."

"Happy to help!" said the pig. "My name is Porkins."

"Dave," said Dave.

PORKINS

"Well met, Dave," said the pig.

"I don't want to be rude," said Dave, "but I've never met a pig who can talk before."

"That's because I'm not a pig," said the pig, "I'm a pigman."

"Ah, ok," said Dave. He decided not to point out that he'd never heard of a pigman before either.

"Would you like something to eat?" Porkins asked.

"Yes please," said Dave, "I'd love some baco—I mean, anything. Any food would be great."

Porkins led him down some torch-lit tunnels until they reached an iron door, set into a flat, gray stone wall. A sign next to the door said: *Porkins's House.*

Porkins pulled a switch next to the door and it swung open. Dave followed him inside.

Porkins's home was surprisingly cosy, with lots of pictures on the stone walls and wooden furniture. Dave sat down as the pigman cooked some mushroom stew in the furnace.

When the stew was ready, the two of them ate at the wooden table. After Dave finished, Porkins made him some pumpkin pie. When the meal was finally over, Dave was stuffed.

"Phew," said Dave. "I ate like a pig! Uh, no offense."

But Porkins didn't seem to take offense at anything. He was always happy and smiling.

"How come you live underground?" Dave asked him. "Or is that something all pigmen do?"

A dark look crossed Porkins's face.

"I'm the only pigman left, I'm afraid," said Porkins sadly. "I moved underground as it reminds me of my home."

Dave wanted to ask Porkins what had happened to the other pigmen, but Porkins looked so sad that he decided now wasn't the time.

"I'm from a village," Dave said, "on the surface. I'm on a quest to hunt down the ender dragon."

"Why?" Porkins asked. "Did it do something bad?"

"Well, no," said Dave, "but it's a dragon, and it's a hero's job to slay dragons."

"Fair enough," said Porkins. "Can I come with you?"

Dave was taken aback.

"It's going to be very dangerous," he told the pigman. "I mean I'll probably have to fight all sorts of monsters on the way. And then there's the dragon."

"That's fine," said Porkins, "it all sounds spiffing, actually. I've been bored out of my mind living by myself. An adventure sounds just the ticket!"

"I mean, you'll need a sword," said Dave. "And as I said, it will be very dangerous."

Dave had always thought of adventures as something you did on your own: a hero out in the wild with just his sword to protect him. As nice as Porkins seemed to be, Dave thought he'd just get in the way.

"Will this do?" Porkins asked. He opened a chest and pulled out a sword with a shimmering blue blade.

Dave's mouth dropped open.

"Is that... is that..." he mumbled, unable to get his words out.

"Diamond!" said Porkins, happily. "There's not much to do down here except mine. I've got a spare if you'd like it."

He pulled out a second diamond sword and handed it to Dave.

"T-thank you!" said Dave.

"No problem," smiled Porkins. "I'm sure you'd do the same for me, as a friend."

Dave grinned. Maybe having a companion on his quest wouldn't be so bad after all.

That night they stayed at Porkins's house. Dave slept on the spare bed ("no-one's ever used it before!" Porkins happily informed him), then in the morning Porkins made them breakfast (Dave stopped himself from asking for bacon, just in time).

Porkins packed a rucksack (Dave noticed there were a lot of diamonds, coal and other blocks in there) and then they set off on their journey.

CHAPTER FOUR
Carl

"I think this way leads back to the surface," said Porkins. "Although it's been a while, so I might be wrong."

They were making their way through a vast underground cave system. Porkins had plenty of coal and Dave had a few bits of wood left in his bag that hadn't fallen into the lava, so they made some torches and placed them down as they went along.

"Are there monsters in these caves?" Dave asked.

"Oh yes, lots!" said Porkins happily.

Suddenly a pack of flying creatures burst out from the darkness, flapping past Dave.

"Monsters!" he yelled. "Help me!"

The creatures flew off, back into the darkness.

Porkins laughed.

"Don't worry, those were just bats. They're harmless."

"Harmless. Right," said Dave, feeling his cheeks glow red. "I knew that."

Then they heard a sound coming from the darkness:
"BUUUUURR!"

"Zombies!" said Dave. "I'd know that sound anywhere."

He and Porkins pulled out their diamond swords.

Suddenly zombies came out of the darkness, surrounding them on all sides. Dave's hands were sweaty and he was nervous, but then he remembered that he had a diamond sword. A diamond sword!

"Rrraghhh!" he yelled, running at the zombies. He hit one in the head with his diamond blade and it was immediately destroyed. One hit was all it took for each zombie, and he and Porkins cut through them like butter.

Finally the zombies were all slain, leaving just piles of rotten flesh behind—which Dave stuffed into his backpack. He didn't know if you could craft anything with it, but he thought it might come in useful later.

"That was fun!" said Porkins.

"Yeah," said Dave, grinning. "It was, actually."

Then he heard a sound that chilled him to the bone: "HIIIISSSSS!!!"

"HIIIISSSSS!!!"

"Creeper!" Dave yelled. A green creature with black eyes and a gaping mouth emerged from the shadows.

Dave pushed Porkins out of the way, and the two of them fell off a cliff edge as the creeper exploded behind them.

For the second time in two days, Dave found himself falling—but this time he landed in water. He and Porkins were washed away by an underground river, Dave trying desperately to grab onto the sides and get out, but the water was moving too fast.

Dave wasn't very good at swimming, and tried desperately to keep his head above water as the current swept them down into the darkness of the caves.

Suddenly the river ended, and he found himself falling again—and landed in a lake. He splashed around, trying to find the shore, but the lake seemed to be huge. In the dark he could hear a waterfall, where the river flowed through the ceiling into the lake.

He kept swimming, terrified of what kind of creatures could be below him in the dark water, until he reached the shore, and clambered out.

"Porkins?" he yelled. There was no answer. He was all alone.

Dave reached into his bag for a torch, but his bag was gone. A cold trickle of fear ran down his spine. He was deep underground, in the dark, with no torches and no tools. What was he going to do?

Then, just as he thought things couldn't get any worse, he heard the sound he feared the most:

"HISSSSSSSS!"

He was too shocked to run, so just stupidly covered his face with his hands. But after a few seconds there was no explosion.

Then the noise came again, it sounded like it was right next to him:

"HISSSSSSSSS!"

But still no explosion.

"Oh come on," said a voice nearby. "why isn't this working?"

Another voice came out of the darkness, this one further away: "Come on, blow him up!"

"I'm trying," said the first voice. "HISS! HISS! HISSSSS! I'm not exploding."

There was laughter—three or four voices, it sounded like.

"What kind of creeper can't even explode?" said a third voice.

"Shut up!" said the first voice. "I'll do it, ok? I just need some time."

"You've had your chance," said the third voice, "and you failed. Let me try. HISSSSSS!!!!"

Dave ran. He couldn't see where he was going, but he had to get away from the creepers.

"Now he's getting away!" one of them yelled. "Great job, Carl!"

Dave stumbled through the dark, feeling his way along the walls. He ran and ran until he was sure he must have lost them.

But they can see in the dark, he thought unhappily, *and I can't.*

What was he going to do? He could be wandering these caves forever and never find his way out, but he had to try.

He walked on for what seemed like hours, keeping his ears peeled for monsters and hoping desperately to come across some light.

He wondered what had happened to Porkins. Had he managed to get out of the river before it flowed into the lake? Or had something terrible happened to him?

Dave thought about trying to build some tools in the dark, but everything required wood. He tried punching stone, but it took forever to destroy it with just his fists, and without using a pickaxe it didn't drop any cobblestone, so he couldn't have made stone tools anyway.

No, his only hope was that he'd come across a passage that led back to the surface. But he was so deep now that it didn't seem very likely.

"Hello," said a voice.

Dave jumped.

"Who's there?!" He reached for his sword, but remembered he didn't have one.

"Don't worry," said the voice, "I'm not here to blow you up."

"You—you're a creeper?"

"Yeah. I'm the one who tried to blow you up by the lake. Sorry about that."

Dave was confused—and still quite terrified.

"So if you don't want to blow me up, what do you want?"

"My friends have kicked me out of their gang," said the creeper, sounding sad. "They say a creeper who can't explode is no creeper at all. So I thought I'd join you."

"Join me?"

"Yes. Look, I'll level with you. You look like a bit of an idiot, but I've lost all my friends and I've got no family—"

"What happened to your family?"

"They blew themselves up. Obviously. That's what every creeper should do. But for some reason, I can't."

"Why would you want to blow yourself up anyway?" Dave asked.

"Because that's what creepers do!" said the creeper, annoyed. "Anyway, no creepers will let me in their gang now, and you're the only non-creeper I know, so I'm going to join you."

"Right," said Dave. He didn't know what was worse—a creeper who wanted to blow you up or one that wanted to be your friend. But then an idea struck him.

"Can you help me find my way to the surface?" he asked the creeper.

Probably not," said the creeper. "But I can try, I guess. Just follow me."

"I can't see you," said Dave. "I can't see in the dark."

"Right," said the creeper. "Just follow my voice then. I'm Carl, by the way."

"Dave," said Dave.

"That's a stupid name," said the creeper. "Trust me to get stuck with a Dave."

CARL

CHAPTER FIVE
Captured by Zombies

"Keep going," said Carl, "follow my voice."

Dave had been following Carl the creeper for hours through the darkness. He kept thinking about Porkins, and hoped the pigman was ok. As annoying as he was, he'd been better than Carl the creeper: who was constantly moaning.

"The surface is overrated anyway," said Carl. "Dunno why you'd want to go up there in the first place."

"That's where I'm from," Dave told him. "I'm on a quest to kill a dragon."

"Sounds like a pretty stupid quest to me," said Carl.

Suddenly Carl stopped, and Dave walked straight into him.

"Shush," said Carl.

"What is it?" Dave asked.

"Zombies up ahead. I can hear them."

Dave could hear them too now, making their usual "BUUUURR" sounds. It sounded like there were a lot of them. He could see the slight glow of torchlight too, up in the distance.

"We'll have to go the long way round," said Carl.

Then, amongst the zombie sounds, Dave heard something else:

"I say chaps, this is all very spiffing!"

His heart sank.

"They've got Porkins," he said.

"Who's Porkins?" asked Carl.

"He was traveling with me. He's a pigman."

"What's a pigman?"

"It's a bit like a pig, but a bit like a man as well."

"Well," said Carl, "whatever he is, he's going to be zombie food in a few minutes. We need to go the long way round, or we'll end up being the same."

"We can't leave him!" said Dave. "He's my... my sort-of friend."

Carl sighed.

"Well, you can go rescue your sort-of friend by yourself," he said. "I'm staying here. If you survive, come back and find me."

"I thought you were in my gang?" said Dave. "Gangs stick together, I always thought."

The creeper sighed again.

"Ok, ok, I'll help your stupid pig friend. Although by the time we get there he'll probably be roasted with an apple in his mouth."

"Then we'd better move quickly," said Dave.

He and Carl crept forward towards the torchlight. Dave could just about see now, and he got his first glimpse of Carl. Carl was a normal creeper, but about a head shorter than they usually were.

They finally reached the edge of a cliff, and below them a big group of zombies were gathered around a campfire. Tied up with rope, sitting against a wall, was Porkins. As ever, he was smiling.

"Is dat fire ready yet?" one of the zombies asked. "I'm starving."

"Me too," said Porkins. "What are we eating?"

"What an idiot," Carl whispered to Dave.

"Fire ready now," another zombie said. "Let's get cooking."

Four of the zombies waddled over and picked Porkins up. They tied him to a pole.

"Is this a prank, chaps?" Porkins asked. "This is terribly fun, but I'm afraid I must be off soon—I need to find my friend Dave. He's a villager, I don't suppose you've seen him?"

"If we see him, we eat him too," said a zombie.

"Eat him?" said Porkins, confused. "Why would you... oh dear."

His face fell, as he finally realized what was about to happen. The zombies carried him towards the fire.

"I must say, I doubt I'll taste very nice," said Porkins nervously. "Very tough meat, I suspect."

"Well, what now?" whispered Carl. "We don't have any swords."

Dave had been thinking the same thing. How were they going to save Porkins without ending up cooking on the fire as well? Then he looked at Carl and had an idea.

The zombies placed Porkins's pole above the fire, and started to turn it.

"I must say, this is a bit too hot for my liking," said Porkins. "If anyone can hear me—HELP!!"

"Get away from him!"

The zombies all turned round. Dave was holding Carl the creeper out in front of him.

"Get away from him, or I'll blow us all to smithereens!" said Dave.

"I hate to remind you," Carl whispered to him, "but I can't blow anyone to smithereens. I can't explode!"

"Yes," Dave whispered back, "but they don't know that."

He moved forward. The zombies started to back away.

"That's it," said Dave, "keep away."

"Dave!" said Porkins happily. "I knew you'd come for me! Everyone, this is my best friend Dave."

"Well, I don't know about best friend," said Dave, "we've only known each other a day..."

"Only a day, but I know he's going to be my BFF," Porkins told the zombies. "Now Dave old chap, would you mind getting me down from this spit? It's a bit hot. I think there's some sand in my bag."

Dave saw that Porkins's bag and—to his delight—his own, had been left in the corner of the room. He put Carl down and ran over to Porkins's bag, taking out a block of sand, then ran back and placed it on top of the fire, putting it out. He started to untie Porkins.

The zombies were still watching cautiously from the corners of the room.

"Get out of here," Dave told them, or my creeper will blow you all to bits!"

The zombies stayed where they were.

"I'll sort this out," said Carl. He slithered towards the zombies. "HIIIISSS!"

At the sound of the hissing, the zombies all ran, pushing and shoving each other in a mad dash to escape. Within a few seconds there was no sign of them, leaving just Dave, Carl and Porkins in the torch-lit room.

Dave finished untying Porkins. Porkins let go of the pole and landed on his feet. He gave Dave a hug.

"Thank you Dave!" he said. "You really are a hero! That dragon doesn't stand a chance."

He turned to Carl.

"And thank you too, little man," Porkins said. "I don't think I've had the pleasure?"

"This is Carl," said Dave. "He's a creeper. A friendly one. Sort of."

"What do you mean, 'sort of'?" said Carl. "I'll have you know that for a creeper I'm amazingly friendly. I didn't blow you up, did I?"

"You did try to," said Dave.

"A friendly creeper," said Porkins, grinning, "what fun! I just know we're all going to be such good friends."

"I've never wanted to blow someone up more in my whole life," said Carl.

They had no idea where they were, but with the torches from Dave's bag and Carl being able to see in the dark, they headed off on their quest to find the surface.

It didn't take long before they saw rays of light up ahead.

"Daylight!" said Dave happily.

He ran on ahead, until he came out of a cave and found himself on a mountain overlooking a lush green valley below. After being underground for so long, it was the most beautiful sight he'd ever seen.

Porkins and Carl came out behind him.

"Isn't it wonderful?" Dave said.

"No," said Carl. "Not really."

CHAPTER SIX
The Portal

After chopping some trees down for wood, they built themselves a little cabin by a lake—to protect them from monsters at night and give them somewhere to plan their next steps.

Dave looked through the book Old Man Johnson had given him. He had no idea where he was and had no ender eyes left, so he'd have to make some more if he was going to find his way to another stronghold.

He looked up the recipe for ender eyes. To make one you needed an ender pearl and some blaze powder.

"Where do you get ender pearls from?" Dave wondered. A shiver of terror went through him when he saw the answer: they were dropped by slain endermen.

Since he was little, Dave had been terrified of endermen. He'd never seen one in person, but he'd heard the legends. Endermen came in the night, carrying away naughty children in their long, black arms. It was said that their flesh was so dark that at night you could only see their empty white eyes, and if you made eye contact, they'd rush over and suck out your soul.

The thought of killing one enderman, let alone several, was not something that Dave was keen on. But if it was the only way, then he had no choice: he'd promised himself he'd slay the ender dragon before Steve, and he intended to keep that promise. Anyway, he had a diamond sword now. If he could get some diamond armor as well, nothing would be able to stop him. At least that was what he hoped.

Blaze powder seemed even more complicated to acquire. According to the book, it was made from blaze rods, which were dropped by creatures called blazes when slain. Dave had never heard of blazes, but he'd heard of the place they came from: *The Nether*.

There were plenty of legends about the Nether as well. According to the stories Dave had heard, it was a vast, hellish landscape of endless lava, populated by gigantic gray floating creatures called ghasts. If they spotted you, they'd blast you with fire.

The book gave detailed instructions of how to get to the Nether as well. To create a portal to get there you needed a block called obsidian, which was found deep underground.

As Dave went to sleep that night, he thought about all the work they were going to have to do to get ender eyes, and cursed Steve for stealing the ones he'd originally had. He wondered where Steve was now. With the head start he'd had, he might have already reached the End and killed the dragon.

The next morning Dave made breakfast for the others, then told them his plan.

"First of all, we need to do some mining," he said. "We need diamonds for armor and tools, and obsidian for building a nether portal."

"A nether portal?" said Porkins, looking shocked. "You want to go to the Nether?"

"I don't want to go, I have to go," said Dave. "I need blaze rods."

"I—I can't go with you, old chap," Porkins said. "I can't go to the Nether." For once he didn't look cheery—in fact, he looked sad.

"What's the matter?" said Carl, mockingly. "Scared of ghasts?"

"I come from the Nether," Porkins said. "Until a few years ago, I lived there. But then something horrible happened."

Porkins looked as if he was going to cry.

"You don't have to tell us what happened if you don't want to," Dave said, putting a hand on his shoulder.

"No, tell us," said Carl. "I love horror stories."

"My people, the pigmen, have lived in the Nether for generations," Porkins said. "It's a hard place, but we had a good life there. Until three years ago when a strange man came to visit us. Do you know the hero Steve?"

"All too well," said Dave.

"Well this man looked just like him," said Porkins. "Apart from his eyes were white. He called himself Herobrine."

As Porkins said the word *Herobrine* a shiver went down Dave's spine, and at the same moment the wind pushed open the door to their cabin, whistling eerily. He went over and closed it. He'd never heard that name before, but something about it chilled him to the bone.

HEROBRINE

"My people were always being attacked by ghasts," Porkins went on, "and the man promised he could make us stronger, so we'd be able to fight back. Our leaders agreed, and Herobrine gave us all a potion to drink.

"I was the only one who didn't trust this chap Herobrine, so I never drank mine. But everyone else did. By morning, Herobrine had gone, and my people had been transformed into mindless zombies.

"Even my own father didn't recognize me anymore, he just looked at me blankly with his dead, zombie eyes. I ran as fast as I could, until I found a nether portal inside an old fortress and used it to come to your world. I've been here ever since."

Porkins's eyes were red and wet by the time he finished his story. Dave handed him a block of wool to wipe his face with.

"Thank you," said Porkins. "I hope you understand why I can't go with you. I can't stand to see my people like that—reduced to being mindless zombies."

"I understand," said Dave. "Carl and I will go by ourselves."

"Hey," said Carl, "I don't remember volunteering for that! I'm not going to the Nether."

"What's the matter," Dave asked with a smile, "afraid of ghasts?"

Carl frowned.

"Very funny," he said.

Over the next few days, they set to work mining for diamond and obsidian. Each morning they noticed that a few blocks had been moved around in the night, which Carl said was a clear sign that there were endermen about. Dave didn't fancy facing endermen without a full suit of armor though, so at night they all stayed inside the cabin.

One night it rained, and they heard screaming outside.

"It sounds like someone's in trouble," said Dave, grabbing his sword. "We've got to help them!"

"No," said Carl, "those are endermen. Water kills them, so when it rains they keep teleporting to find somewhere dry to hide."

"I hope they don't teleport in here," said Dave, nervously.

Within a week, they'd managed to get enough diamond so that

they all had diamond swords and pickaxes. After a couple more days they had enough obsidian to build a portal.

Dave placed the obsidian blocks in place, creating the portal.

"Now we just need to light it," he told the others. "It's late now, let's wait until tomorrow."

Even unlit, Dave could sense something dark and mysterious coming from the portal. The sun was shining brightly, but the obsidian was as dark as night. He wasn't looking forward to going through it, but he had no choice.

In the morning, Dave used some flint and steel to light the portal, following the instructions in his book. Instantly a rippling purple forcefield appeared inside it. When he cautiously stepped closer he could hear strange noises coming from within.

"Well," he said to Porkins, "I guess this is it. We'll see you when we get back."

Porkins sighed.

"I'm coming with you," he said. "You and Carl are all the family I've got, old chap. I'm going to help you."

Dave gave Porkins a hug. It seemed like the right thing to do.

"Well," said Dave, "I'm glad to have you with me."

"Can we stop all this lovey-dovey stuff and get on with this?" Carl said. "The quicker we get in the Nether, the quicker we can leave!"

So they all stood in front of the portal, their weapons at the ready for whatever they might find in there.

They were an unlikely trio, Dave thought to himself, a villager, a pigman and a creeper, but Dave felt safer knowing he was with friends.

"Ok," said Dave, "here goes nothing."

He stepped into the portal...

CHAPTER SEVEN
The Nether

"Run, chaps!" Porkins yelled.

Dave barely had time to get his bearings before Porkins grabbed him by the hand and started running.

Dave looked round and saw the biggest mob he'd even seen: a huge, floating white block with tentacles, its red eyes fixed on Dave and his friends.

A ghast, Dave knew. From the tales he'd heard about them he knew they were not to be messed with.

With a flick of its tentacles the ghost flung a firebolt at them. It landed just short, the huge explosion hurting Dave's eardrums.

Where's Carl? Dave wondered suddenly, but then he saw that Porkins was carrying him. The creeper was so small that Porkins was holding him with one arm.

"Lovely home you have here," Carl yelled at the pigman. "Oh yes, the Nether is a great place!"

Porkins ignored him.

"Through here," Porkins said, running down a small passage in the rock. "It won't be able to follow us."

Dave followed Porkins through the small hole. He looked round and saw the ghost behind them, too big to fit in the passageway. It screamed in frustration and started hurling firebolts at the rock.

"We'd better get a move on or it'll blast its way through to us," Dave said. He and Porkins followed the narrow passageway until they were sure they'd lost the ghost. They kept going and eventually came to another opening. Dave walked out and got his first proper look at the Nether.

An endless cavern stretched out before him. The sky was nowhere to be seen, but somehow the cavern was perfectly lit. Even when they'd gone through the narrow passageway, Dave recalled, it hadn't been too dark.

The cavern was made of a reddish block Dave was unfamiliar with, but every so often there were patches of other blocks, including some glowing blocks that hung in clusters from the ceiling. The most striking thing, however, was the sea of lava that stretched out in every direction. He could see fires raging in the distance: the reddish blocks themselves seemed to be burning.

It was a truly dismal place, but Dave knew that it was Porkins's home so he kept his negative thoughts to himself.

Carl, however, wasn't so kind.

"This place is a dump," Carl said. "I mean, I used to live in a cave, but at least it wasn't full of lava."

Dave heard a strange noise in the distance.

"What is that?" he asked Porkins. "It sounds like... it sounds like crying."

"Ghasts," said Porkins solemnly, pointing at some white blobs in the distance. Dave hadn't noticed them before.

Unlike the one who'd attacked them when they came out of the portal, these ghasts had closed eyes. They looked almost like they were crying.

"They stay like that until they attack," Porkins told them. "My friends and I used to listen out for their crying to make sure they never took us unawares. Before Herobrine..."

Dave had never seen Porkins like this. Normally the pigman was jolly and chipper, always smiling. But coming back to the Nether seemed to have drained all the happiness out of him.

The pigmen had lived here once, Porkins had told Dave and Carl. Then a man named Herobrine had tricked them into becoming mindless zombies. As far as Porkins knew, he was the last normal pigman left.

Dave had a look round the cavern, but he couldn't see any zombie pigmen, thankfully.

"Come on then," Carl said, "what are we looking for? Let's get what we need and leave here as soon as we can."

Porkins sighed sadly.

"We'll need to find a fortress," the pigman told them. "That's where the blazes are."

"Were the fortresses where your people lived?" Dave asked. "Before... you know."

"No," said Porkins, "me and my chaps were a nomadic people."

"What's that mean?" Carl asked. "Were you gnomes?"

"Nomadic," Dave said, "not gnome-madic. I think it means they moved from place to place, with no fixed home. Is that right?"

"Yes," said Porkins with a smile, "we roamed across the land, collecting mushrooms and avoiding ghasts. It was a good life."

Porkins looked wistfully across the lava, the smile still on his face. The memory of the old days seemed to have brought a bit of the old Porkins back: the jolly pigman who Dave had first met.

Suddenly they heard a sound nearby. To Dave it sounded like a pig squealing, but there was something off about it. It was deeper than the sound a pig normally made, and a bit more... *rotten.*

Dave looked to his left and saw a huge crowd of zombies gathered together on a rocky plain below them. No... at first they looked like zombies, but they were different somehow. A lot of their flesh had melted off to reveal the bone or turned green, but Dave could tell they had once looked just like Porkins.

Zombie pigmen.

"Does anyone else not see all the zombies?" Carl whispered. "We need to get out of here!"

"No," said Porkins sadly. "They won't harm us. They're my people."

And he walked towards the crowd of zombie pigmen.

CHAPTER EIGHT
The Pigmen

At first Dave thought Porkins was crazy, but then he realized he was right: the zombie pigmen kept themselves to themselves as Porkins walked slowly through them. They seemed slightly less mindless than normal zombies, but they still seemed to have little clue what was going on. As Porkins walked through them they just looked at him with mild curiosity and made grunting sounds.

Dave found it hard to imagine that these creatures had once been like Porkins, intelligent pigmen who could speak. The noises they made now sounded more like pigs, with the occasional zombie sound thrown in as well.

"Come on," Dave said to Carl, "let's follow him."

"You two idiots are gonna get me killed one day, I just know it!" Carl sighed.

"You're a creeper!" Dave said. "I thought your dearest wish was to blow yourself up?"

"Yes," said Carl. "Blow myself up. Not get eaten by zombie pigmen or get destroyed by a ghast."

"Fair enough," said Dave.

Dave and Carl walked nervously through the horde of zombie pigmen. A couple of the pigmen gave them curious looks, but most didn't even notice them.

"Meet my people," Porkins said sadly. "I'm not sure if I knew these chaps—hard to tell with their flesh all rotted off. But they were my people, nonetheless."

"I'm sorry," Dave said.

What else was there to say?

"Let's keep going and find a fortress," Porkins said. "There are quite a few throughout the Nether, ruins of an ancient civilization.

Some of my people used to say that the blazes are all that's left of the Old People who built the fortresses. Either the Old People transformed into blazes or the Old People created the blazes and the blazes wiped them out. The stories differ, depending who you ask. Either way, the blazes are the only things that live in the fortresses now. Well, there are rumors of other creatures living in the depths, but I've never seen them."

"How hard will they be to slay?" Dave asked. "The blazes I mean."

"I've never slain one myself," Porkins said, "but from what I hear, it shouldn't be too hard. Especially with our diamond swords."

The three of them walked on through the Nether, making sure to keep out of sight of the ghasts that floated above. There was something depressing about the Nether, Dave thought. It was the fact that it was all so similar—wherever he looked there were lava seas and red blocks, there was no variety. No different biomes.

There were no days or nights either, and Dave found it impossible to keep track of time. Eventually he, Porkins and Carl all began to feel sleepy, so they dug themselves a small cave in the rock, so they could sleep without being disturbed by ghasts.

Dave wished he had brought a bed with him; the three of them had no choice but to sleep on the hard floor. It took Dave a long time to get to sleep, but somehow he managed it. He dreamed of the green hills of his home—the home Steve had so callously destroyed—and of his dad's cooking. He hoped that wherever they were, his parents and his fellow villagers were ok.

In his dream he was just about to tuck into a nice porkchop when he was suddenly woken by someone picking him up.

"What are you doing?" he yelled, waking up to find himself surrounded by zombie pigman. One of them had picked him up and thrown him over its shoulder. Other zombie pigman had grabbed Carl and Porkins as well.

"Let us go, you fiends!" Porkins yelled. "Unhand us this instant!"

"Yeah, let us go you freaks!" Carl said.

In response the pigmen just snorted, and carried them out of the cave.

CHAPTER NINE
Caught

Even if he could have struggled free, Dave and his friends were surrounded by hundreds of zombie pigmen, all marching in the same direction.

"Where are they taking us?" Dave asked Porkins, who was being carried by the zombie pigman next to him.

"I've no clue, old bean," Porkins said. "Maybe to cook and eat us?"

"Thanks Porkins," Carl said, rolling his eyes. "Very reassuring."

As far as Dave could see, the pigmen had left his and Porkins's bags and all their weapons behind in the cave. He tried to keep track of the route they were taking, so he could go back for the bags when (or *if*) they escaped, but everything in the Nether was so similar that he soon lost his bearings.

They came round a corner and suddenly Dave forgot about the bags. In fact, he forgot about everything. Up ahead was the biggest building Dave had ever seen. Colossal pillars rose out of the lava, holding up wide bridges that seemed to go nowhere. Dave supposed the bridges must have led somewhere at one point, but that must have been a long time ago. The bridges led away from a huge building built into the rock.

At first Dave thought the fortress was black, but then he realized it was a very dark purple. It seemed to eat the light. It was a dark and foreboding place and Dave had no desire to enter it, but it seemed like he had little choice—that seemed to be where the pigmen were bringing them.

A nether fortress, Dave thought. Whatever he'd been expecting a nether fortress to look like, this wasn't it.

"Seriously chaps," Porkins said to the zombies, "put us down and we'll say no more about this. I used to be one of you, you know. Or rather, you used to be one of me."

The zombie pigmen ignored him.

They were almost at the fortress. Dave could see where the pigmen were bringing them now: a small doorway in the rock that surely led up to the fortress. If they were going to get out of this they had to act fast. But what could they do?

Then Dave saw a ghast floating high above them, and he came up with a plan.

"Hey you!" he yelled up at the ghast. A few of the pigmen looked round at him, snorting in confusion.

The ghast didn't look as if it had heard him, so he shouted again:

"HEY YOU!"

This time it heard him. In a second its sad, crying face transformed, its eyes glowing red with anger.

The ghast shrieked, swooping down towards them. The pigmen started running about in terror. As dumb as they were, they knew to run from a ghast.

The pigman carrying Dave dropped him, then fled for its life, snorting wildly. Dave looked round and saw Porkins and Carl had also been dropped.

"Run!" Dave shouted at them.

"Always with the running," Carl sighed. "Before I met you two I only ever walked. I miss walking."

The three of them dodged out of the way just in time to avoid being blown up by a fireball from the ghast. They ran away from the fortress, running down a narrow passageway in the rock.

"I think we're safe," Dave said. He stuck his head out of the entrance.

The ghast was firing fireballs at the fleeing pigmen, who were running off in every direction, squealing and screaming.

"What now, old bean?" Porkins whispered. "There's the fortress, but it looks like the zombie chaps live there now."

"If only we had our weapons," Dave sighed. "I tried to keep

track of the route the zombie pigmen took us, but it was no use. We'll never find our way back to that cave."

"Don't be so sure," Porkins grinned. He poked his squishy pig nose. "A pigman's sense of smell is second to none—and I can smell the baked potato you left in your bag, even from here!"

"Hey," said Carl. "That's *my* baked potato, not Dave's."

"It doesn't matter whose baked potato it is," Dave said. "That's great, Porkins! Please, lead us back to the bags!"

Porkins trotted off happily, Dave following behind.

"My baked potato," Carl muttered to himself.

CHAPTER TEN
Entering the Fortress

Porkins's nose was as good as he promised: soon he, Dave and Carl were back at the cave where the zombies had captured them.

They checked their bags and saw that, thankfully, nothing had been touched.

"Come to Daddy!" Carl said, taking a big bite out of his baked potato. In a couple of bites he'd devoured the whole thing.

"Ah lub baked botatohs," he told them, his mouth stuffed full of potato.

"I can see that," said Dave. "Although isn't it a bit cold?"

"So what now?" Porkins asked. "Do we storm the fortress, swords in hand?"

"I guess," Dave said. "But Porkins, If we did that we'd probably have to slay some zombie pigmen. I can't ask you to do that."

Porkins sighed sadly.

"Yes you can," he said. "Those *things* aren't my people anymore, they're just mindless zombies. My people are gone."

"Either way," Carl said, "we can't just march in there and cut through hordes of zombies. Even with our diamond swords we'll be outmatched."

"Another thing I've been wondering," Dave added, "is will there be any blazes left? If the pigmen have taken over that fortress, surely they would have slain them all."

Porkins thought for a moment.

"Maybe we should keep going then chaps, find another fortress."

The others agreed that this was probably a good idea.

According to Porkins, the zombie pigmen didn't usually stay in fortresses. There was no point in trying to sneak into this fortress when they might find an empty one somewhere else.

Before they left the cave, Dave checked his backpack.

Good, he thought to himself, *it's still there.*

Before they entered the nether portal, Dave had packed some spare obsidian in his bag, in case they couldn't find their way back to their original portal. According to his crafting book, you could build portals in the Nether as well. Where it would bring them was anyone's guess, as the book said time and space flowed a bit differently in the Nether, but at least they would be able to get back.

They left the cave and made their way around the lava sea, making sure to keep to the shadows. The last thing they wanted was to be spotted by more pigmen—or a ghast.

As they came close to the fortress—the one the pigmen had taken over—they could see zombie pigmen marching along the walkways and at the small windows. Dave and his friends kept low and out of sight, and finally came to another small passageway through the rock.

"What does your nose tell you about this route?" Dave asked Porkins. Porkins stepped forward and took a sniff.

"I can't smell anything funny," he said. "No pigmen or ghasts, anyway."

"That's good enough for me," said Dave.

Dave led the way, his diamond sword at the ready. Even in an underground tunnel like this, it never got dark in the Nether, so they had no need for torches.

They walked and walked, following the twists and turns of the underground passage, until finally they found themselves coming up to a corridor made of purple brick.

"Nether brick," Porkins whispered. "Crumbs, we must have ended up underneath the fortress. Let's go back the other way."

Dave was about to agree with him, when suddenly he heard a sound up ahead: a deep, almost robotic groan.

"What's that?" he wondered aloud. It didn't sound like a ghast or a pigman.

"If I'm not mistaken," said Porkins excitedly, "I think that's the chap we've been looking for—I think that's a blaze!"

CHAPTER ELEVEN
Blazes

They crept slowly down the purple corridor. There were no windows, and Dave guessed they must be deep underneath the fortress.

"There's no sign of any pigmen," he whispered.

"Oh I'm sure they'll turn up," said Carl. "They'll turn up, you'll yell *run!* and we'll all have to run for our lives again. That's the way these things normally pan out."

They came to a place where the corridor split off in different directions. Porkins sniffed the air.

"This way," he said.

They followed him down the corridor.

"Wait a minute," Dave said to the others. He stopped to look at a carving on the wall.

The carving looked very old, and it had worn away or been broken in a few places. The Nether brick itself had been carved. Dave assumed it must have been made by the people who built the fortress, however many years ago that was.

In the carving were creatures with long arms and legs. They looked a bit like the pictures of endermen Dave had seen in his book, although in the carving they were wearing clothes. As far as Dave knew, endermen never wore clothes.

The creatures were all kneeling down, as if they were praying, and in the middle of them stood a man.

Steve, Dave thought. *That's Steve! How old is he?*

But no, it couldn't have been Steve. There was something about the figure—its blank eyes—that creeped Dave out.

"That's the scoundrel who tricked my people!" Porkins said,

looking at the carving. "That's Herobrine!"

Herobrine. The last time Porkins had said that name, Dave had felt a strange sense of fear he couldn't explain, and this time was no different. He leaned forward, getting a closer look at the carving, when suddenly there was a noise from down the corridor: another strange groaning sound. A blaze.

The sound was louder this time—they were getting closer. There seemed to be several creatures groaning back and forth, and making strange metallic sounds.

"I think there's a few of them," said Porkins.

"Woop-di-do," said Carl miserably.

Up ahead was a small open doorway on the side of the corridor. They all looked through, being careful to keep quiet.

Through the doorway the floor dropped down, and they found themselves looking down on a small room. It had what looked like a cage in the middle, with three of the strangest creatures Dave had ever seen floating around it, dancing around the cage in circles.

Each blaze had a yellow head, floating on top of a body of smoke. Strange yellow poles floated in the smoke too, though if they were limbs or weapons or what, Dave didn't know.

They had eyes, but no mouths or noses. Dave thought their heads looked a bit like Steve's, and he found himself thinking about what Porkins had told them about blazes:

Either the Old People transformed into blazes or the Old People created the blazes and the blazes wiped them out. The stories differ, depending who you ask.

Could the blazes have been some old race that had become monsters? It seemed possible to Dave, but now was no time to be thinking about history. They had a job to do.

"What's that cage in the middle of the floor?" Dave whispered to Porkins.

"It's a spawn," Porkins whispered back. "That's where blazes come from—or so I've heard. If we kill those blazes, more will come from the spawn."

"That's great!" said Dave.

"Why would that be great?" asked Carl.

"Because," said Dave, "that means we can get all the blaze rods we need here."

"Unless we get killed by blazes," said Carl.

"Unless we get killed by blazes," Dave agreed.

CHAPTER TWELVE
Swords at the Ready

According to Porkins, blazes could throw fireballs, so Dave decided they needed a better plan than just to jump down into the room swinging their swords about.

Porkins was the only one with a bow (Dave was annoyed he hadn't thought to build bows for him and Carl before they entered the Nether) so he was going to stay up here and fire arrows at the blazes. Meanwhile Dave was going to jump down and fight the blazes with his sword and shield. Carl was going to cheer them both on.

"Moral support is very important," Carl told them. "My cheering could make all the difference."

Dave hoped that by fighting the blazes both on the ground and with arrows from above they would confuse them, making them easier to defeat.

"We'll keep slaying them as they come out of the spawner until we have plenty of blaze rods," Dave told the other two. They were sitting a short way down the corridor, so the blazes couldn't hear them.

"How are you gonna get out of that room when you're finished?" Carl asked.

"I've got some wood in my bag," Dave said, I'll prepare some stairs.

"Not wooden stairs," Porkins told him, "they might get set alight. You'd be better off using this," he tapped the purple wall, "nether brick stairs."

Dave, Porkins and Carl started digging at the walls, making sure Dave had plenty of nether brick blocks. Then he put a crafting table down (he still had one in his bag) and crafted some stairs.

"Right," said Dave, "I guess we'd better get to it. There's just... there's just one thing. Porkins... how good are you with that bow and arrow?"

"Not too shabby, old chap," Porkins said.

"Good," said Dave. "Just, um, make sure you hit the blazes with your arrows and not me."

They walked back to the doorway.

"Ready?" Dave asked.

The other two nodded. Dave held his sword and shield tightly. His palms felt sweaty, and it wasn't just from the heat.

"ATTACK!" Dave yelled. He jumped down into the small room. The blazes turned in shock to stare at him, then they floated towards him, angry looks on their faces.

Dave held his shield up just in time to block a fireball. At the same time an arrow whizzed over him, hitting one of the blazes right between the eyes. It screamed and span around wildly, and Dave took the opportunity to run forward and slash it with his sword.

The blaze screamed a final time, then exploded in a puff of smoke. All that was left was a glowing yellow rod on the floor.

Dave ran forward and threw the blaze rod over his shoulder into his backpack. He turned just in time to see the other two blazes floating towards him, and another one was forming in the spawner, growing in size.

Two more of Porkins's arrows flew down, hitting each of the blazes in the face. Dave ran forward again and chopped them both into dust. As soon as the other blaze emerged from the spawner, Dave sliced it open with his sword.

Before long Dave had collected loads of blaze rods—so many that his rucksack was almost full.

"Right, that's enough now," Dave yelled, "I'm coming back up!"

He laid down some nether brick stairs and ran up to the doorway.

"What happened to you?" he asked Carl with a grin. "I thought you were meant to be cheering us on?"

Carl shrugged.

"You seemed to be doing alright on your own," the creeper said. "So I thought I'd leave you be."

"I say, we ought to destroy those stairs," Porkins said. "To stop the blazes coming after us."

"Good idea," Dave said. He pulled his pickaxe out, but suddenly they heard a flurry of snorting and footsteps around a bend in the corridor.

"Zombie pigmen!" Dave yelled. "Run!"

"I knew it," Carl sighed. "I knew this was going to end in running!"

They began to run away from the sounds, but then a huge crowd of pigmen ran out from a passage in front of them. They turned round and saw zombie pigmen behind them too. There was no way out.

"We're trapped," Dave said. "Swords at the ready!"

Dave tried to appear brave for Porkins and Carl, but he knew this had to be the end. Even with their diamond swords, they had no chance of defeating this many pigmen.

"Tally ho, chaps," Porkins said sadly. "It's been fun. A real adventure."

"I should have stayed in my cave," said Carl.

But then something strange happened. Instead of charging at them, the pigmen just stood there.

"Why aren't they attacking?" Dave wondered.

Suddenly the zombie pigmen in the corridor in front of them stepped to the side, putting their backs against the walls to clear some space. Then, the biggest, fattest pigman Dave had ever seen walked between them.

But it wasn't the pigman's huge belly or massive height that caught Dave's eye. It wasn't even the golden crown it wore on its head. It was that fact that it was a *pigman*. Not a zombie pigman, but a regular pigman. Just like Porkins.

Porkins stepped forward, his mouth hanging open in amazement.

"Trotter!" he said. "Is that you?"

"Hello hello, my boy!" the huge pigman said with a smile, his deep voice booming down the corridor. "Yes it's me. And it's *King* Trotter now."

Dave noticed that the huge pigman was holding a golden staff with an emerald on the top. He tapped the staff on the ground and the emerald began to glow.

"Seize them," the big pigman said, the smile disappearing from his face. "Seize them and bring them to my chambers."

"Trotter, what's going on?" Porkins yelled, but suddenly he, Dave and Carl were surrounded by zombie pigmen.

"What's going on is that you're my prisoners, chaps," the big pigman said. "And soon enough, you'll be my slaves."

CHAPTER THIRTEEN
The King of the Pigmen

The three of them were marched down endless nether brick corridors by the zombie pigmen. Every so often they would go up some stairs, and eventually Dave could see the Nether outside the windows. They were no longer underground.

Finally they were marched into a large room. Instead of being made of nether bricks, the walls were made of solid gold blocks, and there was a golden throne in the middle. The big pigman—*Trotter*—was sitting on the throne, waiting for them.

"So good to see you, Porkins," he said. "Welcome to my throne room."

"Who is this fatso?" Carl asked.

"His name is Trotter," Porkins said angrily. "Trotter the Rotter we used to call him—he never was very trustworthy."

"Well, it's King Trotter now," Trotter said, a nasty smile on his face. "And you'll learn to obey me soon enough."

"How come you didn't turn into a zombie, you scoundrel?" Porkins asked.

"The same reason you didn't, old boy," Trotter said. "Because I didn't drink any of this..."

He tapped his staff on the ground and two zombie pigmen marched over, holding a cauldron of bubbling green liquid.

"The potion Herobrine gave us!" Porkins gasped.

"Yes," Trotter said. "Herobrine came to see me, long before he visited the rest of the pigmen. He told me he was going to trick the pigmen into drinking this potion, so they'd turn into zombies. He offered me this magic staff, saying it could control zombies. With it I could rule all of the Nether!"

"And you accepted his offer," Porkins growled. "You betrayed your people! You really are a rotter, sir. A rotter and a cad!"

"And a king," Trotter grinned. He tapped his staff and the emerald glowed green once more.

"Hold the prisoners still," Trotter told the pigmen. Dave felt two pigmen grab his hands and hold them behind his back. "It's time for them to take their medicine."

Three zombie pigmen walked up to the cauldron with bottles, scooping up the green liquid.

"They're going to turn us into zombies!" Dave gasped. "Don't drink it!"

But a zombie pigman squeezed his nose and he couldn't help opening his mouth.

"I told you you'd be my slaves," Trotter grinned, leaning back in his throne. "Herobrine gave me this power so that I could build an army in the Nether, ready to fight for him when the time comes. Soon all the realms will be his to rule, and I will command the Nether for him. Praise Herobrine. Praise the Infinite Void."

"Oh my," said Porkins, "we're really in the soup now."

Then they heard sounds coming from down the corridor—the sound of fighting and pigmen squealing.

"Wait a minute, old bean," Porkins said to Dave. "Did you ever destroy those stairs? The ones that led up from the blaze spawn room?"

"Oh," said Dave, suddenly remembering, "I don't think I did."

"What's all that noise?" Trotter growled. There was a hint of nervousness in his voice. He stood up, picking up a huge golden sword. "I say, you out there," he yelled to the zombie pigmen out in the corridor, "what's going on?!"

Suddenly a hoard of blazes burst into the room, spinning wildly. The pigmen were screaming and grunting, doing their best to fight them off.

In the confusion, Dave pulled away from the pigman holding him. He pulled his sword out of his belt and started slashing wildly, attacking the pigmen holding Porkins and Carl.

"Let's get out of here!" he told them.

"You!" Trotter roared. He was ignoring the chaos around him and looking straight at Dave and his friends. "You did this!"

The huge pigman ran towards them, his sword swinging wildly.

"I never thought I'd be the one to say this," said Carl, "but... RUN!"

CHAPTER FOURTEEN
Escape

They ran out of the throne room. The corridors were full of pigmen and blazes fighting—more of each than Dave could count.

They started running down the corridor, trying their best to push through the crowds.

"COME BACK HERE!!"

Trotter burst out of the throne room, sending blazes and pigmen flying.

"YOU CAN'T RUN FROM ME!" he yelled, smashing his way through the crowds of fighting blazes and zombie pigmen towards Dave and his friends.

"We're done for!" Carl moaned.

"Not necessarily," Dave said. He stuck his head out of a window. There was nothing but lava below, so they couldn't jump down, but then he spotted a ghast, floating nearby.

"Hey!" he yelled at the ghast. "Come on! Come and get us!"

It worked. The ghast's eyes went red and it flicked a fireball at them from its tentacles. Dave, Porkins and Carl dodged out of the way of the window just in time, but Trotter wasn't so lucky. As he ran past the window the fireball came through and hit him.

The huge pigman screamed in pain, and Dave and his friends took the opportunity to run off down the corridor.

"I've got obsidian," Dave told them. "We just have to get somewhere safe and create a portal, then we can get back home."

They suddenly found themselves inside a huge nether brick chamber. The room was full of cauldrons, all full of bubbling green liquid.

"Looks like Herobrine gave Trotter plenty of supplies," Porkins said bitterly.

"Come on," said Dave, "that ghast blast won't have stopped him for long."

He was more right than he knew: at that moment Trotter burst into the room, sword in hand.

"Come on Porkins, old chap," he snarled. "It's your old pal Trotter. I just want to talk."

He charged towards them. Dave braced himself, expecting to be cut in two by Trotter's huge sword, but then Porkins stepped forward.

"You've taken enough from me, already!" Porkins yelled. "You're not taking my new friends as well!"

He kicked over a cauldron. The green liquid spilled across the floor and Trotter ran right into it. The huge pigman slipped over and fell to the floor, squealing in pain.

"It'll... take more than that... to stop me!" Trotter snarled, getting to his feet. But before he could charge again, Porkins kicked another cauldron over, and another...

As the green liquid stung his feet, Trotter roared, stampeding around like a mad bull, sending cauldron after cauldron falling to the floor. Soon the ground was thick with green liquid, and the huge pigman fell to his knees.

"What... What have you done to me?!" he yelled.

He's turning into a zombie, Dave thought. The green liquid was doing its job: turning the huge pigman's flesh green and exposing the bone underneath.

"My mind..." Trotter squealed. "I can't... I can't think straight..."

"Come on, it's time to go," Dave said.

The others could see he was right. Trotter was confused now, but soon he'd be a mindless zombie—the biggest zombie pigman who ever lived. They didn't want to be around when that happened.

The three of them ran out of the room, leaving Trotter behind.

They ran down endless corridors, deeper and deeper into the fortress, until finally they came across a room big enough to build a nether portal in.

Dave rummaged in his bag and pulled out his crafting book. He wanted to make sure he got this right—obsidian blocks took a long time to break, so they couldn't afford to make a mistake.

"Four blocks across, five up," he read, trying not to forget, "four across, five up."

He pulled out the obsidian and quickly built the portal. Then a sound came from down the corridor:

"RRROOOAAAR!!!!"

They could hear huge footsteps running towards them.

"I don't want to hassle you Dave, but hurry up!" Carl yelled.

Dave pulled out his flint and steel and lit the portal.

But nothing happened.

He stood back and checked the portal, starting to panic.

"Four across, five high!" he said. "Why's it not working?!"

He tried lighting the portal again, but still nothing happened.

Porkins, who was looking out into the corridor, turned round.

"Come on, old chap!" he said. "Trotter's coming!"

"The portal's not working!" Dave yelled.

Porkins's eyes suddenly went wide.

"That's because those are nether bricks!" he gasped. "You're meant to use obsidian!"

Porkins was right, Dave realized with a start. In his haste to build the portal he'd used the wrong blocks!

"Well come on!" Carl yelled. "Build a new one!"

Dave rummaged in his bag and pulled out a handful of blocks—they were *definitely* obsidian this time.

Four across, five up," he whispered to himself.

He quickly built the portal.

"Done!" he said happily.

"Well light it then, squid for brains!" Carl screamed.

"We've got company!" Porkins yelled.

Porkins ran from the doorway of the room just in time, as suddenly Trotter was there, trying to squeeze through and grab them. He was still wearing his golden crown, but that was the only bit of him that was the same. He was a mindless zombie now, his flesh going green in places and peeling and his eyes dim.

"RRRRAGGGHH!!!!!" zombie Trotter roared at them. There was an endless horde of zombie pigmen behind him, all trying to get through the doorway, but Trotter was so big he was blocking it. He was desperately trying to push through—and he was succeeding.

Dave pulled out his flint and steel once more. This time the portal shimmered into life when he lit it; the purple barrier appearing before them. He'd never seen a more beautiful sight.

"Come on!" Dave yelled.

He grabbed Carl, picked him up and threw him through the portal.

"Hey!" Carl had time to yell, before he disappeared into the purple liquid. Porkins ran forward and jumped through as well. Once his friends were safe, Dave jumped through after them, leaving the Nether behind.

CHAPTER FIFTEEN
Snow

Dave found himself face down in something cold. He sat up and saw he was kneeling in thick snow. After the sticky warmth of the Nether the snow felt refreshing, but he knew he had no time to enjoy it.

He stood up and looked around. All he could see was the portal next to him, the purple light glowing dimly in the dark. It was night time now, and it was snowing fiercely. He could barely see anything.

"Porkins?" he yelled. "Carl?"

"Over here, old chap!"

Porkins was nearby, his head poking out of the snow.

"We need to destroy the portal," Dave yelled, "before—"

Suddenly Trotter burst through the portal, snorting and roaring. He reached a huge zombie hand out to grab Dave, but just missed him. Just like the doorway, the portal was too small for Trotter to get through, but he was pushing with all his might and it wouldn't be long before he made it.

"Destroy it!" Dave yelled to Porkins. The pigman was to the side of the portal, in exactly the right place. Porkins whipped out a diamond pickaxe and starting hacking away at an obsidian block.

Dave waded through the snow, trying to get as far from Trotter's reach as he could.

"Carl?" Dave yelled. "Are you ok?"

The tiny creeper stuck his head out of the snow.

"No thanks to you," he said miserably.

"RRRROOOARRR!!!"

Trotter was almost free now. Porkins was hacking away at the obsidian block for dear life.

Then suddenly it broke. The portal flickered for a moment, and then was gone. Trotter was cut in half at the waist, the half of him that was already through the portal falling into the snow.

"You think he's dead?" Carl asked.

"ROOOAAAARR!!"

Zombie Trotter raised his head, his eyes focusing on Dave. He began pulling himself through the snow with his arms, dragging his severed body along.

"ROOOAAAARR!!"

"Stop right there, you brute!" Porkins shouted. He raised his bow, but before he could fire Trotter swung his fist at him, sending Porkins flying. Porkins landed in the snow, disappearing from view.

"Porkins!" Dave yelled. Trotter turned back to him, baring his teeth.

Dave picked up Carl and started trudging through the snow as fast as he could, but Trotter was gaining on him. Even without legs the zombie pigman was able to pull himself through the snow faster than Dave was able to wade through it.

Suddenly Dave felt a huge hand grab him. He fell into the snow, dropping Carl. Trotter lifted Dave into the air.

Trotter opened his mouth wide. Dave tried to break free of the zombie pigman's grasp but he was too strong.

He's going to eat me! Dave realized in horror.

Trotter licked his huge lips, his rotten breath stinking up Dave's nostrils.

Then, from nowhere, an arrow appeared between Trotter's eyes. The zombie pigman yelled in pain, dropping Dave into the snow.

Dave looked up as another arrow, then another, then another, struck the zombie pigman. Trotter yelled and flailed his fists around in frustration, trying to find his unseen attacker. Soon Trotter was so full of arrows that he looked like a hedgehog, and with a final "RROOAAR!!" he slumped down in the snow, narrowly avoiding squashing Dave.

There was a *poof* and Trotter was gone. All that was left of him was a crater in the snow, some rotten flesh and a gold ingot.

Dave got gingerly to his feet. He couldn't see any sign of Porkins or Carl, but he could see something: a rider on horseback coming towards him through the snow.

"Thank you," Dave gasped, realizing the rider must have been the one who fired the arrows.

The rider and his horse were covered from head-to-toe in diamond armor. The rider pulled to a stop in front of Dave, his horse rearing up on its hind legs.

Wow, Dave thought. *Now this is what a *real* hero looks like.*

"Thank you, sir," Dave said. He'd never used the word *sir* before, but it seemed like the right thing to say. "I owe you my life."

The rider removed his diamond helmet.

"No worries, bro," he said. "All in a day's work for a hero!"

"No," Dave said, falling back into the snow. "No, no, no, no, no, no, no! Not you! Anyone but you!"

It was Steve.

EPILOGUE

The man in the blue shirt climbed off of his horse. In front of him lay a huge crater, a few half-destroyed houses around the rim.

This had been a village once, he knew, before it had been destroyed by an explosion.

He knelt down and touched the earth, using the magic the witches had taught him to replay what had happened.

He saw images flashing past his eyes, like reading a storybook: a small, uninteresting village surrounded by hills; another man in a blue shirt building a statue of himself as villagers watched; an explosion.

The man in the blue shirt scowled. He knew who the other blue-shirted man from the vision was: *Steve*. He'd never met Steve, but many people had confused the two of them over the years. He and Steve looked exactly alike, he was told, apart from one feature: their eyes. The man in the blue shirt had completely white eyes.

Herobrine, people called him, although he couldn't recall where the name had come from. He was certainly no hero.

He walked to the edge of the crater. His heart skipped a beat with excitement as he saw what lay below, through a crack in the ground.

A stronghold.

It had been so many years since he'd seen one. He'd thought the Old People had destroyed them all, but two days ago one of his witches had received a vision:

"One of the Old People's fortresses has been uncovered," she'd told him. *"A portal to the End has appeared!"*

Herobrine floated down through the ceiling. The stronghold was in ruins, and the portal was beyond repair, but it gave him hope.

If one stronghold survived, he thought to himself, *there must be more.*

For so long he had thought he would never find his way back to the End, but now there might be a way. If he could find another stronghold, with a working end portal, he could finally complete the mission he'd begun so long ago.

The Old People had perfected travel between all the realms, building fortresses in the Nether, cities in the End and kingdoms under the sea. Herobrine had taught them his magic, and in return they had taught him their own. But when they had learned what he really wanted—his true plan—they had betrayed him.

He had paid them back, of course. There were no Old People left anymore; Herobrine had taken care of that.

He touched the smooth surface of one of the ender portal blocks. Even broken he could feel strong magic coming from it. Using his own power he reached out into the past, to see how it had broken.

A vision came to him: the stronghold closed off from the world, completely in darkness. The portal was complete and working. Suddenly there was a massive explosion from above, caving in the roof and breaking the portal, then Steve and some villagers came down through the roof.

Steve, Herobrine thought angrily, *that fool destroyed the portal.*

The vision continued. The villagers all gathered round the broken portal, speaking words Herobrine couldn't hear. Looking into the past wasn't an exact science, even with his power.

Then one villager, he looked younger than the rest, started speaking. Everyone stopped what they were doing and listened to him. The villager led them all back outside and threw something into the air. Herobrine used all his magic to try and hear what the boy was saying, but he could only make out a few words:

"*I'll find the End Portal... slay the ender dragon...*"

Herobrine took his hand off the broken ender portal and the vision came to an end.

Could it be true? Could that young villager have discovered a way to find ender portals?

Herobrine closed his eyes. He reached out with his magic, trying to find the information he sought. *The boy's name... what is the boy's name...*

The boy had lived here, this had been his home. The boy was gone, but Herobrine could feel his presence still. People moved from place to place, building their feeble structures, but the ground and the rock remembered.

What is his name? Herobrine asked again. *Tell me his name!*

Finally, the ground whispered back an answer. It was a short answer; a short name.

Herobrine floated back out of the stronghold, landing on the grass on the edge of crater. Two of his witches were waiting for him.

"Well?" one of them asked. "Did you find what you were looking for?"

"Dave," Herobrine whispered. As he spoke the grass for miles around withered and died and the leaves fell from the trees. A nearby herd of cows were suddenly spooked, and ran away as fast as their legs would take them.

"I want you to find someone," he said softly. "A villager. His name... is *Dave.*"

BOOK 2

Ice and Fire

PROLOGUE

Herobrine sat upon a throne of bedrock. The small castle at the top of the mountain was all built of bedrock—the only blocks in the world that couldn't be destroyed or mined. Even the most enchanted of diamond pickaxes wouldn't even make a dent on its walls. The castle had been built by the Old People, who had once ruled the three realms. They were all gone now. Long gone.

"What news do you have for me?" Herobrine asked the witch in front of him. "Have you found the villager yet?"

"No, Master," the witch said nervously. "The villager named Dave still eludes us. But we've sent word to all the witches loyal to our cause. Everyone is looking for him—he won't be able to hide much longer."

"I hope for your sake that's true," said Herobrine. "And what word from the Nether? I haven't heard from that fool Trotter in too long."

"Um, we um, think he may have been slain, Master."

The witch pulled something out of her robes: a gold staff with an emerald on the top. Herobrine recognized it immediately: it was the magic staff he had given a pigman named Trotter. Herobrine had turned the pigmen of the Nether into zombies, all except Trotter. The magic staff was to let Trotter control the zombie pigmen. Herobrine's plan had been to let Trotter rule the Nether as he wished, if he promised to lend his zombie army to Herobrine when needed.

"We think Trotter may have been slain," the witch repeated. "There were signs of a battle."

"No matter," said Herobrine, "I'm sure I'll be able to find someone else to rule the pigmen. This wretched world is full of people as greedy and ambitious as Trotter. Is there anything else?"

"No, Master," said the witch.

"Then go then," said Herobrine. "And next time, bring me better news. I want this Dave found."

"Yes, Master."

The witch climbed onto the window ledge, equipped her elytra and flew off into the sky.

Herobrine walked to the window. From up here, high up in the mountains, he could see for miles around. Biome after biome stretched out before him.

Somewhere out there was a villager named Dave who knew the secret to finding end portals. He was out there, and Herobrine was going to find him.

CHAPTER ONE
Nothing but Snow

Dave had been cold for the past two days, and, he suspected, he'd be cold for many more days to come.

"Come on bros," Steve called from up ahead. "Get a move on!"

"It's alright for him," Carl said bitterly. "He has a horse. Why don't I have a horse?"

As annoying as Dave thought Steve was, he had to remember that Steve had saved their lives. A huge zombie pigman had been about to eat Dave when Steve had arrived in the nick of time. He'd filled the giant pigman full of arrows and saved the day.

Also to Steve's credit was that he'd stuck around to help them. Dave had expected Steve to ride off on his horse as soon as they were safe, but no—Steve said he'd stay with them until they got out of the snow biome.

"The snow can be dangerous, bros," Steve had told them. *"Especially for noobs like you."*

At first Dave had been amazed that they'd bumped into Steve at all. The last time Dave had seen Steve, Steve had been riding away on his horse, off to kill the ender dragon. Dave had been heading in the same direction—but without a horse.

Eventually Dave realized it must have been their trip through the Nether that had put them ahead of Steve. Time and space flowed differently in the Nether, Dave had read, so the small distance they'd traveled in the Nether had been the equivalent of a much bigger distance in the real world. Well, that was Dave's theory anyway.

It was starting to get dark, so Steve lit a fire and they all sat around it. There was no shelter—all they could see were endless flat plains of snow in every direction.

"How you doing, little boys?" Steve asked the three of them. "You've had a tough couple of days."

Dave was outraged.

"Steve, we're not little boys—we're grown men!"

"Oh, sorry, bro," Steve said. "No offense. I hope you've all learned your lesson though—going on adventures is only for heroes. Still, on the plus side, at least you all got to meet me—the legendary Steve!"

"Steve," Dave said, "we've met before."

"Sorry, bro," Steve said. "I meet a lot of people. It's hard to keep track of all the names."

"You blew up my village!" Dave snapped. "You blew up my village and stole my ender eyes and you can't even remember my name!"

"Oooooh!" said Steve. "I remember you now, dude. Wallace, isn't it?"

"It's Dave!"

"Dave, of course bro. I remember now."

Dave was seething with rage. After all that had happened, how could Steve not remember him?

"I must say," said Porkins, "this is all frightfully exciting. Off on an adventure with a famous hero. Even in the Nether we've heard of you, Steve."

Steve grinned.

"Glad to hear it, Porkchops," he said. *Porkchops* was the nickname he'd given Porkins. The pigman didn't seem to mind, but Dave thought it was ridiculously rude.

"Do you even know where we're going?" Carl asked Steve. "We've been walking for two days now. When will this biome end?"

Steve laughed.

"I love this guy," he said to Porkins and Dave. "A friendly creeper! That's hilarious! You know, little dude, I almost killed you when I first saw you—I thought you were coming to blow me up!"

"Yes, I remember," Carl said bitterly. "You almost cut me in two with your sword."

Steve built them a very basic wooden house and some beds, and they all went to sleep. In the morning, Steve put the beds in his backpack, but left the rest of the blocks.

"I've got more wood than I know what to do with," Steve told them. "I'll just build a new house tomorrow night."

Dave imagined all the houses Steve must have left behind him over the years. A trail of abandoned houses in the middle of the wilderness.

They continued their journey. By midday they could see huge blue towers in the distance.

"Is that a city?" Dave asked Steve. He was imagining a city of ice skyscrapers.

"Nah, those are ice spikes," Steve said. "I dunno why they grow like that. Ice is weird."

As they got closer they could see the ice spikes more clearly: massive blue columns reaching up into the sky. Dave had to squint and put his hand up to stop the sunlight reflecting off the ice hurting his eyes.

"Good grief," said Porkins. "What a wonderful sight!"

Finally they reached the ice spikes. It was only when walking underneath them that Dave really got a sense of how huge they were. He reached out and touched the base of one of the spikes. It was cold, of course, and as hard as stone.

"Wow," he said, and he saw his breath appear in front of his eyes as mist.

It was so cold in the ice spikes biome that Dave wished he had some warmer clothes. But at least he had clothes—Porkins and Carl were naked. Carl said the explosives inside his body kept him warm no matter the temperature outside, but Porkins was suffering. He had grown up in the Nether, so wasn't used to this sort of cold.

"I-I-I'll be o-o-ok old chap," Porkins shivered. "A little cold never hurt anyone."

But Dave could see Porkins was just putting on a brave face.

"Steve," he said, "we need to find some warmer clothing, or Porkins is going to freeze."

"A frozen pork chop!" Steve said. But no-one laughed.

"Are there any animal mobs in the snow that drop wool or leather?" Dave asked Steve.

"Rabbit hides," Steve said. "Four rabbit hides make one leather. Then we can use the leather to make your friend some armor. We just have to slay a whole bunch of rabbits."

He did some quick maths in his head.

"Hmm, two leather each for boots, then the tunic needs eight..."

"Steve," said Dave, "what are you—"

Steve held a finger up to silence him.

"Ninety-six rabbits!" Steve exclaimed. "If we slay ninety-six rabbits we should have enough leather to make your friend a full outfit."

"Good lord, that seems a bit much," said Porkins. "I'm a bit chilly, I'll admit, but ninety-six rabbits getting the chop... that's a bit harsh."

"Here comes one now," Carl said. They all turned to see what Carl was looking at. Something white and fluffy was coming towards them out of the mist.

"That's rabbit number one," Carl grinned. "Get your sword out, Porkins. Only ninety-five left after this."

"That's a big rabbit," Porkins said.

"I don't think it's a rabbit," Dave said. He drew his sword.

Finally the creature emerged from the mist—Dave was about to charge it with his sword, but then stopped. It was a polar bear—but only a baby one.

"Aw, what a cute little chap!" Porkins said. He ran forward and rubbed the top of the bear's head. "You're a good chap, aren't you. A very good chap."

"WHAT A CUTE LITTLE CHAP!"

"It would make a nice coat," Carl said.

"Carl!" Porkins said, outraged.

"Maybe we should get out of here," Dave said. "What if its mum and dad are nearby?"

"Don't worry my man," Steve said. "There's four of us here. If anything comes at us we can face it together!"

ROOOOAAARRRR!!!!!

They all looked round and saw a huge white bear charging towards them through the mist. This one was no baby.

"Every man for himself!" Carl yelled, as he ran off in the opposite direction.

CHAPTER TWO
Bear!

"ROOOOAAARRRR!!!!!"

Dave froze like a cow in torchlight. The bear was almost upon him, but he hadn't even drawn his sword.

But Steve had no such problem. He whipped his sword out and charged at the bear head on.

"No!" Dave heard Porkins yell.

Porkins dived forward and tackled Steve to the ground.

"What are you doing, bro?!" Steve yelled.

"You can't kill it!" yelled Porkins. "Not in front of its cub!"

Dave had forgotten about the little bear, but before he had time to think about it he heard Porkins scream. The mother bear was in front of Porkins and Steve, standing up on its back legs and getting ready to attack.

Dave pulled out his diamond sword. He didn't want to slay the bear, but it looked like he had little choice—if the bear wasn't stopped it would eat Steve and Porkins—and almost certainly have him and Carl for dessert.

"Over here, you... bear!" he yelled.

The polar bear, still standing up, turned to look at Dave, its teeth bared. Then it got back on all fours and charged right for him.

ROOOOAAARRR!!!

Dave froze again. He tried to get his sword ready, but his hand was trembling.

This was a terrible idea, he thought to himself. *This was a terrible, terrible idea!*

The bear was almost on him now. Dave brought his sword up to block its attack, but suddenly he felt his hand go numb from nerves, and the sword fell from his fingers. He watched in horror as it plunged into the snow.

It was too late to pick the sword back up. Dave just closed his eyes and braced himself for the bear's attack.

"It's Steve time!"

Dave opened his eyes and saw Steve run in front of him, blocking the bear's path. But Steve, idiot that he was, didn't even have his sword drawn!

Then, moving more quickly than Dave would have thought possible, Steve started to build. He built a wall of wooden blocks to shield Dave and himself from the bear. Dave could hear the bear scratching and pounding on the other side, roaring with frustration.

The bear wasn't stupid though, and Dave soon heard it making its way round the side of the wall—but Steve was too quick for it. He built a wall round the side, then another, then another, completely trapping the mother bear and her cub inside.

"There you go," Steve said proudly to Porkins, "I didn't kill it."

Porkins got back to his feet. Carl, who had run as far away as his tiny creeper legs could carry him, made his way back towards them.

"That was awesome," Carl grinned. Dave was shocked—Carl never normally had a kind word to say about anyone.

"But we can't just leave them in there," Porkins said.

"How come?" Steve asked.

"Because they've got no food, old chap!" said Porkins. "And they need room to run around and be free."

Steve thought for a moment.

"I have an idea!" he said. He started building—replacing two of the wall blocks with an iron door (quickly so that the polar bears couldn't get out) then getting some red powder out of his bag and adding it to some contraptions Dave didn't recognize.

"What's all that stuff?" Carl asked.

"Redstone," said Steve. "I'll create a circuit, leave a trail of redstone, then we can flip a switch and open the door from a safe distance."

Dave had read a little about redstone in his crafting book, but he'd never tried building anything. Steve was using the redstone like he'd done this a million times before. It looked really complicated to Dave, but Steve seemed to have no problem.

"Come on, bros," Steve said, "we need to get a safe distance away."

They followed behind as he led them away from the polar bear enclosure, leaving a trail of redstone across the snow. He led them to a small ledge in the shadow of an ice spike, then he put down a lever. An unbroken trail of red powder led all the way across the snow to the metal door.

"Would you like to do the honors, Pork Chop?" Steve asked Porkins.

"How fun!" said Porkins, taking hold of the lever. "Tally ho!"

Porkins pulled the lever. There was a couple of seconds delay, then the metal door opened. Dave and the others watched as the polar bear and her cub cautiously stuck their noses out of the door, then, seeing that the coast was clear, they began to walk off across the snow.

"Nice one, Steve," Carl whispered.

"Yes, well done old chap!" Porkins added.

"Yeah, well done Steve," said Dave. He tried to smile, but he found it difficult. Dave didn't feel happy for the polar bears or happy they'd all survived. He just felt jealous. Jealous of Steve.

CHAPTER THREE
Finding Shelter

Dave hated feeling this way, but he couldn't help it. Steve was effortlessly heroic, whether fighting off giant zombie pigmen or trapping polar bears, and that made Dave jealous. He had thought that he'd return from his adventure as a great hero, but once again he'd been overshadowed by Steve.

It didn't help that Porkins and Carl spent the rest of the day talking with Steve, listening to his stories as they walked through the snow.

"This one time I fought a skeleton riding a spider!" Steve told them. "I blocked its arrows with my shield—*thuck thuck thuck!*—then ran over and chopped its head off. Both of them!"

"Yeah right," said Dave bitterly. "Skeletons don't ride spiders."

"This one did, little dude," Steve insisted. And he went on telling his story.

Even Carl, who normally just made sarcastic comments and complained, was fawning over Steve—asking him about the mobs he'd slain and the treasure he'd found.

By the time night began to set in, Dave was thoroughly miserable.

"Ok bros," Steve said, "looks like I ought to build us a house for the night."

"Sounds good, old bean," said Porkins, smiling. The pigman was a lot happier now: after the polar bear incident, Steve had rummaged around in his bag and found he did have some leather after all. There was enough of it to make Porkins a tunic, some pants and some boots, so he was much warmer now.

Steve was getting ready to lay the wooden blocks down for the house when Dave spotted something in the distance.

"What's that over there?" he asked the others. "It looks like some sort of building."

Hidden in the mist was a small domed structure. Dave and the others walked forward until finally they could see what it was: a little building made of blocks of snow.

"Hey it's an igloo," Steve said. "I love these little things!"

Dave rolled his eyes. Of course Steve had seen one before— Steve had seen *everything* before.

But he hasn't been to the End, Dave thought to himself. *And he hasn't slain an ender dragon. I can be the one to do those things first!*

Steve led them into the igloo.

"It's a little cozy, but it'll do for a night," Steve said.

There was only one bed in the igloo, but Steve got three more out from his backpack. It was a bit cozy, but at least they all had somewhere to sleep.

As they all lay in bed, trying to get to sleep, Dave had a sudden thought.

"Steve," he said, "how many of my eyes of ender do you have left?"

"Eyes of what-now?" asked Steve.

"Eyes of ender," Dave repeated, trying not to lose his temper. "Ender eyes. Those green eye stone things you stole from me back at the stronghold."

"I'm still drawing a blank, dude."

"They show the way to ender portals!" Dave snapped. "I had some but you stole them all off me and rode away on your horse!"

"Oh those," said Steve. "I sold them for Emeralds. Well, an emerald. A villager in a desert biome gave me one emerald for the whole lot. Pretty sweet deal, huh?"

Dave was furious.

"Do you know how hard they are to make? How difficult the ingredients are to get? I would have given you an emerald to keep them! I would have given you a hundred emeralds!"

"Little bro," Steve said, "you need to learn to bargain."

"So how are you planning on finding another portal?" Dave snapped.

"Yeah, I was wondering that," said Steve. "The past couple of weeks I've just been riding around, hoping to come across some more of those end eye things, but no luck. Could you tell me how to craft them?"

Dave couldn't help but smile. So Steve, who knew so much, didn't know the recipe for eyes of ender. That meant he'd never find another stronghold—Dave would be the first to find another end portal and slay the ender dragon!

"Sorry," Dave told him, "I've forgotten the recipe."

Dave pulled the covers around him tighter, getting nice and snug. He couldn't help but smile: finally he had an advantage over Steve!

And then he heard the banging.

"Can anyone else hear that?" he asked the others.

"All I can hear is you not letting me get to sleep," said Carl.

"I can't hear anything, bro," said Steve.

"That's because you're talking!" snapped Dave. "Just listen!"

Remarkably, the other three shut up for once and did listen.

It was unmistakable now: a very faint noise:

Bang bang bang bang...

"I... I think it's coming from under the floor," said Carl, sounding terrified.

CHAPTER FOUR
Under the Igloo

They all peered over the sides of their beds, looking at the floor.

"Maybe there's a cave under the igloo," Porkins whispered. "A cave full of ruddy zombies!"

The noise was coming from under the plush white rug. Still lying on his bed, Dave reached over and pulled the rug slowly up...

"There's something here," Dave said. He pulled the rug to the side, revealing a wooden trapdoor.

"A secret base!" whispered Porkins. "What fun!"

"Cool!" said Steve. "Let's have a look!"

"Wait!" said Dave. "It could be dangerous!"

But Steve wasn't one for waiting. Before Dave knew it, Steve was through the trapdoor, climbing down a previously-unseen ladder.

Dave, Porkins and Carl jumped out of their beds and dashed over to the trapdoor, watching as Steve made his way down the ladder.

"What fun!" said Porkins, and he started climbing down too.

"After you," Carl said to Dave.

Dave rolled his eyes, but then started climbing down the ladder as well.

"Help!" he heard a voice say from below. It didn't sound like either Porkins or Steve. "Please help me!"

"It's ok bro," Dave heard Steve saying. "The heroes have arrived!"

Dave reached the bottom of the ladder. He was in a small stone room, a chest on one side, a table covered in strange equipment on the other, but that wasn't what caught his attention.

At the far end of the room were two tiny prison cells, sealed off from the rest of the room by metal bars. Inside one cell was a villager. Inside the other cell was a zombie. But not just any zombie—it looked like a cross between a zombie and a villager. A *zombie villager.*

Dave was shocked. He'd heard that villagers could get infected by zombies, but he'd never seen a zombie villager with his own eyes. It looked just like a normal villager, but with green skin and ragged clothes.

"BUUUUURRR!" said the zombie villager.

"Please," said the normal villager. "You have to let me out!"

Steve took out a diamond pickaxe and started hacking away at the bars. Before long the villager was free.

"Thank you!" the villager said. "Thank you, Thank you!" Then: "Hey, I know you—you're Steve, right?"

Steve grinned. "The one and only."

"Wow," said the villager. "It's so awesome to meet you. You're almost as big a hero as Ripley."

And with that, the villager dashed up the ladder, yelling "I'm free, I'm free!"

Steve looked confused. Maybe even a little hurt.

"Who's Ripley?" he wondered.

"BUUUUUUR!" said the zombie villager.

Dave took another look round the room. For the first time he noticed a sign above the two prison cells—two arrows, each facing in opposite directions.

"What do those arrows mean?" he wondered.

Steve took a look at the sign. "I guess it's showing that villagers can turn into zombies."

"That explains the arrow going from the zombie to the villager," Dave said, "but not the arrow going the other way."

"Whatever," said Steve. "Let's see if there's any loot!"

He opened the chest and started rummaging through.

"There's a lot of junk in here," he said, throwing items over his shoulder. "Ah nice, a golden apple!"

He held up the most beautiful apple that Dave had ever seen. Instead of having red skin, the apple had skin that looked like solid gold. Dave could see his own face reflecting back at him.

"I wonder what it tastes like?" Steve said. He opened his mouth, ready to take a bite.

"WAIT!" Dave shouted.

"What's the matter, old chap?" Porkins asked.

Dave went over to the table. On it were a few scraps of paper with scruffy writing and diagrams on them.

"Well, can I eat it or not, bro?" Steve asked.

Dave looked through the papers.

"I think we may be able to turn the zombie back into a villager," Dave said. "It's hard to read this writing, but I think these are instructions. Steve, what ingredients were in that chest? I think we've got to do some brewing."

With Steve's help, Dave brewed a potion. It was his first time using a brewing stand, but, naturally, Steve knew exactly what to do.

"Ok," Dave said, looking at the bottle in his hand, "this is a Splash Potion of Weakness. We have to throw it over the zombie to weaken him, then feed him the golden apple. If these notes are correct, he should turn back to normal."

"Who was doing all these zombie experiments anyway?" Porkins wondered. "You don't think it was Herobrine again?"

"I guess if this works we can ask this guy," Dave said, nodding his head towards the zombie villager. "It's a shame his friend ran off so quickly."

"Do you... do you think this would work on zombie pigmen

too?" Porkins asked, his voice cracking slightly. Dave knew that Porkins wanted more than anything to turn his people—the pigmen—back to normal.

"Maybe," Dave said. He had no idea if it would or not, and he didn't want to get Porkins's hopes up too much.

"There's only one problem," Steve said. He took the apple and tried to push it through the bars. "The apple's too big to fit through."

"Then we'll have to break the bars," Dave said. "Porkins, you throw the potion over the zombie, then Steve, you break the bars with your pickaxe. Then I'll... I'll give the zombie the golden apple."

"You're just going to hand it to him?" Porkins asked nervously. "You really think that'll work, old chap?"

Dave wasn't sure at all. But they had to try. If an innocent villager had been turned into a zombie they had to save him. Or her. It was hard to tell if the zombie was a boy or a girl.

"Ok," said Dave, "everyone ready?"

Everyone was.

"Porkins, throw the potion!"

Porkins thrust his hand forward, splashing the potion through the bars, all over the zombie.

"BUUUUUURRR!!!"

The zombie flailed around for a bit, but then it calmed down again. It looked sleepy, like it could barely keep its eyes open.

"Steve, break the bars!" yelled Dave.

Steve smashed through the bars with his diamond pickaxe. Dave braced himself, ready for the zombie villager to rush out, but it just stayed in its cell, staring at the floor.

"Buuuuur..." the zombie muttered sleepily.

Dave gingerly stepped forward, holding the golden apple out in front of him.

"H-here you go," he said to the zombie. "Would you like a snack?"

The zombie villager lifted its head and looked curiously at the apple.

"Come on," Dave said. "Take it. It's for you."

The zombie slowly lifted its hand.

"That's right," said Dave. "A lovely golden apple!"

Finally the zombie took the apple.

"Buuur?" It said.

"Now eat it," Dave said. "It's lovely!"

The zombie took a bite, it's teeth crunching through the apple's golden skin. From the outside the Apple had looked like solid gold, but it looked like it was as soft and easy to eat as a normal apple.

The zombie villager's face lit up, and it took another bite. Then another, then another, until the apple was all gone."

"Nothing's happening, bro," Steve whispered.

"Buuur?" The zombie said.

Then, suddenly, its body started twisting and contorting,

flailing around and smashing into the walls of the cell.

"What's it doing?" Porkins asked. "Is it trying to dance?"

"No," said Dave, "I think it's transforming."

He was right. The zombie's green skin was fading to pink, and the noises it was making sounded less zombie now and more villager.

"BUUUURRR!!" It groaned. "BUUUURRR! BUUUURRR! BUUUU—ooow, what's happening to me?!"

Finally it collapsed on the ground, breathing heavily.

"Did it work?" Porkins asked.

The villager raised its head—a zombie no more.

"Where am I?" the villager asked. It was a woman, probably just a couple of years younger than Dave's mother. Dave felt a sudden pang in his chest—he hoped that wherever his mom and dad were they were doing ok.

"You were, um, turned into a zombie," Dave told her. "Do you know who did this to you?"

"No idea," the woman said. "The last thing I remember was going for a walk in the snow with my husband and then I was here, in front of you."

"I say, so you don't remember being a zombie at all?" Porkins asked.

"Nope," said the woman.

"There was another villager in the cell next to yours," Dave said, "but he ran off as soon as we freed him, so we couldn't ask him if he knew who did this."

The woman's face darkened.

"The other villager... was he wearing blue robes?"

"Er yes," said Dave.

"That rat!" the woman snarled. "That's my good-for-nothing husband! Are you telling me he just ran off and left me?!"

"Afraid so," said Dave.

"I'll kill him!" said the woman. "I'll make him wish he was never spawned!"

"Wait," said Porkins suddenly, "can you hear something? Up in the igloo?"

They all listened.

"It's Carl," said Dave. "It sounds like he's talking to someone."

They all climbed the ladder. Carl and the villager—the one who'd run away when they freed him—were sitting on one of the beds eating baked potatoes and chatting away.

"Hello!" said the villager happily when he saw Dave, Porkins and Steve come up the ladder. "I was just talking to your little friend here. He's ever so funny!"

Suddenly the villager's face dropped as he saw the woman villager come up the ladder behind the others.

"Oh," said the villager, looking terrified, "hello dear, so good to see you."

"You ran off and left your own wife as a zombie!" the woman villager yelled. "What kind of husband are you!"

"I didn't know it was you dear, I swear!" said the man villager, backing away across the room.

Carl rolled his eyes.

"Why can't we ever meet some nice, normal people?" he asked Dave.

CHAPTER FIVE
Phillip and Liz

So the six of them continued the journey through the snow. The man villager, unfortunately, knew nothing about who'd captured them: just like his wife, the last thing he remembered before waking up in the cell was walking through the snow. As far as he could tell, he and his wife had been down in the igloo's secret basement for around two days when Dave and his friends found them, and no-one else had been down to the cellar in all that time.

"Unless they came down when I was sleeping," the villager said. "I am a deep sleeper."

The man villager was called Phillip and the woman villager was Liz. They lived in a town nearby, and they told Dave and the others they'd get a warm welcome there.

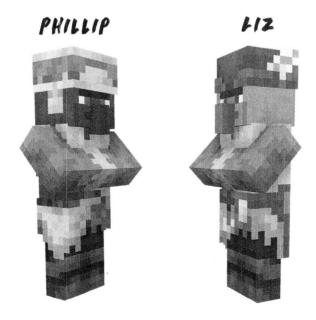

PHILLIP   LIZ

"Of course I recognized you straight away," Liz said to Steve. "The legendary Steve! There's a huge statue in our town of you, made of solid gold! We put it up after you saved us from that creeper attack, all those years ago."

"Of course," said Steve, "how could I forget!"

Although it sounded to Dave like Steve didn't remember at all.

"Although it's not as big as the new statue," Phillip told them, "the one of Ripley."

Liz rolled her eyes.

"My husband is always on about Ripley. Ripley this, Ripley that—it's all he ever speaks about!"

"What is Ripley?" Dave asked.

"You mean you've never heard of Ripley?" said Phillip, sounding amazed.

"Nope," said Dave.

"Why, he's our town's hero!" Phillip said. "He's an even bigger hero than Steve! Uh, no offense."

But Steve did look offended. It made Dave smile, seeing Steve uncomfortable like this. Everywhere Steve went people told him what a great hero he was, and now this villager was saying there was an even *bigger* hero.

"I'd sure like to meet this Ripley," said Steve bitterly. "Then we'll see who the best hero is."

"Ripley is amazing!" Phillip went on, oblivious to Steve's annoyance. "He defeated a horde of skeletons the other week. Then he fought off a spider attack. Then he obliterated a zombie invasion. A lot of bad guys have been trying to have a pop at our village recently, but Ripley beats them every time!"

"Is Ripley a villager?" Dave asked.

"Yep," said Phillip happily. "The greatest villager who ever lived!"

Dave couldn't believe it. *A villager hero!* He had to meet this Ripley.

By late afternoon they could see Phillip and Liz's town in the distance. It was built at the foot of a huge mountain. It looked much bigger than Dave's old village, with tall wooden houses and cobbled streets lit by lamps.

By the time they made it to the town it was night. The town was bathed in a sheen of pale blue moonlight. It was one of the most beautiful sights Dave had ever seen.

"Welcome to Snow Town," Phillip grinned.

"It's absolutely spiffing!" said Porkins, looking on in amazement.

They had almost reached the edge of the town when two villagers on horseback rode out to meet them.

"Who goes there?" one of the riders asked.

"Barry, it's me!" said Phillip.

"Phillip!" said the rider. "We've been looking for you and Liz for days. Where've you been—it's been a week!"

"Has it really been that long?" said Phillip. "Well, it was quite an adventure, I can tell you."

"Yes, yes," said Liz. "It was all such marvelous fun. I got turned into a zombie and abandoned by my husband. What an adventure!"

"I didn't abandon you!" insisted Phillip.

"And who are you?" the rider said, turning to Dave and his friends before he could get caught up in Phillip and Liz's argument. "A creeper!" he yelled, catching sight of Carl. He drew an iron sword. "Stay back!"

"No," said Dave, "he's our friend—I promise."

The guard didn't look convinced.

"A friendly creeper? I've never heard of such a thing."

"Well, you have now," said Carl. "Do you mind putting that sword away?"

The guard reluctantly sheathed his sword.

"My apologies," he said. "These are dark times. Our town has been besieged by monsters of late. If it wasn't for Ripley—"

"Bro," said Steve angrily, stepping forward, "I don't want to hear another word about this Ripley!"

"Steve!" the rider exclaimed. "I'm sorry sir, I didn't see you there. What an honor!"

Steve grinned.

"Always nice to meet a fan."

"Come on Barry," said the second rider, "let's take them in. It looks like a storm's on its way."

He was right, Dave saw. It had started to snow again.

The two riders led Dave and the others into the town. Dave, Porkins and Carl looked round in amazement at the beautiful wooden buildings: huge lodges with sloped roofs and balconies. When they reached a fork in the cobbled street, Phillip and Liz turned to speak to them.

"Well, our house is down here," Phillip said. "I suspect you'll want to stay at the inn, so we'll say our goodbyes for now."

"Thanks again for saving me," Liz said. "You four really are heroes."

"Although not as much as Ripley," Phillip added.

Liz rolled her eyes. The two of them made their way down a cobbled street.

"If I hear you say one more word about Ripley—" Liz said, and then she and Phillip disappeared around a corner.

"Come on," one of the riders said to Dave and the others. "The inn is this way."

They followed the riders down a narrow street, then suddenly they came out into a huge town square, surrounded by important-looking stone buildings. But it wasn't the fancy buildings that caught Dave's eye: it was the statues.

In the middle of the square was a huge gold-block statue of a man holding a sword: it was clearly meant to be Steve. But next to it, almost twice the size, was a statue made of diamond blocks— this one was of a villager, also holding a sword. The size of the villager statue made the smaller Steve statue look like it was of a little kid.

"Dude!" said Steve, sounding outraged. "How come that statue's bigger than mine?"

"That's Ripley," said one of the riders, "our town's hero."

The riders led them to a large inn on the other side of town. It took a lot of convincing by Dave for the inn-keep to let Carl in ("he'll blow my inn to pieces!" she insisted), but eventually they managed to hire a couple of rooms. Dave, Porkins and Carl didn't have many emeralds, so they all had to share a room. The inn-keep gave Steve the best room she had for free—as he'd apparently saved her from zombies when she was a little girl.

"What an adventure this is!" Porkins said, when he, Dave and Carl were finally alone in their room. Dave and Porkins both had beds and Carl, as he was so small, was sleeping in an open drawer.

"I guess," said Dave. His passion for adventure had worn a bit thin over the past few days. He'd liked it when it was just him, Porkins and Carl together, but Steve was ruining things. He was so good at everything that Dave and the others might as well have been spectators.

"Dave, old bean," said Porkins, "do you think that golden apple technique would work on my people? Maybe that's how I can finally turn them all back into normal pigmen."

"Maybe," said Dave. "I tell you what—let's collect as much gold and apples as we can, and when we've got enough, we'll return to the Nether and try it out."

"A spiffing idea!" said Porkins happily. "Very spiffing indeed!"

Soon the pigman and Carl were both fast asleep, leaving Dave to his thoughts.

We need to find some endermen, Dave thought to himself. *If we're going to build more eyes of ender, we need ender pearls.*

With all the distractions of recent days, Dave hadn't thought about his quest to slay the Ender Dragon in a while, but he hadn't given up. Their trip to the Nether had provided them with plenty of blaze rods—even if they'd nearly died getting them—so now all they needed were ender pearls, then they could build eyes of ender and find their way to another fortress.

It all sounds so simple, Dave thought—Although he knew by now that nothing about his adventure was ever simple.

CHAPTER SIX
The Wither

Dave was woken by the sound of explosions. He sat up in bed and saw Porkins and Carl were awake too. Porkins was looking out of the window.

"What's going on?" Dave asked.

"The town is burning!" said Porkins.

Dave jumped out of bed and ran over to the window. He could see the endless wooden rooftops of Snow Town stretching into the distance, and in the middle of them a fire was burning. Every few seconds an explosion would go off, sending blocks of wood flying into the air.

"We have to help," Dave said. "Come on!"

"Do we really?" asked Carl. "This bed is so comfy." But once Dave gave him a stern look he got out of bed and joined them.

Dave opened the door of their room and the first thing he saw was Steve, dressed head to toe in his diamond armor.

"Don't worry little bros," he said. "I'm on my way. Steve to the rescue!"

"Stop showing off and just get moving!" Dave yelled.

So the four of them ran out of the inn and down the cobblestone streets towards the fires. Carl only had little legs, so he rode on Porkins's shoulders.

"I can't believe we're running *towards* the danger," said Carl. "Everyone knows you run *away* from danger—that's the normal thing to do!"

"A creeper afraid of explosions?" said Dave, grinning. "Who would have thought?"

"Hey, we like to explode on our own terms," said Carl.

"Creeper culture is very complex—I wouldn't expect a villager to understand."

They finally reached the fire. A group of buildings had been destroyed; their blocky ruins still burning. In the middle of the destruction were a group of villagers, holding bows and iron swords and looking very nervous.

"Why have they got swords?" Dave wondered. "Are they planning on chopping the fire's head off?"

But then his question was answered, as a huge monster floated out of the ruins of a burning building.

Dave had seen pictures of this type of monster before, but seeing one in the flesh was quite different. Its body was like a long, black spine, oily and slimy looking. It had no arms and legs, but floated through the air without wings. And on the top of its shoulders were three oily black skulls.

A wither

The wither's middle skull—the largest—opened its jaws wide, making a horrible screaming sound, and a ball of fire spat from its jaws. The fireball hit the ground near the villagers, causing a huge explosion but—thankfully—missing them.

Suddenly the wither turned, facing Dave and his friends. It opened its mouth and spat out another fireball—although Dave realized that they weren't fireballs after all, but skulls!

"Take cover!" Dave shouted. He, Porkins, Carl and Steve all dived out of the way as the skull hit the ground and exploded.

"Steve, do something!" said Carl. "Have you fought one of these things before?"

"No," said Steve, "but how hard can it be? I'm Steve!"

Steve ran forward in his diamond armor, clutching his diamond sword. Dave had to admire Steve's bravery, even if his common sense left a lot to be desired.

"Have at thee!" Steve yelled. He swung his sword at the wither, but it rose into the air, dodging his swing.

"Think you can escape me up there?" Steve yelled. He took off his backpack and rummaged around, looking for something. "Uh oh," he said, "I don't suppose anyone has a spare bow? I think I left mine back at the inn."

"Porkins, do you have your bow?" Dave asked.

"Sorry old bean," said Porkins, "I left it back at the room!"

The wither screamed again, spitting out skulls in all directions. Dave dodged an explosion just in time, hiding behind the broken wall of a ruined building.

Then he heard the hooves.

"It's Ripley!" Dave heard someone yell. "We're saved!"

Dave peered over the wall and saw a horseman riding towards the wither. Both horse and rider were clad in diamond armor. The horse reared up and the rider aimed his bow at the wither. The rider's armor and bow were all pulsating with purple light—enchantments.

The rider fired an arrow at the wither. The wither screamed in frustration and fired a barrage of flaming skulls back, but the rider was too quick, pulling at the reigns of his horse and dodging out of the way just in time.

Next the rider jumped off of his horse to the ground, and fired more arrows at the wither, his fingers working the bow so fast that Dave could barely keep track. Arrow after arrow hit the wither, each one making it scream with pain and fury.

The wither, perhaps realizing that ranged attacks weren't working, flew down towards the rider, but the rider was ready—he drew his sword and sliced the wither's heads off: one, two, three. The wither flailed around headless for a few seconds, then it—and its three severed heads—all went *poof* and were gone. All that was left was a shining star-like object. The rider picked it up and pocketed it, then took off his helmet.

It was a villager.

CHAPTER SEVEN
Ripley

"Ripley, you saved us!" one of the villagers yelled happily. Soon the diamond-armored villager—Ripley—was surrounded by a crowd of grateful people.

"Thank you Ripley!" another villager said. "You're the best!"

Ripley smiled. It wasn't an arrogant smile, like the one Steve always wore, but a nice one. A *kind* smile.

"Is everyone alright?" Ripley asked. "Did everyone get out ok?"

It turned out that everyone had. The wither had appeared suddenly in the center of the village, no-one knew where from.

"It could have teleported in from the Nether," one villager suggested.

"Withers don't come from the Nether," said Porkins. "Only wither skeletons."

"Where *do* withers come from?" Dave wondered, but nobody knew—not even Steve.

A jolly, fat villager in crimson robes soon waddled over, bowing down before Ripley.

"You've saved us again!" the fat villager said. "We'll build another statue of you, Ripley—twice the size of the old one!"

Ripley laughed. "There's no need, Mr Mayor, honestly."

The mayor suddenly noticed Steve.

"Well I never!" he said. "Is that... Steve?!"

"The one and only, bro," said Steve, stepping forward. "You know, I would have taken care of that monster myself, but sometimes I like to let others have their chance too. It's only fair."

THE MAYOR

"Two great heroes in our little town!" The mayor said excitedly. "What an honor! We'll have a banquet tonight to celebrate—everyone is invited!"

Everyone cheered.

"Oh," said the mayor, "and, er, someone fix those broken homes please."

That night the mayor was as good as his word—putting on a banquet in the square for the whole town. Long tables had been set out around the two statues, and there was a table of honor at the front, which Dave and his friends somehow found themselves on.

"You must try this, it's delicious," the mayor told Dave,

passing him a bowl of meat. "Only the best food for our honored guests."

Dave was about to take a piece of meat when he caught sight of Porkins, sitting next to him.

"Oh yummy!" said Porkins, taking the bowl. "This looks lovely!"

"Uh, I wouldn't if I were you," said Dave. "It's pork."

"Oh," said Porkins, looking sheepishly at the meat, his face turning a little pale. He quickly passed the bowl on.

Carl had been seated next to Ripley, near the center of the table. Apparently, Dave had overheard someone say, the mayor loved the novelty of a talking creeper so much that he wanted him close enough to talk to.

Carl was on good form, chatting away happily with Ripley and the mayor. One person who didn't look happy, however, was Steve. He'd been placed right at the end of the table, next to a fat boy who looked like he must be the mayor's son—or, at the very least, a nephew.

Then Dave felt a hand on his shoulder. He turned around and, to his surprise, saw Ripley standing behind him.

"Dave, isn't it? Can I have a word?"

Dave nodded, feeling unnaturally nervous.

Ripley led Dave away from the feast, down some narrow streets until they reached a tiny park, with a balcony that overlooked the endless icy plains below. In the distance Dave could just make out the ice spikes he and the others had walked through a few days ago.

"This is a beautiful view," said Dave.

"It is," agreed Ripley. "Dave, I was talking with your friend Carl earlier. He told me about the quest you're on—to kill a dragon."

"Oh," said Dave, feeling slightly embarrassed. He suddenly expected Ripley to tell him how stupid the idea was; that Dave should stick to being a normal villager.

"I think it's a brilliant idea," Ripley said. "So many villagers are content to lead boring, meaningless lives. We need more villagers like you, Dave. Heroes and adventurers."

"Uh thanks," said Dave, surprised. "But I'm no hero. I can barely use a sword."

"There's more to being a hero than fighting," Ripley said. "Your friend Steve needs to remember that."

"Steve's not my friend," Dave told Ripley. "He blew up my village with TNT. No reason—he just thought it would be fun to watch it explode. It was a miracle no-one was hurt."

"That sounds like Steve, alright," Ripley said. "If he's not your friend, how did you end up traveling with him?"

Dave told Ripley about his adventure so far: about Steve stealing his eyes of ender, meeting Porkins and Carl then going to the Nether, before Steve defeated the giant zombie pigman in the snow.

"As much as I dislike Steve, he has saved my life. More than once," Dave said.

Ripley nodded.

"No-one would doubt Steve's fighting prowess, but keep an eye on him," he told Dave. "Steve doesn't care about friends or about treating people with respect. I know he seems harmless, but he sees villagers as animals, not as equals."

Dave thought Ripley was probably right.

"So how did you get into the hero business?" Dave asked Ripley. "And how did you get so good at fighting?"

"It wasn't easy, I can tell you," Ripley grinned. "Villagers aren't natural fighters, as you probably know yourself. It all started about a year ago, when our town was attacked by zombies. Most people wanted to flee, saying there was no way we could defeat them without Steve, but I decided to take a stand. I crafted myself a sword, a bow and some arrows and took the fight to the zombies. It was a close thing, but somehow I defeated them. Ever since then I've been training and honing my skills. Here, let me show you something."

Ripley led Dave back down the path, this time going a

different route and ending up outside a small wooden house.

"This is my home," said Ripley. "It's not much to look at, but wait til you see what I've got in the basement."

They went round to the side of the house, where a trapdoor had been built into the floor. Ripley opened the trapdoor and descended down a ladder. Dave followed. He felt a bit of a fool, following a stranger into their mysterious basement, but there was something trustworthy about Ripley.

Down, down, they went. It was almost pitch dark now, but Dave kept going..

"Nearly there," he heard Ripley say below him.

Suddenly Dave felt his feet touch solid ground.

"Ripley?" he called. It was so dark that he couldn't see a thing.

"Check this out," he heard Ripley say.

There was the *clunk* of a button being pressed and suddenly there was light.

"Wow," said Dave.

CHAPTER EIGHT
The Underground Room

They were inside a huge underground room—much larger than the house above. The walls were lined with iron blocks, and all around the room were levers and contraptions and structures.

In the middle of the room was a wide open space, an arena, with a selection of weapons leaning against a stand.

"What is all this?" Dave asked.

"This is my training room," said Ripley, smiling. "Let me show you."

Ripley went over to the weapons rack and picked up a weapon Dave hadn't seen before: it looked like a giant fork made of diamond. Next Ripley pressed a button, and suddenly four devices around the side of the arena were spitting out eggs of different colors. When the eggs hit the ground they turned into mobs.

Suddenly Ripley was surrounded by creepers and zombies, but he seemed completely unfazed.

He threw the diamond-fork-thing through the air and its three prongs lodged into a zombie's forehead. The zombie disappeared with a *Burrr!* and the fork-thing whizzed through the air, back into Ripley's hand. He threw the fork again, this time at a creeper, then grabbed a sword. Another creeper slid up to him and started hissing, but Ripley was too quick—slicing it to pieces with his sword before it could explode.

Ripley moved faster than Dave would have thought possible, hacking and slashing as more and more mobs tried to attack him. Finally all the mobs were dead, and Ripley stood victorious in the middle of piles of gunpowder and zombie flesh.

"Wow," said Dave, "that was incredible."

"That's only easy mode," Ripley grinned. He pressed another button and suddenly the blocks at the center of the arena slid away, revealing a pool of lava below. "A bit of lava always makes training sessions interesting," he grinned. "This whole town is built above a lava lake."

"Did you build all this yourself?" Dave asked.

Ripley nodded. "All my own designs. A year ago I'd never even heard of redstone, but I read every book about it I could find. It's amazing what you can build. I knew that if I was going to be a hero I couldn't be content with just learning to fight—I had to learn to craft as well. Potion brewing, enchanting, knowing how to craft armor and weapons—I taught myself everything."

Dave was impressed.

"This is what I'm most proud of though," Ripley said. He pressed a button and a panel slid open, revealing a villager who looked just like Ripley. "Meet Robo-Ripley," he said.

"Wait," said Dave, "you're telling me that's a robot? It looks so real!"

"Yep," said Ripley proudly, "it's a robot powered by redstone. He makes an excellent sparring partner. Watch."

Ripley took a sword from the rack and threw it to Robo-Ripley, who caught it without even looking.

"Engage battle mode," said Ripley.

Robo-Ripley raised its sword and put its legs shoulder width apart, taking a fighting stance.

"*Battle mode initiated*," said Robo-Ripley. "*Kill mode off.*"

"Kill mode?" asked Dave nervously.

"I thought it might make things interesting if it was actually trying to kill me," said Ripley. He grinned. "But so far I've never been brave enough to leave kill mode on."

Ripley ran forward and sliced at the robot with his sword. Robo-Ripley dodged and parried Ripley's blow with its own sword. The two of them fought an epic battle, sword clashing against sword, until finally Ripley hit the robot's sword so hard that it flew out of its hand.

Ripley raised his sword, holding the sharp point up to the robot's neck.

"I win," said Ripley.

"*Surrender mode activated,*" said the robot.

"So what now?" Dave asked. "Are you going to stay in Snow Town?"

"Not forever," Ripley said, putting his sword back on the rack. He pressed a button on Robo-Ripley's back and it returned to its cupboard, the wall closing shut behind it.

"Hopefully I've taught some people in town that villagers can be heroes too," said Ripley, "that's all I ever wanted: to inspire the next generation of villagers to be more adventurous than our parents were; to show them that they don't have to rely on Steve to save them. That statue the mayor built of me in the town center is a bit embarrassing, but it'll be worth it if it inspires a few baby villagers to grow up to be heroes. Now I want to go to new places—

to teach villagers across the world what it means to be a hero."

Dave was inspired.

"Maybe you could come with us?" Dave said. "Imagine: two villagers defeating the ender dragon before Steve! How great would that be!"

"I was hoping you'd ask that," Ripley said. "I'd be honored. As soon as I heard about your quest, I knew I had to join. Thank you, Dave."

Dave suddenly has a thought.

"Your mob spawner things," he said, "I don't suppose you can spawn endermen?"

It had suddenly struck him how much easier it would be to get ender eyes if they could just spawn and kill endermen in this room.

"Afraid not," said Ripley. "I don't have any endermen spawn eggs. How come?"

"Oh, no reason," said Dave.

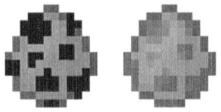

Dave would have stayed the whole night in Ripley's training room if he could, but Ripley said they both ought to get some sleep—it was late after all.

By the time Dave got back to the inn, Carl and Porkins were already asleep. Dave climbed into his bed, his mind racing with exciting thoughts. He'd finally met another villager who thought like him: another villager who thought the world didn't have to revolve around Steve. And, best of all, Ripley had agreed to join them on their adventure!

When he finally got to sleep, Dave had a big smile on his face.

CHAPTER NINE
Zombie Attack!

At the mayor's request, Dave, Steve, Porkins and Carl agreed to stay in town a few more days.

"It's so nice to have guests," the mayor told them. "Especially adventurers!"

Dave got the impression that the mayor liked to keep popular people around him, like Steve and Ripley, to help his own popularity.

Dave spent most of the time in Ripley's basement, training. When Ripley had free time he'd teach Dave to sword fight, using Robo-Ripley as a sparring partner. Dave would spar with the robot as Ripley yelled advice at him.

"Keep your shoulders square!" Ripley would say. "Keep your guard up!"

For Dave it was also nice to be able to relax and not be on the road for a few days. He, Porkins and Carl were given all the best food and were treated to massages, hot baths and whatever else they desired.

"This is the life," said Carl, eating a baked potato as he, Dave and Porkins sat on a balcony overlooking the town. "Maybe we should just stay here and be treated like kings for the rest of our lives!"

"They're only treating us so well because we're friends with Steve," Dave said. Down below he could see the huge statues of Steve and Ripley in the town square.

Maybe one day people will build a statue of me, Dave thought. *When I've killed the ender dragon.*

Suddenly there were screams from below.

"Help!" Dave could hear people yelling. "Someone help!"

"Not again," Carl groaned. "Why are you villagers always in trouble?"

"Come on," Dave said. "Grab your swords—we have to help."

"Why?" Carl asked. "There are already two heroes in town—Ripley and Steve. Why do they need us?"

"He's got a point, old bean," said Porkins. "What can we do? Surely we'd just be in the way."

"Look," snapped Dave angrily, "we're meant to be heroes!"

"I thought we were adventurers?" said Carl.

"It's the same thing!" said Dave.

Carl and Porkins were both looking at him with shocked expressions.

"I'm sorry," Dave said, trying to calm himself down. "I just want to help."

"Ok," said Carl, "let's go then, I guess. Porkins—you can carry me."

The three of them made their way towards the source of the commotion, running along down the narrow cobblestone streets.

"What's going on?" Dave asked a villager fleeing in the opposite direction.

"Zombies!" yelled the villager. "Zombies in the town!"

And he ran off.

Dave, Porkins and Carl kept going until they reached the big town square, where villagers were running from a horde of zombies.

"Look," said Porkins, "they're not normal zombies—they're zombie villagers!"

Porkins was right, Dave saw. The zombies chasing the villagers were zombie villagers—and every villager they caught turned into another zombie villager.

"Come on," Carl said, "get your swords out, let's get this over with."

"We can't kill them," Dave said, "they're villagers!"

Dave had no idea what to do. As far as he knew, the only thing that could cure zombie villagers was using the potion of weakness on them and then feeding them a golden apple, but he had neither of those things.

Suddenly Dave saw the mayor running across the square, his fat belly wobbling. Chasing him was a fat zombie villager Dave recognized as being the mayor's son.

"Heeeelp!" The mayor yelled. "My son is trying to eat me!"

"Wow," said Carl. "It sure is tough being a parent."

"MY SON IS TRYING TO EAT ME!"

Suddenly a figure clad in diamond armor jumped down from the rooftops.

"I'll save you, Mr Mayor!" said the figure, raising its sword. It was Steve.

He ran towards the mayor's son, screaming a battle cry.

"IT'S STEVE TIME!!!!"

"No!" Dave yelled. "It's not a normal zombie!"

But Steve didn't hear him, he was too busy getting ready to swing his sword.

"Steve no!" said the mayor, looking on in horror. "That's my son!"

Suddenly Ripley ran forward, blocking Steve's diamond sword with his own. He was also clad in diamond armor.

"What are you doing, bro?" Steve said angrily. "I'm trying to stop the zombies!"

"Those are innocent people, you idiot!" said Ripley. "Zombie villagers!"

Steve's face fell.

"I... I didn't know, bro!"

"Idiot," snarled Ripley.

Ripley pulled out a bottle of blue potion and drank it. Suddenly he started moving at super speed, quickly building a structure in the middle of the town square.

That must have been some sort of speed potion, Dave thought.

Ripley finished building his contraption: it was a small rectangular structure made of dispensers. He flipped a switch on the side and all the dispensers started firing out hundreds of potion bottles.

"Take cover!" Ripley yelled to Dave and the others.

They quickly hid behind a bench, peering over to watch as the potion bottles from the machine flew through the air and smashed against the zombies, covering them with liquid.

"What is that potion?" The mayor asked.

"Splash potion of weakness," said Dave. "Look, the zombies are calming down!"

The zombies were no longer running around: instead they were slowly lurching from side to side, as if they might fall asleep at any moment.

"Right, phase two!" yelled Ripley. He flipped another switch, and the machine stopped firing out potions—and fired out golden apples instead.

"Wow!" said Dave.

The apples landed near the zombies or hit into them. When the zombies saw the apples they looked at them curiously, then picked them up and took a bite.

The golden apples were irresistible to zombies, it seemed, and soon all the zombies were munching down apple after apple.

"They're changing!" said the mayor excitedly. "They're changing back to normal!"

He was right—the green in the zombies' skin was beginning to fade, as they transformed back to normal villagers. They all seemed to be unharmed—if very confused.

"Where am I?" one of the zombies asked. Dave noticed it was Phillip, the villager they'd saved in the igloo. Phillip looked over and spotted Ripley and his machine. "Ripley! Ripley saved us!"

Soon everyone was rushing over to Ripley, hugging him and congratulating him.

"That dude is such a show off," said Steve to Dave, rolling his eyes. "Bro, I was killing bad guys when he was still in diapers!"

And with that, Steve slumped off.

"What's wrong with him?" Porkins asked.

"I think he's jealous," Dave said, unable to hide the happy grin on his face. "Jealous that, for once, he's not the biggest hero in town."

That night there was a big feast in Ripley's honor. Steve didn't even turn up this time. Dave went back to the inn to try and get Steve to come and join them, but Steve wasn't in his room.

"I think he's sulking somewhere," Dave told Porkins and Carl when he returned to the feast.

There was no sign of Steve all that night, but Dave was having too much fun to care. After a night of eating and celebrating, he went to bed with a full stomach and a smile on his face.

In his dreams that night he imagined a feast in his own honor: everyone chanting *Dave! Dave! Dave!* and telling him what a hero he was. His parents were there, and they were so proud of him.

"Dave!" he heard a voice say. "Dave wake up!"

He woke. Porkins was standing over him.

"There's something going on again, old chap," said Porkins nervously. "I heard yelling outside."

Suddenly the landlady burst through the door.

"Come quick!" she said. "Your friend Steve—he's threatening to blow up the town!"

CHAPTER TEN
Steve Turns to the Dark Side

Dave, Carl and Porkins ran as fast as they could towards the town center. When they got there, Steve was standing on the top of his golden statue, surrounded by a huge crowd of villagers.

"You bros had your chance to worship me as you should!" Steve was yelling. "But you chose to worship that idiot Ripley instead, and now you will all pay! I've filled the caves under your town with TNT, and I'm going to destroy it and build an even BIGGER statue of me in its place!"

The villagers started screaming and running. In typical villager-style, they were running around in circles and bumping into things and not doing a very good job of escaping.

"Steve!" Dave yelled. "This isn't you! I know you're angry, but this isn't the way!"

But Steve ignored him. He jumped off of the statue and quickly ran across the square, disappearing down a side street.

"We've got to stop him," Dave said to Porkins and Carl.

"But he's Steve," said Carl, "he's our friend. And besides, he'd whup our butts."

"I don't want a whupped butt," said Porkins. "That doesn't sound very nice."

"EVERYONE LISTEN!"

It was Ripley, standing on a rooftop.

"We need to evacuate the town, before it blows up! This way, to the north gate!"

The villagers stopped running around like idiots and began to head off in the direction Ripley was telling them to go. There were so many that there was a huge queue, everyone pushing and shoving to escape.

"Come on," said Carl, "let's get out of here."

"No," said Dave, "I have to stop Steve. He may be an idiot, but this isn't like him—blowing up an entire town."

"Um, didn't he blow up your entire village?" asked Carl.

"Well, yes," said Dave, "but that was out of stupidity—not malice. It's not like Steve to get angry, and I think if he does this he might never forgive himself."

"Dave!" Ripley yelled down at them from the rooftop. "You three have to get out of here!"

"I can't," Dave shouted back. "I'm sorry Ripley, I have to stop Steve."

Dave ran out of the square, with no real idea of where he was going.

Where could Steve be? he wondered.

Then he remembered what Steve had said—about filling the caves under the town with TNT—and he knew where he had to go. He ran to Ripley's house, opened the door, and slid down the ladder.

When he reached Ripley's basement, the hole in the floor was already open, and Dave could see the lava pool below. He peered over the edge and saw the lava was actually quite far below, in the middle of a huge cave. He also saw something that chilled his bones: the walls of the cave were all lined with hundreds of blocks of TNT—thankfully just out of reach of the lava.

"Steve!" Dave called down into the cave. "Steve, where are you?"

"Over here, little bro!"

It was Steve, but his voice wasn't coming from the cave, it was coming from the room Dave was in—Ripley's basement.

Dave looked up and saw Steve at the side of the room, trapped in a cage made of iron bars.

"Help me, bro!" Steve yelled.

Dave was confused.

"Steve, what's going on? Five minutes ago you were

threatening to blow up the town."

"Bro that wasn't me," said Steve.

"No it wasn't," said a voice from behind Dave. "For once, Steve is innocent."

Dave turned round.

It was Ripley.

CHAPTER ELEVEN
Ripley's Plan

Ripley was standing at the foot of the ladder. On his left side was a villager who looked exactly like him (*Robo-Ripley*, Dave realized) and on his right was an identical copy of Steve.

"You've already met Robo-Ripley," said Ripley, "so meet Robo-Steve."

"It was you!" Dave gasped. "Your robot was the one who threatened to blow up the town, not Steve!"

Ripley smiled.

"I should thank you, Dave," he said. "You gave me the idea when you told me about Steve blowing up your village. I could use my robot to frame Steve, and ruin his name forever. I'd already made my name as a hero by releasing monsters into the town for me to defeat, but my victory won't be complete until villagers across the world all hate the name *Steve*."

"All those monsters…. that was you?" said Dave.

"Of course," said Ripley. "I summoned the wither, I created the zombie outbreak, and plenty more before that. I planned it carefully, of course, so no-one ever got hurt."

"I bet you were the one running zombie experiments in that igloo as well," said Dave.

"Guilty," said Ripley. "I needed to make sure the cure worked before unleashing zombies on the town."

"That's not cool, bro," said Steve. "Not cool at all."

"Why?" said Dave to Ripley. "Why are you doing this?"

"Dave, I thought you of all people would understand," said Ripley sadly. "For too long our people have been held back by our love for Steve. After Snow Town is destroyed, villagers around the world will realize they were wrong about Steve. He's not a hero, he's a villain."

"No he's not!" snapped Dave. "He may be an idiot, he may do stupid things, but when it comes to the crunch he does the right thing. Well, most of the time."

"I'm disappointed," said Ripley. "I like you Dave. I would have come with you on your quest to kill the ender dragon. We could have both gone down in history as villager heroes, but now I'm going to have to kill you. I can't have my secret getting out."

He turned to the robots.

"Kill mode activated," he told them. "And Robo-Steve, once all the villagers have evacuated I want you to activate the TNT and blow up the town. Is that clear?"

"Blow up the town once the villagers are clear," said Robo-Steve, his voice sounding exactly like Steve's. "Affirmative, bro."

"I programmed him to say *bro* a lot," Ripley grinned. "I thought it was the best way to make him sound like the real Steve."

Ripley began to climb back up the ladder as the robots drew their swords.

"I'm sorry Dave," Ripley called from the ladder. "I wish things could have worked out differently."

"I wish your face could have worked out differently!" Dave shouted back.

Ripley shook his head. "Maybe you're more like Steve than I realized. Goodbye Dave."

Dave drew his sword. Both robots—Robo-Steve and Robo-Ripley—we're closing in on him. There was no way he could take them both on.

I'm a hero, he thought, *I can do this!*

No you can't, said another voice in his head. *Even a hero needs friends.*

He knew what he had to do.

Dave turned and ran in the opposite direction. He could hear the robots start to chase him as he pulled out a diamond pickaxe and rushed towards Steve's cage. He raised the pickaxe and swung it at the bars, cutting through them as fast as he could.

"Come on little bro!" Steve yelled. "You can do it!"

Dave looked behind and saw the robots were nearly on him. He swung a final pickaxe blow and suddenly the bars shattered.

"Give me your sword!" said Steve.

Dave threw his sword to Steve. Steve jumped through the broken bars, swinging the sword just in time to block a sword thrust from Robo-Ripley.

As Steve fought off the two robots, Dave ran to the weapons rack to grab another sword. This one was only iron, but it was the only one he could find. He quickly spun around just in time to block a blow from Robo-Steve.

"I've seen you fight, bro," said Robo-Steve. "Fighting me is pointless—your skill level isn't high enough."

"Good job I'm not fighting alone then," said Dave.

Robo-Steve turned round just in time to see Steve swing his sword down, burying the blade in the robot's head.

ROBO-STEVE

"*ERROR!*" the robot said, his voice sounding robotic now. "*CRITICAL ERROR!*"

Robo-Steve collapsed to the floor. The other robot, Robo-Ripley, came running at them, but Steve quickly swung round and kicked it in the chest. The robot staggered backwards, tottering on the edge of the pit that opened up above the lava lake.

"*Extreme danger detected!*" said Robo Ripley—then it fell backwards, down through the cave and into the lava.

"Nice one Steve," said Dave.

"I couldn't have done it without you freeing me from the cage, bro," said Steve. "So I guess you deserve some credit too."

"Come on," Dave said. "Once Ripley realizes his robots are out of action he'll set the explosives off himself. We have to stop him."

The two of them ran towards the ladder, climbing up it as fast as they could.

When they reached the town square, a few villagers were still trying to push their way out down the narrow streets.

"Come on!" Ripley was yelling at them. "You have to evacuate!"

Then Ripley spotted Dave and Steve and the color drained from his face.

"Traitors!" Ripley yelled. "Look everyone, it's the traitor Steve, and he's working with Dave!"

Before Dave could protest, something flew through the air and landed in the middle of the square.

"Oh no," said Dave, "it's still alive!"

It was Robo-Steve. It had a huge cut in the middle of its face from where Steve had hit it with his sword, but it was very much alive.

"*Error overridden,*" said Robo-Steve. "*Mission resumed. Blow up town.*"

The villagers had stopped evacuating to stare at what was going on.

"That's a robot Steve!" one of them said. "Cool!"

"Get out of here!" Ripley snapped at the villagers. "Now!"

The villagers all started to push and shove again, trying desperately to escape the square and the town.

"*Searching memory banks for location of TNT switch,*" said Robo-Steve. "*Must blow up the town.*"

"No!" said Ripley. "You're meant to blow up the town after everyone has evacuated!"

"*Blow up town,*" repeated Robo-Steve.

"Robo-Steve, deactivate!" yelled Ripley.

"*Error, deactivation program corrupted. Cannot deactivate. Blow up the town! Blow up the town!*"

Robo-Steve looked up at the rooftops, suddenly spotting the thing he was looking for.

"*TNT switch location found.*"

Dave followed the robot's gaze and saw that, yes, a switch had been stuck to the roof of one of the buildings.

Ripley must have created a redstone trail from that switch to the TNT, Dave thought.

"No!" Ripley yelled, but the robot ignored him. It did a superhuman jump into the air, landing on the roof next to the switch.

"*Blow up the town,*" the robot repeated, grabbing hold of the switch.

"Blow this up, you rascal!"

It was Porkins. He and Carl had come running back into the town square. Porkins was aiming his bow at Robo-Steve. He fired and the arrow struck true, hitting the robot in the back.

"*ERROR!*" screamed the robot, "*ERROR!*"

It let go of the switch and stumbled backwards, falling off the roof. It landing with a *thud* on the cobblestone ground.

"Well," said Carl, "I'm glad that's all over."

But he'd spoken too soon. Robo-Steve staggered to its feet. Half of its fake skin had torn off, allowing them to see the metal body underneath. One of its robotic eyes had been revealed, and it glowed red.

Blow up town," the robot said. "*Blow up town!*"

"BLOW UP TOWN!"

"You idiot robot," said Ripley. "Not until everyone is evacuated!"

Ripley charged at the robot with a diamond sword, but Robo-Steve was too quick for him. It drew its own diamond sword and stabbed Ripley through the chest.

"Ripley!" yelled Dave.

Ripley fell to the floor.

The robot turned to face Dave. Steve, Carl and Porkins all stepped forward, their swords raised.

"Looks like you're outnumbered, bro," said Steve.

"*Probability of success thirty-three-per-cent,*" said Robo-Steve. "*More power needed. Accessing emergency building supplies.*"

Robo-Steve's chest opened and inside Dave could see a collection of tiny blocks and tools. Robo-Steve pulled out a diamond pickaxe. It ran towards the gold Steve statue in the middle of the square and dug its way through the gold blocks, disappearing into the statue's leg.

"What's it doing?" said Dave. "Hiding in the statue?"

"Oh no," said Ripley.

Dave had forgotten about Ripley: he was on the floor, clutching the wound on his chest. Dave ran over to him.

"It's ok," Dave said, "we'll get you some healing potion."

"No," said Ripley. "We have to stop the robot! It must be using the redstone supplies I gave it."

"Using the redstone for what?" asked Dave.

Suddenly there was a tremendous noise of scraping metal and breaking cobblestone. Dave looked around and saw one of the most terrifying sights he'd ever seen in his life.

The giant golden Steve statue had come to life...

CHAPTER TWELVE
Statue Fight

"Oh my!" said Porkins. "This doesn't look good, chaps!"

"It's Robo-Steve," said Ripley, "he's controlling the statue from the inside using redstone."

The huge gold statue stumbled towards them, each footstep shaking the ground. It was getting used to walking, each step taking a long time.

"Do you have any redstone?" Ripley asked Dave.

Dave shook his head.

"I've got some bro," said Steve.

Ripley gave Steve a look of pure hatred.

"Fine!" he snapped. "Give me everything redstone-related you have—including any switches, buttons and repeaters. Quickly!"

Steve took off his bag and quickly handed all his redstone to Ripley.

"Now get me inside the other statue!" roared Ripley.

"Are you sure about this?" said Dave. "You're hurt, you need help."

"This is all my fault," said Ripley. "I was so focused on my hatred for Steve that I put the whole town in danger. I need to put a stop to this."

Dave took out his pickaxe and started hacking away at a diamond block at the foot of the giant diamond Ripley statue.

"Hurry!" said Ripley. "We're running out of time!"

He was right. The gold Steve statue was getting used to walking now, taking more confident steps. It was nearly upon them.

"Come on guys," Steve said. "I may be the greatest warrior

who ever lived, but even I might have trouble fighting a statue!"

The diamond block broke and Ripley crawled inside the diamond villager statue.

"Get everyone out of the town!" Ripley yelled to Dave. "I'll hold Robo-Steve off as long as I can."

"Good luck, Ripley," Dave said.

"Go!" Ripley roared.

"Come on," Dave said to the others, "time to go!"

Dave and his friends ran out of the square and down a side street. Up ahead they saw some villagers, still pushing and shoving each other to get out of the town.

"Haven't villagers ever heard of queuing?" Porkins said. "No wonder it's taking them so long to evacuate—they keep pushing each other!"

"Maybe they just need to push a bit harder then," said Dave. "Carl, do you mind?"

Dave picked up Carl.

"Hey!" said Carl angrily. "What are you playing at?"

Dave ran forward, holding Carl out in front of him.

"Help!" Dave yelled. "This creeper is going to explode!"

The villagers started screaming and pushing to get away.

"A creeper!"

"Let me through! Let me through!"

Before long all the villagers had pushed their way out of the town. Dave and his friends followed them.

The villagers had gathered a short way up the mountain, on a cliff overlooking the town. They were all staring intently at something going on in the town, and Dave knew exactly what it must be.

Dave pushed through the crowd and peered over the edge of the cliff. Below, in the town square, the two giant statues were fighting: the gold Steve statue, controlled by Robo-Steve, and the diamond villager statue, controlled by Ripley. The huge statues were slashing at each other with their swords, each mighty blow shaking the mountain.

The statues had already left a trail of broken buildings in their wake, and Dave knew it wouldn't be long before they disturbed the TNT underneath the town.

"Everyone keep moving!" Dave yelled. "We have to get as far from the town as possible!"

But before he could get the villagers to move any further, there was a mighty explosion: *DOOM BOOM BOOM BOOM DOOOOM!!!!*

Blocks flew threw the air and Dave had to clutch his ears to block out the sound.

When the explosion finally stopped, Snow Town was gone. All that was left were a few half-destroyed buildings and a crater with a lake of lava at the bottom.

At least we got the villagers out, Dave thought. *Apart from poor Ripley.*

"My town!" said the mayor, falling to his knees. "My beautiful town!"

Most of the villagers were in tears now: the only home they had ever known was completely destroyed. Dave knew how they felt.

"I know this is bad, but you can build a new town," Dave told them. "A better town than before."

The mayor pointed at Steve.

"You!" he said. "You did this!"

"It wasn't Steve," said one of the villagers sadly. "It was Ripley. He had a Steve robot, I saw." It was Phillip, Dave realized: the villager they'd rescued from the igloo. The one who'd been such a big Ripley fan.

His wife Liz went up to him, but instead of having a go at him she put her arms around his waist.

"At least everyone's safe," Porkins said to Dave. "You did a ruddy good job, old bean."

"Yeah, I guess you're more of a hero than I thought," added Carl. "You're an idiot, but also a bit of a hero."

"Thanks," smiled Dave. Coming from Carl, that was a

compliment.

Steve came over to Dave as well.

"Well done bro," he said. "You did well back there—that was quick thinking using the little creeper dude. Maybe one day you'll be as big a hero as me!"

"Thanks," smiled Dave.

Suddenly something fell from the sky, landing with a *thud* between Steve and Dave. The creature raised its metal head, its eyes glowing red.

It was Robo-Steve.

CHAPTER THIRTEEN
Robo-Steve's Last Stand

All the fake Steve skin and clothes had peeled off, and now Robo-Steve was nothing but metal. Somehow it still had its diamond sword.

"*Destroy town,*" it said, looking at the terrified villagers. "*Destroy! Destroy! Destroy!*"

"Not on our watch," said Steve. "Come on Dave, let's show this rust bucket who's boss.

Dave and Steve raised their swords.

"Let's do this, bro," said Dave, smiling.

"Hey!" said Steve, with a grin. "That's my word!"

The robot ran at them, swinging its sword wildly. Dave blocked the first blow, the diamond of the robot's sword clanging against the iron of his.

Steve swung his sword at the robot's back, but it was too quick, jumping out of the way so quickly that Steve's blow nearly cut Dave in half.

The robot swung his sword upwards but Steve quickly blocked the hit, his diamond sword clashing with the robot's.

"*Destroy!*" the robot hissed. "*Destroy destroy DESTROY!!*"

"Come on Dave and Steve!" Dave heard Carl yell. "Kick that robot's butt!"

Dave looked round. Porkins, Carl, the mayor and the whole town were watching the fight, the villagers all cheering them on. He'd been so engrossed in the fight that he hadn't noticed.

"A little help here, bro!" Steve yelled.

Steve was fighting off a furious flurry of sword blows from Robo-Steve, the robot's hand moving so fast that it was hard to see.

Dave ran forward and swung his sword at the robot's back, but it was too quick, and brought its own sword round to block the blow.

"*You two are no match for my superior skill,*" the robot hissed.

Suddenly an arrow pierced the robot's right eye. The robot stumbled backwards, strange metallic noises coming from its mouth.

Dave turned round. Porkins was holding his bow, getting another arrow ready.

"You may be strong, old chap," said Porkins to the robot, "but we fight as a team."

Robo-Steve pulled the arrow from its eye and ran towards Porkins with its sword, ready to strike him down, but suddenly it tripped—over something small and green on the floor.

"Sorry buddy," Carl said, as the robot clattered across the ground, "I didn't see you there."

"*DESTROY!!!*" Robo-Steve screamed jumping to its feet. It tried to swing its sword at Carl, but Porkins fired another arrow at its head, striking its other eye.

The robot staggered backwards.

"*ERROR! FATAL ERROR! ACTIVATING EMERGENCY TELEPORT!*"

The robot's body started to hum, then there was a flash of purple and it disappeared.

"Is it gone?" Porkins asked.

The villagers all cheered, running forward and lifting Dave and his friends into the air.

"Well they certainly think it is," said Carl. "And if it comes back, we'll whup its butt again."

CHAPTER FOURTEEN
Goodbye Again

Steve built a big house for the villagers with his remaining materials. It was a bit cramped—with all the beds packed tightly together over three floors, but it would do until the villagers rebuilt their town.

"Thank you, you four, for all you've done for us," the mayor said, as he and the other villagers went to see Dave, Steve, Porkins and Carl off. The four of them had all been given new horses.

"I still can't believe Ripley tricked us," the mayor said angrily. "He made fools of us all."

"He changed his ways at the end though," said Dave. He didn't know why he felt the need to defend Ripley, after Ripley had nearly killed them all, but he did.

So Dave and the others said their goodbyes, then rode off, leaving the people of Snow Town behind.

They rode on until night, when they finally reached the end of the snow biome. Dave was overjoyed to finally see grass again.

Dave built them a small house to shelter in with some nether brick he had left over. They all went to sleep pretty quickly, but halfway through the night Dave was woken up by someone moving around.

"Who's there?" he called into the darkness.

"It's just me, little bro," Steve whispered.

Steve and Dave went outside. Steve had his backpack on.

"So you're leaving?" Dave asked.

"Yeah bro," said Steve. "This has been fun, but I'm more of a lone traveler. Besides, I've still gotta beat you to that dragon!"

Dave grinned.

"The race is on," he said. Then, reluctantly, he added: "Steve, do you want me to tell you how to make eyes of ender?" You won't get very far in finding an ender portal without them.

"Nah," said Steve, "I'll work it out. Or I'll randomly stumble into one. You know me."

"You probably will," said Dave with a smile.

"Right," said Steve. "I, uh, guess this is it, bro."

The two of them had an awkward hug, then Steve climbed up on his horse.

"Keep it Stevey," said Steve, giving Dave a salute.

"Good luck," Dave said.

Steve grinned. "Bro, when you're as good as me, you don't need luck."

With that, Steve pulled on the horse's reigns and galloped away. Dave watched him go, until he disappeared behind some trees.

"Where's Steve?" asked Carl, sticking his head out of the house.

"He's gone," said Dave. "You know how heroes are. They love working alone."

"Fair enough," said Carl. "So what now?"

"Now, Dave said, a smile on his face, "we go endermen hunting."

"I wish I hadn't asked," said Carl.

CHAPTER FIFTEEN
Return to the Nether

Porkins crept towards the zombie pigman, as Dave and Carl watched from behind a block.

Dave never thought he'd be back in the Nether so soon, but here he was. After their adventure in the snow, Porkins was understandably anxious to find out if golden apples could cure zombie pigmen the same way they cured zombies.

The zombie pigman looked at Porkins curiously. The two of them were both pigmen, but the zombie pigmen had been corrupted, turned into mindless beasts by the mysterious Herobrine. As far as Porkins knew, he was the last pigman who *hadn't* been turned into a zombie.

Porkins slowly pulled out a bottle from his backpack, taking his time so he didn't frighten the zombie. Zombie pigmen were normally fairly calm—unless they thought they were under attack.

"This is the tricky part," Dave whispered to Carl. "He's got to splash the zombie with the potion, but if it thinks it's being attacked it'll attack back—and all its friends will join in too."

"Thanks for the running commentary," said Carl, rolling his eyes. Before he met Carl, Dave wouldn't have thought it was *possible* for a Creeper to roll its eyes, but somehow Carl did it all the time.

Porkins edged forward. He was barely a block away from the zombie pigman now. He uncorked the potion... then jerked the bottle forward, covering the zombie pigman in liquid.

"SQUEEE!!!"

The zombie pigman flapped its arms and squinted its eyes. All the other zombie pigman turned to watch, and for a second it looked like they all might attack, but then the potion-covered pigman relaxed again.

"The potion is weakening him, calming him down," Dave whispered.

"Enough with the commentary!" said Carl.

Porkins reached into his backpack and pulled out a golden apple, then held it out in front of him, offering it to the zombie pigman.

"Here you go, old chap," said Porkins. "A delicious apple, all for you!"

The zombie pigman looked at the apple suspiciously. For a second it looked as if it was going to turn and walk away, but then it snatched the apple out of Porkins's trotter and started stuffing it into its mouth.

In a few big bites, the apple was gone. The zombie pigman burped loudly.

"Charming," said Carl.

Porkins walked over to Dave and Carl, joining them behind their rock.

"And now we wait!" he said excitedly. And wait they did. They waited and waited and waited, but the zombie pigman just kept shuffling around like a zombie.

Eventually Porkins went back over to it.

"Can... you... understand... what... I'm... saying... old... chap?" Porkins asked. The zombie pigman looked at him blankly.

They tried the process with five more zombie pigmen— spraying them with Splash Potion of Weakness and then feeding them a golden apple—but each time it seemed to make no difference.

"Blast it all," said Porkins sadly. "I really thought it would work."

Finally Porkins admitted defeat, and the three of them headed back to their nether portal. When they emerged on the other side it was the middle of the day, the sun shining brightly overhead.

Dave had built the portal in the middle of a vast plain biome. There was grass in every direction.

"Maybe we should just stay here," said Carl. "Build ourselves a nice house, spend every day lying in the sun. It would make a nice change from running for our lives."

Dave grinned. "You're welcome to stay if you want," he told the creeper. "I'll even build you a house. We could put up a statue of you outside, made of green wool."

"No thanks," said Carl, "I've had enough of statues to last me a lifetime."

"Talking of houses, we should build ourselves one," said Porkins. "The sun will be going down soon, chaps."

So Dave and Porkins built a basic wooden house, while Carl relaxed in the sun. It wasn't much, but it had three beds and would protect them from hostile mobs.

"I thought you were meant to be hunting Endermen?" said Carl to Dave as they all climbed into their beds.

Carl was right. Dave had all the blaze rods he needed, after their adventure in the Nether, and now he needed ender pearls—and the only way to get those, according to his books, was to kill endermen. Only with both the pearls and the rods could he make eyes of ender—the magical trinkets that showed the way to ender portals.

"Tomorrow," Dave said. "We'll start tomorrow."

It started raining outside. Occasionally Dave could hear a strange wheezing sound, like a creature in pain.

"Those are endermen," said Carl. They don't like the rain so they keep teleporting to escape."

Dave looked out of the window. Occasionally he saw strange dark creatures appearing then disappearing.

"Sometimes after storms you find a few ender pearls on the ground," said Carl, "from endermen who got killed by the rain."

"So water kills them?" asked Dave.

"Yup," said Carl. "You never know, you might get lucky—if enough endermen get killed tonight, we could end up with all the pearls we need."

After the long day they'd had, Dave soon found himself falling asleep. In his dreams he was a fierce knight in diamond armor, fighting a dragon.

When he woke, it was still dark. In the dark he could hear something making a strange noise.

His heart stopped. He knew what that noise was.

He opened his eyes slowly, looking down at the floor. As his eyes adjusted to the moonlight he saw two thin, long, black sticks. *No,* he thought, *not sticks—legs.*

An enderman was inside their house.

CHAPTER SIXTEEN
Dave vs Enderman

Dave's first instinct was to look up at the enderman, but he quickly remembered what a bad idea that would be. He'd never seen an enderman in person before, but he knew from the books he'd read and the scary stories he'd been told as a child that if you looked at one in the eye, it would attack you.

The enderman made some more strange noises and started walking slowly around the tiny house. Dave watched as it leaned down and pulled up one of the cobblestone blocks from the floor.

Dave looked across the room at the two other beds. Thankfully Porkins and Carl were still asleep.

What do I do? he thought desperately. *What do I do?*

His bed was next to the door, so if he was careful he could probably get out and shut the door behind him before being caught—but that would just leave Porkins and Carl alone with the enderman.

The house was only small with one room, and the enderman was standing right in the middle of the floor, so there was no way he could wake Porkins and Carl and sneak them out. No, he only had one choice: he was going to have to kill the enderman.

Dave had no idea how easy or difficult it was to kill an enderman, but he had a diamond sword and knew how to use it. The only trouble was, his rucksack was on the other side of the room.

The enderman dropped the cobblestone block, then leaned down to pick up another one. Seeing that this might be his only chance, Dave slowly climbed out of bed, trying hard not to make any noise.

"Potatoes..."

It was Carl, talking in his sleep. The enderman made a curious noise, turning its head to look at Carl.

Please don't wake up, Carl, Dave thought. With the enderman distracted, Dave crawled across the floor towards his bag.

"Baked potatoes..." muttered Carl.

Dave finally reached his bag. Being as quiet as he could, he slowly opened the zip. Then he slipped his hand inside, feeling around for his sword. A jolt of pain rushed through him and he pulled his hand out of the bag. Blood was running down his arm— he'd cut a finger on the blade of his sword. Dave put the finger in his mouth, sucking it and trying his best not to make a sound.

"What's going on?" muttered Carl. "Who's making those weird noises?" Dave watched in horror as Carl opened his eyes, looking right at the enderman.

"Arrrgggghh!!!" said Carl.

The enderman screamed, a long, horrible, sound that hurt Dave's ears, its mouth opening wide.

Dave reached into his bag again, grabbing the hilt of his sword, ignoring the pain in his finger.

"Heeeelp!" yelled Carl.

The enderman ran forward towards Carl, still making the horrible screaming sound. Dave swung his sword at the creature's legs. The enderman screamed in pain then turned to face Dave, screaming in his face.

It was Dave's first proper look at it. The enderman was a tall, thin creature, with jet black skin and soulless pink eyes. When it opened its mouth he could see through the back of its head.

The creature rushed at Dave, who quickly swung his sword, burying the blade between the creature's eyes. With one final, horrible scream it fell to the floor, then *poof* it was gone.

Carl was breathing rapidly, terror still in his eyes.

"You ok?" Dave asked him.

"Not really," Carl replied.

The creeper jumped out of bed. He leaned down and picked

up a tiny green ball. *An ender pearl*, thought Dave, recognizing it from his crafting book.

"One down," said Carl. "And all it took to get it, was me almost getting killed."

There was a grunting from across the room. Porkins was snoring.

"And he slept through it all," said Carl to Dave. "Typical."

CHAPTER SEVENTEEN
The Ender Hunters

In the morning, Dave, Carl and Porkins went outside. As Carl had suspected, there were some ender pearls left on the ground, from endermen who had been killed by the rain. There were only three though, leaving Dave with a grand total of four pearls.

"Well, it's a start," said Dave. "Now, let's make an eye of ender."

According to the old book Dave had found in the stronghold under his village, using eyes of ender was the only way to find ender portals. All you had to do was throw them into the sky and they would show you which direction to go.

Dave took a blaze rod out of his bag and cracked it in half, creating two piles of orange blaze powder. Then he took one of the piles of blaze powder and an ender pearl and held them next to each other. With a *pop* both the pearl and the powder disappeared, and in their place was a strange green eye.

"Yes!" said Dave. "It worked!"

"Did you think it wouldn't?" asked Carl.

"After all the things we've been through, nothing would surprise me," said Dave. "But the good news is that now we have a way of finding the End. We can finally go and fight the ender dragon!"

"Oh I'm so happy," said Carl, who didn't sound very happy at all.

"I think it's splendid news, old bean!" said Porkins. "So what do you have to do with that eye thing?"

"This," said Dave. He threw the eye of ender into the air. It hovered in place for a moment, then flew off across the sky.

"That's the direction we have to go," said Dave. He looked up at the sky. "Judging from the position of the sun, that's south west—so let's keep heading south west. We don't want to have to use more ender eyes than we need to, we've only got three pearls left."

So off they went, following the route the ender eye had taken. Soon they found themselves walking near to a little village, nestled at the foot of a mountain.

"Shall we go and check it out?" Dave asked the other two. "It might be nice to sleep in a proper inn and have a good meal."

"I dunno," said Carl, "the last time we stopped at a town we nearly got killed by giant statues and blown to bits by TNT."

"They might have baked potatoes," said Dave.

Carl's face lit up. He'd run out of potatoes a while back, and Dave knew he was desperate to have more of his favorite food.

"Alright," said Carl. "Although I know I'll regret this."

There were only five buildings in the whole village, but the inn was fairly busy nonetheless, with lots of villagers eating, drinking and chatting.

"We get a lot of visitors here in Little Orchid," the landlady told them, "travelers always stop here before crossing the mountains. We even had the famous Steve stop here once!"

"Never heard of him," said Dave.

There were no rooms free, but the landlady let them sleep in the stable with the horses. Dave set up the three beds he always kept in his backpack, and the three of them settled down to get to sleep.

"What's the point of staying the night with a bunch of smelly horses when we could just build a house of our own?" said Carl.

"I don't think they're smelly," said Porkins, who was quite fond of the horses. He leaned out of his bed and rubbed one of the horses' noses. "You're not smelly, are you dear chap?"

"Now you're gonna smell of horse too," said Carl.

At breakfast the next day, Dave went over to the landlady for a chat.

"Are there any areas around here where there are a lot of endermen?" he asked her.

The landlady shivered.

"Why would you want to go near endermen?" she asked. "You're not one of those Ender Hunters, are you?"

"Ender Hunters?" said Dave.

The landlady nodded at some villagers sitting in the far corner of the inn. They were wearing cowboy hats.

"Ender Hunters," she said. "They go hunting for endermen so they can sell the pearls. It's a dangerous job, make no mistake."

Dave's eyes lit up. If these *Ender Hunters* sold ender pearls, maybe he, Porkins and Carl wouldn't even need to hunt any more endermen themselves.

Dave went over to the Ender Hunters. There were four of them, and as Dave came up to them they gave him a suspicious look.

"What can we do for ya, partner?" one of them asked Dave. He was a short villager with a black beard.

"I hear you sell ender pearls," said Dave. "Can I buy some?"

The ender hunters all laughed.

"Ok, little man" the short villager said. "If you've got the money, we can sort you out. It's a thousand emeralds for one pearl. But we can do you a special deal—two thousand emeralds for two."

"A thousand emeralds!" said Dave, shocked.

"Or two thousand for two," said the short villager, grinning.

"That's the same price!" said Dave.

The short villager thought for a moment.

"Oh yeah," he said. "I guess it is."

"How can it possibly be that much?" said Dave. "Who could afford that?!"

"We normally sell to the rich folk up in Diamond City," said another of the ender hunters—a fat villager with a tiny hat. "Theys got more money than sense, them folk. They like to wear the pearls as jewelery, or just use them as ornaments in their fancy houses."

"There's no way you could do me a deal?" asked Dave.

"How much you got?" asked the short villager.

"Um," Dave rummaged around in his bag, "seven emeralds."

The villagers all laughed.

"I tell you what," said the short villager, "I know a way you could get all the ender pearls you want."

"You do?" said Dave excitedly. "What is it?"

Five minutes later, Dave came back and joined Porkins and Carl at their table.

"What was that all about?" asked Carl. "Why were you speaking with those weirdos?"

"Um, I've got some good news," said Dave. "I've signed us all up to be Ender Hunters!"

"What the heck is an Ender Hunter?" asked Carl.

CHAPTER EIGHTEEN
Hunting Trip

"Pleased to meet y'all," said the short villager to Porkins and Carl. They were gathered outside, by the stable. "I'm Biff, the leader of our little group." He pointed at the fat villager. "This here is Boff, my deputy, and those other two are Boof and Bop."

"So your names are Biff, Boff, Boof and Bop?" said Carl.

"That's correct," said Biff.

"Doesn't that get confusing?"

"No, sir."

"Riiiiight," said Carl.

THE ENDER HUNTERS

BOP

BIFF

BOOF

BOFF

The Ender Hunters only had two spare horses, so Porkins took one and Dave shared the other with Carl.

"I don't think you'd be able to ride too well with them tiny little legs, anyway," Boff said to Carl.

"Whatever you say, Boof," said Carl.

"I'm Boff," said Boff.

"Wait a minute," said Boof, "I thought I was Boff."

"No," said Bop, "you're Bop."

Carl rolled his eyes. "Let's just get moving, shall we," he said.

So off they went. Biff led the way, the others following behind, as the horses rode down a path between the mountains. Dave had never ridden a horse before, but he soon got used to it, using his legs and the stirrups to control the direction the horse was traveling. There wasn't a cloud in the sky, the sun beating down on them from overhead.

They stopped for the night by some trees.

"Shall I build us a house?" said Dave.

Biff scoffed.

"A house! Why, you three really are city folk, ain't you?"

"I'm from a village," said Dave.

"I'm from the Nether," said Porkins.

"I was born deep underground, where there's no light or fresh air, and every day is a struggle for survival," said Carl.

"Yup," said Biff. "A bunch of city boys. Real men, like us, sleep under the stars."

"Aren't you worried about mobs attacking you in the night?" said Dave.

"Nah," said Biff. "Our old leader, Bogg, used to worry about that, but not me."

"What happened to him?" asked Porkins.

"He was slain by mobs in the night," said Biff.

So they all slept under a tree. Dave found it hard to get to sleep without the protection of a roof over his head and the comfort of a bed, but somehow he managed it.

In the morning they set off again. They rode through the mountains until, around lunchtime, the mountains ended and they saw a huge desert biome stretching out before them.

"Wow," said Dave, who had never seen a desert before. "It's so... yellow."

"Desert biomes is the best place ta hunt endermen," said Biff. "Big, open plains with nowhere for the varmints to hide. We'll set up a base, and wait for nightfall. You three all have swords, right?"

"Yep," said Dave.

"Good," said Biff. "Remember the deal—you get to keep half of all the pearls you get. The other half goes to me and my men."

The four Ender Hunters built a sandstone hut in the middle of a wide expanse of desert. Flat plains of sand stretched off into the distance in every direction.

"This here is the home base," said Biff. If you get injured or need a place to rest, come back here. I'll fill a chest full of cooked chicken and fish.

"So what's the plan, then?" asked Carl. "Are you just gonna run around with your swords killing endermen all night?"

"That's right," grinned Biff. "What's tha matter, little creeper—you scared?"

"Well, yes," said Carl. "Isn't there some way we can trap them? Something we can build?"

"You city folk and your fancy ideas!" grinned Boff, the fat Ender Hunter. "Bock always used to say that too. *Isn't there any way we can trap the endermen? Any way we can farm them?*" He laughed. "Hunting them down with a sword is perfectly safe."

"What happened to Bock?" asked Porkins.

"He was slain by endermen," said Boff.

They spent the rest of the afternoon in the hut. The sun was so bright overhead that Biff said they should stay in the shade, to avoid getting sunstroke.

"I dunno why you worry about sunstroke," said Boff. "You sound just like Boop."

"What happened to Boop?" asked Porkins.

"Let me guess," said Carl. "He died of sunstroke?"

"No," said Boff, "he retired to spend more time with his wife."

"Oh," said Carl.

Eventually the sun began to set. "Time to get ready boys," Biff told them.

They all equipped themselves in armor. All of the Ender Hunters had gold armor. Dave had his diamond armor, Porkins stuck with his leather armor, and Carl didn't put any armor on at all.

"I'll stay and look after the base," he said. "It's a very important job."

Dave was about to put his diamond helmet on when Biff put a hand on his arm.

"No, partner," he said, "we wear these." And he handed Dave a tiny orange block. Dave turned the block over in his hands and saw a face on it.

"It's a pumpkin with a face carved into it?" he said, feeling confused.

"A carved pumpkin," said Biff. "Endermen attack when you look at them, but with one of these on your head, they won't even *know* you're looking at them."

"Nice," said Dave. The pumpkin grew to full size in his hands, then he equipped it on his head.

"It's hard to see out of though," he said.

Biff chuckled. "You'll get used to it. This way you can attack one enderman at a time, without accidentally looking at all his buddies and have them attack you too."

When it was finally dark, Dave, Porkins and the four Ender Hunters went outside. Biff laid a few torches down so they could see a bit, but mostly they were surrounded by darkness—the only light coming from the moon.

Porkins pulled out his bow.

"Fraid that won't do you much good, piggy," Biff said. "Endermen can see arrows coming—they teleport out of the way."

"Ah," said Porkins, sounding a bit worried. Dave knew that Porkins preferred to use his bow when he could. He wasn't a fan of hand-to-hand combat. Porkins pulled out a diamond sword instead, and switched his leather armor for diamond.

"Right," said Biff, "everyone wearing your pumpkin?"

They all were.

"Then let's go!"

CHAPTER NINETEEN
Pearls

As Dave ran towards the darkness, sword in hand, he could barely see anything in front him. The combination of the pumpkin on his head and the lack of light made it very difficult to see where he was going, but he could just about make out some pink dots in the distance.

Enderman eyes.

Suddenly the endermen came into view, lit by the moonlight. There were about five of them, and they looked at Dave curiously. Nearby, hidden in the darkness, Dave could hear yells and enderman cries as the Ender Hunters and Porkins fought other endermen.

"Take that you dastardly cad!" he heard Porkins yell.

Endermen, it seemed, were unlike zombie pigmen—they didn't all swarm over when one of them was attacked.

Dave pulled out his sword.

"Yaaaa!" he yelled, running at one of the endermen. He slashed at it with his sword, and suddenly a transformation took place: the enderman opened its mouth and screamed, charging at Dave with its long, dark limbs.

"Oh crumbs," said Dave. He swung his sword again, forcing the enderman back. It kept coming and coming, moving at incredible speed, as Dave forced it back with sword blow after sword blow. Finally, with one final, ear-splitting scream, the enderman was slain, falling to the floor and disappearing with a *poof*. Dave picked up the ender pearl it dropped, putting it in his rucksack. The remaining endermen were looking at him curiously, as if nothing had happened.

Dave spent the rest of the night slaying enderman after enderman. By the time the sun started coming up, he'd got around fifteen pearls, to add to the four he already had.

"Come on," said Biff, coming over to him, "the night's over, that's enough hunting."

They spent the next five days out in the desert. During the day they'd hang out in the hut or go and fetch water, and at night they'd hunt endermen. There wasn't much to do during the days, so they'd tell each other stories about their adventures.

"I can't believe you've met the legendary Steve," Biff said, as Dave was recounting how Steve had helped them defeat Robo Steve in the snow. "He was always my hero growing up."

On the morning of the sixth day, Dave awoke to find Biff and the other Ender Hunters packing up their stuff and dismantling the hut.

"That's enough ender pearls for now," he said. "We'll be able to make a pretty penny down at Diamond City. You should come with us, become a real Ender Hunter. You'll live longer than you will hunting dragons."

"Thanks," said Dave, smiling, "but we'll stick to our quest."

"Suit yourselves, partner," said Biff. "Maybe we'll see you on the road again. Oh, and you can keep them there horses."

The Ender Hunters said their goodbyes and rode off, leaving Dave, Porkins and Carl with the two remaining horses.

"Well, there they go," said Carl. "Biff, Diff, Jiff and Niff. Or whatever their names were."

"They were nice chaps," said Porkins. "How many of those pearls do we have now?"

Dave did a quick count.

"Forty five," he said. "That should be more than enough."

"They're beautiful little things, aren't they?" said Porkins, studying one in his hand."

"Hey Porkins," said Carl, "you reckon you could hit that cactus over there? You're a good shot with an arrow, but how about pearl throwing?"

"Watch and see," grinned Porkins. "Your old pal Porkins is a terrific shot—even if I do say so myself!"

He threw the pearl and, true to his word, it hit the cactus. Porkins grinned, but then suddenly he was gone—disappearing into thin air.

"Where is he?!" said Dave.

Then he heard a familiar voice nearby: "Owwww!"

Somehow Porkins was on top of the cactus. He jumped off, clutching his behind. Carl was laughing hysterically.

"What happened?" said Dave, feeling very confused.

"Throwing the pearls makes you teleport," said Carl, wiping away a tear of laughter. "I found out the other day when I accidentally dropped one."

"You little blighter," said Porkins, coming back over. He was pulling cactus needles out of his back.

"That was funny," grinned Carl, "you've got to admit."

"Hmph," said Porkins.

"Right you two," said Dave, "let's see where we have to go next."

He took out some blaze powder and an ender pearl from his bag, fusing them into an eye of ender, then he threw the eye into the air. It hovered for a moment, then zoomed off towards the horizon.

"That way," said Dave.

So they all got on their horses and rode off.

CHAPTER TWENTY
The Witch

It didn't take them long to leave the desert biome, and they soon found themselves traveling through a swamp. They rode across the discolored grass, along banks of large, shallow lakes and underneath hanging vines. Occasionally they'd come across strange blue flowers, which Dave picked, just in case they were useful for crafting.

As night began to fall, Dave was about to build a house when he saw some lights up ahead.

"It looks like a village or something over there," he said to Porkins and Carl.

"Or something that wants to eat us," said Carl.

Against Carl's wishes, they went and had a closer look. The lights were coming from a small hut, standing on wooden legs in the middle of some shallow water. Dave could just make out a villager, picking mushrooms on the shore nearby.

"Hello there!" he called. The villager turned round. She was wearing a pointy hat and robes.

A witch! Dave thought. The only other witch he'd ever seen had been his grandmother, and that had been a long time ago, when he was very small.

"Hello dearie," the witch said with a smile. "It's nice to see a friendly face, I don't get many visitors all the way out here."

Carl and Porkins walked over to Dave.

"Watch out!" the witch yelled. "It's a creeper!"

"Oh, that's just Carl," laughed Dave. "Don't worry, he's friendly."

"Relatively speaking," said Carl.

The witch invited them all into her hut, and she set about cooking them some dinner in a cauldron.

"Is creeper stew ok?" she asked.

Carl's face went white. The witch giggled. "Just a little joke," she said, "it's actually pumpkin."

"Will it protect us from endermen?" laughed Porkins.

"I don't get it," said the witch.

She dished up the stew and put it down in front of them.

"Yum!" said Porkins, shoving spoonfuls of stew into his mouth as fast as he could.

"So, who are you boys then?" the witch asked, sitting down on the table next to them. "What brings you to my swamp?"

"I'm Porkins," said Porkins, "And this is Carl and Dave."

Dave could have sworn that when Porkins said *Dave* the witch's eyes went wide. It had only been for a second, but she'd definitely reacted to his name.

I must be imagining things, he thought. *I've been on the road too long, I'm starting to see things!*

"And we're on a mission to kill the ender dragon," continued Porkins.

"Really," said the witch, "how interesting. Oh my manners, I haven't introduced myself yet—I'm Dotty."

"Nice to meet you Dotty," said Dave. "Thanks so much for feeding us."

"No problem," smiled the witch. "I am curious though—how are you planning on getting to the ender dragon? I thought all the old portals were destroyed?"

"Well," said Porkins, "we have a... Dave knows a..."

Something was happening to Porkins's voice. Dave looked over and saw the pigman's eyes were starting to droop.

"Are you ok, Porkins?" Dave asked, but suddenly he began to feel incredibly tired. "I... I think I need to sleep..." he said. He looked over and saw Porkins and Carl were both already fast asleep. Porkins had fallen face first in his soup bowl. Only Dotty was still awake, and she was grinning.

"That's right, Dave, go to sleep," she said. "Go to sleep…"

And he did.

CHAPTER TWENTY-ONE
Bedrock

Dave woke up in a room with black walls. No, not quite solid black—black with flecks of gray.

Bedrock, he knew. But how could a room be made of bedrock? As far as he knew, the only place you could find bedrock was if you dug as far down as you could get. You couldn't mine it and make rooms out of it.

He was in a small cage made of iron bars, and when he looked across the room he saw Porkins and Carl in similar cages. Both of them seemed to be just waking up now too.

"What's going on now?" said Carl. "How do we always end up in these situations?"

"Gosh my head hurts," said Porkins.

Dave reached round to grab a pickaxe from his backpack—but his backpack was gone.

"Does anyone have a pickaxe?" he yelled to his friends.

Porkins reached round, then realized his backpack was gone too.

"My stuff!" the pigman said. "Some blighter has nicked it!"

"I think the same 'blighter' has taken all our stuff," said Carl.

"Your items have been confiscated," said a voice. "But if you cooperate, you may have them back."

Dave could have sworn they were alone in the bedrock room, but now there was a man in here with them, and behind him were a group of witches. One of the witches, Dave was dismayed to see, had his bag, and was flicking through the ancient book he'd found in the stronghold, back when he'd begun his adventure.

"There's nothing in here," the witch said, sounding annoyed.

"Nothing about how to get to the End."

Then he noticed Dotty, the witch whose hut they'd eaten at, leaning against a wall and grinning at them.

"You!" said Dave.

"Yes, me," she grinned. "My master has been looking for you, Dave. And lucky me, you just wandered right into my home. I was just planning to rob you and your friends, to put you to sleep and steal your stuff, but when you told me your name and I realized who you were... well, I knew my master would reward me handsomely for bringing you to him."

She turned to look at the man. For a split second Dave thought the man was Steve. His voice hadn't sounded anything like Steve, but he looked the same. Apart from his eyes—this man had pure white eyes.

"Herobrine!" Porkins gasped, saying what Dave had been thinking. "You rotter! You cad! Let me out of this cage and I'll teach you—"

Herobrine waved his hand and suddenly Porkins stopped talking. But no, that wasn't quite right, Dave realized. Porkins was still talking, but no sound was coming out. It was like his voice had been stopped by magic.

Herobrine walked forward to Dave's cage. As he got closer, Dave felt an immense sense of dread and misery. It was like Herobrine's very presence was sucking all the joy from the room.

"You and your friends are all in identical cages," Herobrine said calmly. Something about his voice made the hairs on the back of Dave's neck stand on end. "Each cage has a trapdoor below it. Below the trapdoor is a lake of lava."

Dave looked down and realized, to his horror, that Herobrine was telling the truth. His cage was only one block wide and he was standing on a trapdoor, and could see the orange glow of lava through the window. There was nowhere to escape to.

"I'm going to ask you a question," Herobrine said, "and if you refuse to answer, or lie to me, the trapdoor below your creeper friend will open, and he'll fall into the lava."

"Hey, that's not fair!" said Carl. "Why can't you drop Porkins into the lava instead?"

Herobrine waved a hand, and suddenly Carl's voice was silenced, the same way Porkins's had been.

"Then I will ask you the same question again," said Herobrine. "And if you fail to answer or lie to me a second time, the pigman will go into the lava. And please don't be under any illusions—I *will* know if you're lying."

Every word that Herobrine spoke made Dave's head hurt. His voice sounded normal, but there was something horrible about it that Dave couldn't quite put his finger on. It was as if Herobrine was only pretending to look like a man and speak like a man, and that underneath was something *inhuman*—something *monstrous*.

"Finally," said Herobrine, "I will ask you the question a third time. If again you fail to give me the answer I want, *you* will go in the lava. Is that understood?"

Dave looked over at Porkins and Carl, who were both terrified.

"Listen," said Dave, "I'll tell you anything you want—please just let my friends go!"

"If you answer me true, all three of you will be released," Herobrine said softly. "You have my word."

Don't trust him! a voice in Dave's head said. And for once it wasn't his own.

Who are you? Dave asked the voice.

It's me, Dave, the voice replied. *I'm sorry it's been so long.*

Grandma? Dave thought. He recognized the voice now—it was his grandmother. Dave hadn't seen her since he was little, but he still knew her voice.

"Is something the matter?" asked Herobrine, sounding like he was getting impatient. "I hope you appreciate the gravity of this situation."

Dave was very confused now. Not only was he captured by the mysterious Herobrine, but now he could hear his grandmother talking to him inside his head.

How are you speaking to me? Dave asked his grandmother. *Is it by magic?*

Dave didn't know much about his grandmother, but he knew she was a witch. When he was little she had always made him laugh by doing magic tricks.

Listen Dave, his grandmother's voice said, *I can't keep this up much longer, speaking to you like this is extremely difficult. Please, whatever you do, don't tell Herobrine what he wants to know. When the trapdoors open, you and your friends will be fine—I promise you. You have to trust me...*

And then her voice was gone.

"Now I will ask you my question," Herobrine said to Dave. "Remember, if you don't answer truly, the creeper dies."

He stepped forward, staring at Dave with those horrible blank eyes.

"How do I find strongholds?" Herobrine asked.

Dave was taken aback. Was that all the question was? He was about to tell Herobrine the answer—that you had to use eyes of ender—but then he remembered what his grandmother had said.

Whatever you do, don't tell Herobrine what he wants to know.

Was he crazy to trust their lives to a strange voice inside his head? Maybe he was, but his grandmother—if it really was her—had sounded so sincere. And the other thing was, he really didn't trust Herobrine. Porkins had told Dave and Carl about how Herobrine had betrayed the pigmen, turning them all into zombies. He didn't seem like the kind of man to keep his word.

"I need an answer, please," Herobrine said.

Dave looked over at Carl. The creeper was yelling something—probably calling Dave an idiot for not just telling Herobrine what he needed to know— his voice was still silenced by Herobrine's magic.

"I'm afraid I can't help," Dave told Herobrine. "I don't know what you're talking about."

"LIAR!" spat Herobrine. His anger came so suddenly that Dave jumped back in terror, but then he became calm again. "Pull the first lever," he said softly.

Dave noticed for the first time that there were three levers on the side of the wall. A witch grabbed one and pulled it.

There was a *click* as the trapdoor below Carl opened. The tiny creeper's mouth opened in shock, and then he was gone.

Dave saw Porkins yelling angrily at him and banging on the bars of his cell. He couldn't hear what the pigman was saying, thanks to Herobrine's magic, but he knew it was nothing nice.

I hope I'm right about this, Dave thought miserably. If he wasn't, and the voice of his grandmother had all been his imagination, then he'd just sent one of his best friends to a very nasty death.

"Now I will ask a second time," Herobrine said. "How do I find strongholds?"

"Look," said Dave, "I hate to disappoint you, but I don't know."

The look Porkins gave him almost broke his heart.

Trust me, Dave tried to tell the pigman with his eyes. *I know what I'm doing, this will all be ok.*

"Second lever!" snapped Herobrine. He'd given up the pretense of acting calm now, and Dave could see the fury all over his face.

The witch pulled the second lever and Porkins fell through. *How could you?* the look on his face seemed to be saying.

Herobrine stepped forward again, looking furious. He was so close that Dave could smell his breath. It smelled of death.

"Last chance," Herobrine hissed. "I know you've discovered a way of finding strongholds. Tell me what it is and I'll let you live. Refuse me again and you go in the lava. Got it?"

"Makes sense to me," said Dave. He was shaking he was so nervous, but he tried not to let Herobrine see.

"For the third and final time," said Herobrine, "how do I find strongholds?"

"Sorry," said Dave, "I'm afraid I can't—"

"PULL THE LEVER!" screamed Herobrine.

"Master," said Dotty anxiously, running over to him, "we can't just kill him, we need to find out what he knows!"

But Herobrine was too furious to listen.

"He refused me," he hissed, "his voice sounding less and less human by the second. "No-one refuses me! NO-ONE! Pull the lever!"

Suddenly Dave found himself falling, through the trapdoor and towards a huge lake of lava far below.

"Oh dear," he said. "I think I've made a terrible mistake..."

CHAPTER TWENTY-TWO
Lava

Dave was falling towards the lava and there was nothing he could do about it.

Well, at least it'll be quick, he thought miserably. If the fall didn't finish him off, the lava would kill him in a few seconds.

But then he felt something grab him under the arms, and suddenly he wasn't falling anymore. He turned round and saw his savior was a witch—a witch flying with wings!

"Your grandmother sent me," the witch whispered.

"You're flying?!" Dave said stupidly.

"Keep your voice down," the witch said. "We don't want Herobrine to know you're still alive. And we're not flying, we're gliding."

Dave looked down and was surprised to see Carl and Porkins standing at the far side of the lava lake, waving at him. There were two witches with them, who, Dave realized, must have caught his friends when they fell through their trapdoors.

"So you're the good witches?" Dave said.

"We're the witches who refused to follow Herobrine," the witch said. "For years he's tried to recruit all the witches to join him, and he's done a good job. Your grandmother leads the resistance—witches who oppose Herobrine and all he stands for. I'm Miranda, by the way."

"Dave," said Dave.

Suddenly there was a blood-curdling scream of anger from behind them. Dave looked round to see a figure swoop down through one of the trapdoor holes.

"It's Herobrine!" Dave said. "And he's got wings too!"

Herobrine was flying after them, going much faster than they were.

"He's using a firework rocket for extra speed!" said Miranda.

They were near the edge of the lava lake now, where Porkins, Carl and the two witches were waiting for them. Dave noticed that there were other witches there as well, maybe ten or eleven. All of these "good" witches were wearing purple robes, unlike Herobrine's witches—who'd been wearing robes that were the same blue as his shirt.

Miranda swooped down and landed next to Porkins and Carl.

"Am I glad to see you guys!" Dave said to them. "Sorry about letting you fall into the lava—but I knew you'd be ok. You see I heard my grandmother's voice inside my head, and she told me we'd all be safe."

Porkins and Carl gave him a funny look. Carl started to speak but stopped when he realized that no words were coming out—the silencing spell was still working, it seemed.

"TRAITORS!" Herobrine yelled, as he swooped down towards them on his rocket-powered wings. The witches all pulled out bottles of potion and started chucking them at Herobrine, but he kept swerving out of the way.

"Hit his elytra!" Miranda yelled. "They're a bigger target!"

The witches did as she commanded, throwing their potions at Herobrine's wings. Herobrine's wings began to break, and he began spiraling down towards the lava.

"You'll all pay!" he screamed as he fell. "I'll destroy you all!"

And then *plop!* He fell into the lava and was gone.

"That was easier than I thought it would be," said Dave.

"Come on," said Miranda, "I don't think that'll hold him for long."

"Hold him?" said Dave. "He fell into lava. He's dead!"

Suddenly there was a gurgling, slurping sound behind him. Dave turned and saw something rising up from the lava. Something big.

"Run!" Miranda yelled. "Everybody into the caves!"

Dave couldn't take his eyes off the huge thing rising up from the lava. *No,* he realized with a jolt of shock. *It's not rising up from the lava—it *is* the lava!*

With slurping and slopping and a thunderous roar that echoed around the cavern, the lava monster stood up, its body starting to take shape: two arms, two legs, a body and a head with two blank eyes.

It was a giant lava Herobrine.

CHAPTER TWENTY-THREE
Giant Lava Herobrine

The huge lava Herobrine waded through the lava lake towards them. It was so tall that it had to stoop to not bump its head on the roof of the cavern.

"YOU THINK YOU CAN ESCAPE ME?!" it roared.

"Move!" Miranda said, grabbing Dave by the shoulders. He turned and saw Carl, Porkins and the witches running towards a hole in the wall of the cavern. Dave and Miranda followed them, finding themselves in a network of caves.

"Keep moving everyone!" Miranda shouted.

Suddenly the cave walls shook, as the giant lava Herobrine pounded at the wall of the cavern with his fists.

"Don't worry," said Dave, to no-one in particular. "He's too big to fit in here!"

But then his heart fell as he saw lava pouring through the cave entrance towards them.

"Keep going!" yelled Miranda. They all started running, the lava quickly catching up with them.

"Up here!" a witch said. They followed her through a narrow passageway that led upwards. They went around some twists and turns and finally found themselves in a small cave with daylight coming in from a hole in the ceiling.

"I think we lost Herobrine," said one of the witches.

"That may be, but you've found us!" said a familiar voice from above.

Dave looked up and saw Dotty and the other bad witches swooping down through the hole in the ceiling wearing elytra wings.

A huge battle broke out, the blue-robed bad witches against the good purple-robed ones. All of them throwing potions at each other or shooting each other with arrows.

"Come on!" Miranda said, grabbing Dave. "You need to get out of here!"

She led Dave, Carl and Porkins down some narrow passageways, until the sound of battle could only be heard faintly in the distance.

"You need to escape through the Nether," she told them. "Herobrine will have all the cave entrances guarded."

"I don't have obsidian," Dave told her. "Those other witches took all our backpacks."

"Take this," Miranda said, reaching into her pockets and pulling out some tiny obsidian blocks and a piece of flint and steel. "That should be enough to get into the Nether and then get out again." She thrust it all into Dave's hands. "Now go!"

"What about you?" said Dave.

"GO!" she yelled. "If Herobrine catches you, he'll force you to reveal how to get to the End. And then we'll all be doomed." She gave his shoulder a reassuring squeeze, then ran back down the passageway, towards the battle.

Dave looked at Porkins and Carl.

"I guess we'd better go then," he said. They both nodded—both of them still unable to speak.

Dave built a rectangle of obsidian, then lit it. The liquid purple portal appeared, as it always did.

"Let's go," he said sadly. He hated the idea of leaving Miranda and the other witches behind after they'd saved their lives, but Miranda had been very insistent. For some reason she, and the other good witches, were willing to lay down their lives to stop Herobrine finding a stronghold and making his way to the End.

Dave stepped into the purple doorway. The liquid of the portal shimmered around him for a second, and then he was back in the Nether, Porkins and Carl following right behind him.

KABOOM!!

Dave was thrust forward by a huge explosion. He fell forward, landing painfully on the netherrack ground. He looked round and saw a crater where the portal had been. Carl and Porkins were on the floor next to him.

"Ow, my head," said Porkins. "Oh, I can speak again!"

"What a pity," said Carl.

"What destroyed the portal?" said Dave, getting to his feet and looking around.

And then he saw the witches. Ten or so of Herobrine's bad witches blocking the path in front of them, sitting on a huge machine made of iron blocks.

"Master Herobrine was right," a witch said gleefully. Dave recognized her as the witch who'd been looking through his backpack—and she still had it, wearing it on her back. "He thought they might try and escape through the Nether!"

"Herobrine is always right," said a tall witch, grinning nastily. "Now boys," she called down to Dave and his friends, "we have a TNT cannon aimed right at you. Come with us and no-one has to get hurt."

CHAPTER TWENTY-FOUR
Return to the Nether (Again!)

Dave needed a plan. He looked at Porkins and Carl, but they seemed as clueless as he was. What were they going to do?

"Come up here, boys," the tall witch said, sounding bored. "We've got another portal, all ready to take you back to Master Herobrine. He's *so* looking forward to seeing you again."

"Is he? That's good," said Dave, trying to play for time until he could think of a plan. Then he spotted a couple of pigmen wandering about near the remains of the portal.

"Actually," Dave told the tall witch. "We don't really fancy seeing Herobrine again. So we're just gonna go."

And he started walking towards the portal.

"What are you doing?!" Carl whispered.

"Trust me," Dave whispered back.

Reluctantly, Carl followed him. Then Porkins too.

"Stop!" the tall witch shouted at them. They heard the squealing of metal as the TNT cannon swirled round to follow them. "We have the cannon aimed directly at you. If you don't come with us, we'll blow you to bits!"

"Nah," said Dave, "I think we're just gonna go."

"I hope you know what you're doing, old chap," said Porkins.

"You know me," said Dave, giving him a smile, "I've always got a plan."

"I'm not sure that's strictly true," said Porkins.

"Ok! You were warned!" yelled the tall witch. "FIRE!"

KABOOM!!!

A blast from the TNT cannon exploded just in front of them.

"I think you missed," Dave shouted up at them.

"This is your last warning!" said the tall witch. "FIRE!!!"

This time the explosion hit the remains of the portal, blowing it to bits and the blast hitting the two zombie pigmen.

"SQUEEE!!!" they yelled as they went flying into the lava.

Suddenly there was a chorus of squealing. Dave suddenly realized there were a lot more pigmen around than he originally thought, all of them now looking agitated, making angry squealing noises and trying to look where the blast had come from.

"FIRE!" yelled the tall witch again.

"Um, are you sure?" said the witch wearing Dave's backpack. "Those pig things don't look happy..."

"I said FIRE!" the tall witch repeated.

The cannon fired again. As Dave had suspected—or at least hoped—the witches wouldn't actually fire at him, Porkins and Carl, as they wanted to bring them back to Herobrine. So the shot whizzed over Dave's head and smashed into the ground nearby, hitting some more pigmen.

This time there was no mistaking where the shot had come from. With a chorus of furious squealing, the pigmen ran angrily towards the witches.

"Uh oh," said the tall witch.

Suddenly there were dozens of angry pigmen attacking the witches from all sides. The witches started throwing potions and a huge battle broke out.

"Now, let's get out of here," Dave said to Porkins and Carl.

The three of them ran as fast as they could, weaving their way through the witches and zombie pigmen. They were coming round a corner when they heard someone shout at them from above:

"Stop right there!"

They looked up. The witch with Dave's backpack, her clothes torn in places from the fight, was on a slope looking down at them, a potion in one hand, ready to be thrown.

"This potion will finish you in one hit," she said angrily. "I promise you that!"

But then a look of shock appeared on her face. She looked

down and saw the tip of a golden sword poking through her belly.

"Oh!" she said. She fell to her knees, and then *poof!* she was gone. The pigman who'd stabbed her ran off the other way to rejoin the fight, and Dave's rucksack fell down the slope, landing by his feet.

He grabbed it, quickly opening it to check the contents. Everything seemed to still be there—all his blocks and, more importantly, his two books. The crafting book that Old Man Johnson had given him, and the ancient book he'd found in the stronghold under his village, all that time ago—the book that had told him how to make ender eyes and find ender portals.

Dave wondered why the witch hadn't found the page about ender eyes when she'd been looking through his backpack. He opened the book and quickly scrolled to the ender eye page.

The page was blank.

Dave scrolled back and forth. He was definitely looking at the right page, but somehow all the writing and images were gone. The pages on either side were packed full of text, but the ender eye page was completely blank.

Then, right before his eyes, the text and images returned, reappearing on the page as if by magic.

It is magic, Dave thought. *The book didn't want Herobrine to know how to find the End.*

It seemed stupid, but compared to some of the crazy things Dave had seen on his adventure, a magic book was fairly low on the crazy scale.

"Are you gonna look at that book all day, or are we gonna get a move on?" said Carl.

They kept moving, walking along at a fast pace. They kept going and going until their feet hurt. There was no way of knowing how much time had passed in the Nether, so Dave didn't know if they'd been going an hour or a day.

"We must have gone far enough now," said Carl.

"I agree, dear chap," said Porkins.

So Dave built an obsidian portal, lighting it with flint and steel.

"Let's hope it brings us somewhere nice," he said, remembering the endless snow biome they'd ended up in last time.

He stepped into the portal.

CHAPTER TWENTY-FIVE
Nothing but Water

When he appeared on the other side, Dave saw clear blue skies, with barely a cloud in sight. He looked down and saw endless ocean in every direction. He was standing on a small obsidian ledge by the side of the portal—the portal had spawned in the sky, far above the water.

Aw well, he thought, *we'll just go back into the Nether and build a portal somewhere else.*

He turned to walk back into the purple liquid, when suddenly a small green thing ran through and bashed into him.

"Oops, sorry," said Carl.

Dave staggered backwards, his feet on the edge of the ledge, using his arms to try and keep balance.

"Arrrrgh!!!" said Dave.

"Uh, just hold on," said Carl. "Porkins will be here in a second—he's got longer arms than me. Well, he's actually *got* arms."

Then Porkins ran through the portal.

"So where are we chaps?" he said, running straight into Carl, then straight into Dave.

"Arrrghh!!!" said Carl.

"Arrrghh!!!" said Dave.

"Oh my!" said Porkins.

And the three of them fell down, down, down, towards the water below.

EPILOGUE

Herobrine was very unhappy.

"What do you mean, they escaped?" he asked the tall witch stood in front of him.

"We went to the Nether to set a trap for them, as you asked," the witch said, her voice trembling. "But they... we were attacked by pigmen."

"Zombie pigmen, you mean?" said Herobrine. "Are you telling me you were outsmarted by zombies?"

"Not outsmarted, outnumbered."

Herobrine strode over and looked down one of the three trapdoors in the bedrock room, at the lava lake below. He'd finally had Dave the villager in his grasp, and he'd let him escape. As furious as he was with the witches, Herobrine was more furious with himself.

He'd become suspicious when Dave had so easily let his friends fall to his death. Herobrine hadn't meant to kill Dave, but he'd lost his temper. Herobrine wasn't used to being defied, and it had made him angry.

Very angry.

When Dave had fallen through the trapdoor, Herobrine had become more suspicious still. It was one thing to let your companions fall into lava, but quite another to sacrifice your own life. Herobrine had stuck his head through the trapdoor to check that Dave really had fallen to his doom, and instead saw the villager flying away, with the help of a traitorous witch.

He'd followed Dave himself, but not before sending his witches to the nearby caves and to the Nether, to cut off any escape routes. But it had all been in vain—as stupid as he looked, this *Dave* had managed to escape from Herobrine's clutches.

"Increase the search," said Herobrine. "I want every witch we have on the lookout. Search the Nether too. And take this."

He held out a golden staff with a emerald on the top.

"Master?" said the witch, sounding confused.

"This staff will let you control zombie pigmen," Herobrine told her. "What is your name, witch?"

"Isabella," said the tall witch.

"Congratulations Isabella," said Herobrine, "you're now in charge of my pigman army. I want you to summon the zombie pigmen and bring them here. They're no use to me in the Nether."

"How many shall I bring?" the witch asked, taking the staff.

"All of them," said Herobrine. "I've been operating in the shadows for too long. It's time to begin my conquest."

"What are you going to conquer?" Isabella asked.

Herobrine smiled.

"The world."

BOOK 3

Adventures Under (and Over) the Sea

CHAPTER ONE
Water, Water, Everywhere...

SPLOOSH!

Dave hit the water and immediately went under. He was so surprised by the impact that he exhaled all the water from his lungs.

Which way do I swim? he wondered, looking around the endless expanse of blue. *Which way is up?*

Then he saw something big and bright. *The sun!*

He swam towards the sunlight, kicking his legs as hard as he could, until, finally, he burst through to the surface, coughing and spluttering.

Treading water, he looked around, but could see nothing but ocean in every direction.

"Carl!" he yelled. "Porkins!"

SPLASH! A tiny green thing came to the surface.

"Blurg!" it said.

"Carl!" said Dave happily. "Are you ok?"

"You try swimming without arms and tell me if you're ok," grumbled Carl.

"Did you see Porkins?" Dave asked him.

"Nope," said Carl. "Can pigmen swim? Maybe he sunk to the bottom. Or was eaten by a dolphin."

SPLOOSH! A pink thing shot up from the water.

"Oh my!" it said. "I thought I was a goner!"

It was Porkins.

"Well, at least we're all safe," said Dave. "Now we've just got to find our way back to land."

Dave looked around, but there was nothing to be seen but ocean. Endless miles of ocean.

"Can you craft us a boat?" asked Porkins. "I'm not sure how much longer I can tread water like this. There's no water in the Nether, so we Pigmen aren't natural swimmers."

"I've got some wood in my bag," said Dave. He was about to unzip his bag, but then he stopped.

"Actually I can't," he said. "My bag is waterproof, but as soon as I open it it'll fill with water. The books will be ruined. I can't even open it to get any wood out."

"Great," said Carl. "So what do we do, just keep swimming until we reach land?"

"I guess we don't really have much choice," said Dave.

"Wait," said Porkins, "there's something strange over there. There are bubbles."

"It's probably killer dolphins," said Carl. "We're all gonna get eaten. Just typical."

Porkins began to swim over to the bubbles.

"Careful," said Dave, but the pigman ignored him.

"Ooo," said Porkins as he swam into the patch of bubbles. "They're nice and warm." Then a look of panic spread across his face. "Oh dear," he said, "I think they're pulling me down, I think

I'm going to—"

And with a *PLOOP* he disappeared under the water.

"Porkins!" Dave yelled. He dived under the water himself and saw Porkins being sucked down by a column of bubbles. Dave swam over to try and grab him, but Porkins was being dragged down too fast.

And that wasn't the worst of it. Far below, Dave could see what was causing the column of bubbles: there was a glowing block at the bottom of the column.

A magma block, Dave realized, to his horror. He'd read about them in his crafting book. If he couldn't get Porkins out of the bubbles in time, he'd be fried up like a piece of bacon.

There was no way Dave could catch Porkins up by swimming, he realized, so he'd have to risk riding the column of bubbles down himself. If he could get to Porkins in time he might be able to push him out of the bubbles to safety.

Dave swam into the bubble column, and could immediately feel himself being sucked down. He was moving so fast he could barely work out which way was down and which was up, but, to his surprise, he realized he could *breathe.* The bubbles were providing him with air.

Getting his bearings, Dave looked down and saw Porkins below him. Dave started kicking his legs, trying to swim down fast enough so that he could catch up to the pigman. Porkins was almost at the magma block now, there wasn't much time left.

I'm coming, Porkins! Dave tried to say, but all that came out of his mouth were more bubbles. He kicked and kicked, slowly gaining on the pigman. Porkins was looking up at him in desperation.

Porkins was barely meters above the magma block now, being sucked down at breakneck speed, but Dave had nearly caught up with him. He kicked and kicked and finally he could just about reach Porkins's legs. He grabbed on tight to the pigman, trying to push them both out of the bubble stream, but the current was just too strong.

Come on, come on! Dave said to himself. He kicked and kicked, until finally he and Porkins burst free from the bubble column. They'd escaped just in time, they were barely two meters above the magma block, but now they had a new problem: they were at the bottom of the ocean and there was no way they could make it all the way to the surface in time without running out of breath.

Dave looked at Porkins. The pigman's cheeks were filled with air, but there was a panicked look in his eyes.

What now? wondered Dave.

CHAPTER TWO
Carl Gets Left Behind

Carl had been bobbing up and down in the ocean for a long time. The bubble column had sucked down Porkins and Dave ages ago, and they'd still not come up for air.

I hope those idiots are ok, he thought to himself. As much as he hated to admit it, he'd grown quite fond of the two of them. All the friends he'd had before had been creepers, and creepers weren't always the nicest people.

Carl had never thought much about the future until recently. When you were a creeper, you didn't have to: you knew that one day you would blow yourself up, and that was the end of that. But ever since he'd failed to blow up Dave, Carl had been wondering what he should do with his life. *If I can't explode, what kind of creeper am I?*

It was getting dark now, and Carl was starting to panic. With no arms, it was hard for creepers to swim, and his little legs were getting tired.

This is what you get for following a villager and a pigman on a stupid adventure, Carl thought bitterly. *You're gonna end up eaten by dolphins.*

It wasn't long before the sun went down and all he could see was the moon. Dave and Porkins had been underwater so long that there was no way they could be alive.

This is why you shouldn't make friends, Carl thought. *They'll only let you down.*

He was finding it harder and harder to keep kicking his little legs, and he was beginning to get sleepy. Then, just as he was about to give up and let himself sink, he saw something floating towards him. Something big and wooden.

Am I seeing things? he wondered. *Or is that... a ship?*

"Over here!" he shouted. "Help! I'm over here!"

For a moment it looked like the ship was going to sail right past him, but then it curved round and came to a stop. It was a huge vessel with big black sails.

A figure appeared on the deck, looking down at Carl. It was a creeper.

"Don't worry, matey, we'll save you," said the creeper, and he threw down a rope. Carl grabbed the rope in his mouth and feet and climbed up. When he reached the deck of the ship he looked around in amazement: the ship was full of creepers.

"Ahoy," said one of the creepers. He had a beard, an eyepatch and a black three-sided hat with a skull and crossbones on it. "We're the famous Creeper Pirates. And you're now our prisoner."

The pirates all pulled out swords.

"Typical," said Carl with a sigh. "Just typical."

CHAPTER THREE
Bubbles and Zombies

Dave and Porkins were desperately kicking their way to the surface. Dave was starting to feel weak now from lack of oxygen. He looked round and saw Porkins looked even worse than him.

We're going to have to go back inside the bubble column, Dave thought to himself. It would suck them down, but at least they wouldn't drown. *But then we'll be at the bottom of the ocean again,* Dave thought. *We'll be back where we started.*

Then Dave had a brainwave. If they could just quickly stick their faces into the bubble stream, they could take a mouthful of air without being sucked down. He grabbed Porkins and gently pushed his face into the bubbles, holding on tightly to him. Then he pulled the pigman back and stuck his own face inside the bubble column. Immediately his lungs filled with air.

The two of them now full of air again, Dave and Porkins began kicking their way to the surface.

I hope Carl is alright, Dave thought to himself. He and Porkins had been underwater so long that the little creeper must have been fearing the worst.

Then Dave saw something that made his blood go cold. Shapes were floating towards them underwater. Hundreds of shapes, hidden in the murky darkness.

Zombies! Dave thought. But how could that be? Zombies couldn't swim underwater, as far as he knew.

Porkins had spotted the underwater zombies too, and was starting to panic. They were all around them: above them, below and surrounding them on all sides.

What do we do? Dave thought. They couldn't try and swim through the zombies, there were too many. He pulled his sword from his belt, but swinging it underwater felt sluggish. There was no way they'd be able to fight their way out.

The zombies were almost upon them now, so close that Dave could see every detail of their rotted bodies. They were different from the zombies he'd seen on land: their skin was a murky blue color and their clothes were brown, like the water had rotted them.

Porkins was looking at Dave with panicked eyes.

He's waiting for me to come up with a plan, Dave realized. *But what can we do?*

His throat and lungs began to hurt.

I need to get some more air from the bubble column, he thought.

And then he realized what they needed to do. The only way to escape from the zombies was to ride the bubble column down to the ocean floor again. Once they were there... well, Dave had no idea what they would do next. But at least they wouldn't get eaten by zombies.

Dave grabbed Porkins's hand, leading him to the bubbles. Porkins was reluctant to go in at first, but then Dave shoved him into the column. Immediately Porkins disappeared from view, the bubbles zipping him away at lightning speed.

Dave turned round. The water zombies were so close they could almost touch him. The water was so thick with them that they were blocking out the sun.

Here goes nothing, thought Dave. He swam into the bubble column, and let the current drag him down.

CHAPTER FOUR
Locked Up

Carl woke up with a sore head. The last thing he remembered was one of the creeper pirates hitting him with the hilt of their sword.

He was locked inside a tiny jail cell, wooden walls on one side and iron bars on the other. From the lurching back and forth he knew he was still on the ship.

As his eyes adjusted to the gloom he noticed that he wasn't alone: There was a creeper with a mop and bucket, in the middle of cleaning the floor.

"Oh hey, you're awake," said the creeper, smiling.

"I sure am," said Carl. "So what is your captain gonna do with me? Make me walk the plank?"

"Oh no," said the mop creeper. "We're gonna hold you ransom then sell you back to your family for emeralds. That's what we always do with prisoners."

"I don't have any family," said Carl.

"Oh," said the creeper. "Then he'll probably make you walk the plank. Sorry."

"Just my luck," said Carl.

"I'm Bill, by the way," said the creeper with the mop.

"Carl," said Carl.

"Well met, Carl," said Bill. "I hope the captain doesn't throw you into the sea too soon, you seem like a nice lad."

"That's very kind of you," said Carl. "Maybe you could open my cell door and give me a boat to escape in, just to make sure."

Bill laughed.

"You're a funny lad, Carl," he said, "a real joker."

BILL

Carl sighed. He didn't even have the energy any more to be scared. Ever since he'd met Dave and Porkins his life had been nothing but a series of unfortunate events. Every time they got out of one mess they got into another. It never ended.

If I get out of this, I'm going to leave those two idiots behind, Carl thought to himself. *I'll find a nice beach, build a house and settle down, all by myself.*

Bill finished his mopping and left, leaving Carl all by himself. Carl tried to get back to sleep, but the motion of the boat was making him feel queasy, so he just sat down and imagined what his life would be like when he was finally free of Dave and Porkins.

CHAPTER FIVE
The Floating Dead

Dave and Porkins swam out of the bubble stream just before they hit the magma block. They'd escaped from the zombies, but they were back at the bottom of the ocean again.

Looking up, Dave could see huge clouds of zombies floating far above them. Thankfully the water zombies seemed as stupid as the land ones, and they seemed to have no idea where Dave and Porkins had gone.

It was dark this far down, but in the distance Dave could just about make out other columns of air bubbles. If he and Porkins could swim from column to column, they could get out from underneath the swarm of zombies, and then come up to the surface in a safe place.

But then, just as Dave thought all their problems had been solved, he saw a horrifying sight: the ocean floor, barely three meters below them, was *covered* in zombies. They were walking along the sand without a care in the world.

They haven't spotted us yet, Dave thought. He was grateful for that. If he and Porkins could swim silently above the zombies, maybe they wouldn't be seen.

He took Porkins's hand and guided him over to their original bubble column. They both took a big gulp of air, then the two of them began to swim towards another column. Porkins seemed to grasp what the plan was pretty quickly.

As they neared the second bubble column, Dave thought there was something off about it: the way the bubbles were acting was different. But he ignored his reservations and kept swimming. He and Porkins couldn't afford to be fussy: they needed air if they were both going to avoid drowning.

There were still zombies far above them and zombies walking along the ocean floor.

There are so many of them, thought Dave.

They were finally nearing the bubble column. Dave kicked his legs harder, eager for a lungful of air. He pushed his face gently into the bubbles, but suddenly something felt different. The bubbles were doing something odd to him and he lost his balance and was swept up into the column.

He was moving at breakneck speed, and it was only then that he realized what was happening.

The bubbles aren't pushing me down, he thought, *they're pushing me up!*

He was hurtling towards the huge swarm of zombies above.

CHAPTER SIX
The Underwater Pyramid

Porkins watched helplessly as Dave went flying up the bubble column.

Oh crumbs, he thought. *Should I follow him?*

Then something flew past his head.

It seemed that the zombies on the seabed below had noticed him at last. They were swimming up towards him, and some of them had weapons. Another weapon—a trident—flew past Porkins, almost hitting him.

The zombies are throwing them! Porkins realized, to his horror.

He pulled his bow and arrows from his belt.

Well, if I'm going out I might as well go out fighting, he thought. But then suddenly he felt something grab him from behind. *The zombies! They've got me!*

But when he looked round it wasn't a zombie after all—it was a villager. A villager wearing some kind of green helmet.

Is that a turtle shell? Porkins wondered.

The villager placed another turtle shell on Porkins's head. As if by magic, the pigman felt his lungs fill with oxygen.

There were other villagers too, Porkins realized. All wearing turtle shell helmets and wielding tridents, they were fighting off the zombies as best they could—even though they were vastly outnumbered.

The villager who had grabbed Porkins now grabbed his hand, pulling him along. The villagers began to swim in formation, swimming through the zombies. Porkins wasn't a great swimmer, but he kicked his legs as hard as he could, just managing to keep up.

The villagers at the front of the formation were using their tridents to fight off any zombies who came too close. At one point a zombie grabbed Porkins's leg, but the villager next to him stabbed the zombie in the chest and it let go.

They swam and swam and, finally, they escaped from the zombie swarm. In front them was one of the most beautiful sights Porkins had ever seen.

On the ocean floor ahead of them were hundreds of huge coral plants. Porkins was amazed at how many colors there were: pinks, purples, reds, yellows and blues, all intertwining with each other.

Porkins was so entranced by the beautiful sight that he almost didn't realize that he was running out of breath. The turtle shell had given him more oxygen, but, it seemed, it wasn't letting him breathe underwater forever.

Just as he was about to start panicking, the villagers swam

towards a strange blue structure built amongst the coral. It was some kind of box, with no roof. As soon as they got near it, Porkins instantly felt his lungs fill with oxygen. But that wasn't all: suddenly he could see more clearly underwater too, and what he saw made his heart skip a beat.

The ocean was teeming with life: tiny schools of brightly-colored tropical fish; dolphins chasing each other; turtles and baby turtles swimming in formation.

They passed the box and inside it Porkins saw a small brown cube, which had opened up to reveal a blue sphere. He had no idea what it was, but it seemed to be letting him breathe underwater and had given him some sort of underwater night vision.

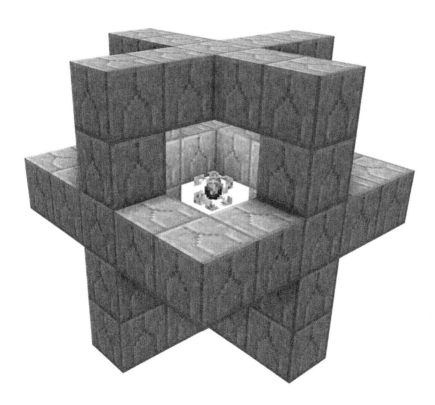

There were no more of the underwater zombies here, Porkins was pleased to see. He could see some weird-looking round green fish with orange spikes in the distance that didn't look too friendly, but thankfully they were far away.

Then, just as Porkins thought the ocean couldn't get any more wondrous, they swam over a ridge and he saw a gigantic underwater city stretching out in front of him. The buildings were all ruins, some in better condition than others, made from strange turquoise blocks. There were shipwrecks too, wooden vessels that had broken up and sunk to the ocean floor long ago.

In the center of the ruined city was a gigantic turquoise pyramid, and that's where the villagers were heading. They swam underneath it, through a ruined entrance, and then along narrow turquoise corridors.

I wonder what kind of people used to live here, Porkins thought to himself. The architecture and the style of the corridors reminded him a bit of the fortresses in the Nether.

Porkins began to panic again. The magical effect from the mysterious thing-in-the-box had worn off, and his turtle shell helmet was losing its power too. If he didn't get out of the water soon he would drown.

The villagers and Porkins began to swim upwards, through a wide passageway, until SPLOOSH! they reached a room full of air.

"Air!" Porkins gasped. "At last!"

The villagers chuckled.

"Come on," one of them said, "this way."

The villagers began swimming across the surface of the water. Porkins trod water, looking around at the room. It was a huge chamber with turquoise stones walls, with the big pool of water in the center.

This must be the top of the pyramid, he thought. High above him the roof sloped upwards into a point.

He splashed across the water. The villagers had already climbed out, and when he reached the side of the pool they pulled him out.

Lots of doorways led off from the pool room, Porkins noticed, and there were stairs too, leading to doorways higher up. Villagers and children villagers were coming out of the doors to stare at him.

"Do you all live here?" Porkins asked one of the villagers who'd saved him.

"We sure do," smiled the villager. "Welcome to Aquatropolis."

CHAPTER SEVEN
Dave Alone

Before he knew what was happening, Dave was hurtling past the swarm of zombies. The bubble column was pushing him towards the surface, and he was letting it.

Hopefully Porkins is following me, he thought. Once they reached the surface they'd be able to find Carl, then the three of them could find some land.

SPLOOSH! Dave broke the surface of the water, gasping and panting. Even though the bubbles had given him air, it was good to get a proper lungful of oxygen.

"Carl!" he yelled, once he'd got his breath back. But there was no sign of the creeper.

Dave looked into the water below, expecting to see Porkins emerge from the bubble column at any minute. He waited and waited, but there was no sign of him.

"What now?" Dave said to himself. He hoped Porkins was ok, but he couldn't stay treading water forever. His arms and legs were starting to get tired, and he knew it wouldn't be long before he'd be feeling sleepy.

Dave was torn. He didn't want to leave Porkins behind, but what else could he do? Either Porkins had found another column of bubbles to supply him with oxygen or... well, Dave didn't want to think of the alternative.

So, reluctantly, he began to swim. He had no idea which direction he was going, but if he kept going he'd have to reach land eventually.

He hoped...

CHAPTER EIGHT
The Pirates

"Wake up sleepy head!"

Carl opened his eyes. Bill the creeper opened his cell door and put a bowl on the floor.

"Mushroom stew," said Bill. "It's good for you."

Carl wasn't the biggest fan of mushrooms, but he was far too hungry to complain. He shoved his face into the bowl and began slurping the soup down.

"Is it ok?" asked Bill.

"Not really," said Carl.

Bill looked sad. "Oh," he said, "I'll try and make it nicer next time."

Carl felt guilty.

"Only joking," he said, "actually it was amazing. One of the best stews I've ever tasted."

Bill's face lit up.

"So glad to hear it!" he said excitedly.

Why am I bothering to be nice to him? thought Carl. *He's got me locked up in a cage.*

But there was something about Bill that made Carl like him. Even if he was a pirate.

"The captain wants to see you," said Bill. "Come on, I'll take you to meet him."

He opened the door of Carl's cell. For a moment Carl considered pushing past Bill and making a run for it, but where would he go? They were in the middle of the ocean.

"Sure," said Carl, "lead the way."

Bill brought Carl up some stairs, opened a trapdoor and led him onto the deck. Carl squinted, the bright sun hurting his eyes.

Waiting for him was a gang of pirate creepers, the captain, with his beard, hat and eyepatch, standing at the front.

"Arr!" said the captain.

"ARR!" the other pirates replied.

"Come on then," said Carl, "make me walk the plank. I haven't got all day."

The pirate captain laughed. "You've got spirit, little landlubber, that you have."

"Thanks," said Carl.

CAPTAIN BLACKBEARD

"I be Captain Blackbeard," said the captain. "And this here's me crew. Normally with a prisoner like you we'd sell you back to your family or make ye walk the plank, but Bill tells me you've got no family."

"They all blew themselves up," said Carl.

"They sound like noble creepers," said Blackbeard. "Any of my crew would also blow themselves up, if I asked it. And they often do, when we go into battle. There's no more honorable death for a creeper."

Carl felt a pang of shame. In truth, he had tried to blow himself up once—to kill Dave when he first met him—but he hadn't managed to do it. *What kind of creeper can't even explode?* he'd been asking himself ever since.

"So I'll offer you a choice," continued Blackbeard. "You can join my crew or walk the plank. Which shall I be?"

"That's a difficult choice," said Carl, "but I think I'll join your crew."

CHAPTER NINE
Aquatropolis

Porkins was led down a wide corridor. Like the chamber with the pool and the underwater passages they'd traveled through, the walls were made from the sleek turquoise blocks.

"What is this material?" he asked one of the villagers.

"Prismarine," the villager replied. "Beautiful, isn't it? We can't take credit for it though—all these ruins were built by the Old People, before they disappeared. The council reckon the ruins are thousands of years old."

"What council?" asked Porkins.

"The Council of Aquatropolis," said the villager. "That's who we're taking you to meet. They're the people in charge."

They came to a large chamber. Sitting on the other side of a big stone table were six villagers in turquoise robes.

"Welcome pigman," said an old female villager with long white hair. "I am Sala, the leader of the council. I hear our people saved you from the drowned."

"Drowned?" said Porkins.

"The zombies," said Sala.

"Ah yes," said Porkins. "Yes your chaps got me out of a real pickle alright. I'm lucky to still have all my trotters. But I left my friend behind—he went up one of those bubble column thingies, near where I was attacked. He's a villager too."

Sala turned to a guard.

"Please look for the pigman's friend," she said. "If he is safe, bring him back to the city."

She turned back to Porkins.

"I'm afraid I don't know your name," she said.

"Porkins," said Porkins.

"Well met, Porkins. We will look for your friend, but please do not hold out too much hope. These are dangerous times to be in the water—an ancient monster, the Kraken, has stirred from the depths and is terrorizing the ocean. Last week it destroyed some underwater ruins full of drowned, freeing them, and now the water is full of them."

"Please find Dave if you can," said Porkins sadly. "I would be very grateful. And Carl too—he's a creeper. We were all in the water together."

"We will try," said Sala. "The people of Aquatropolis always try to lend aid to those who need it. We know what it is like to need help—we came here ten years ago, a group of refugees in need of a home. We cleared the pyramid of guardians, drained the upper levels then set up home here. It's not easy living, but we have created a good life for ourselves here. A safe life. Or at least it was, before the Kraken came."

"What is this Kraken, anyway?" said Porkins. "A monster?"

"Yes," said Sala. "A squid the size of a mountain, with tentacles as thick as tree trunks. It knows no mercy, destroying ships and wiping coastal towns and villages off the map."

"Oh crumbs," said Porkins. "It sounds like a rotter, alright."

"Judging by the ancient carvings we've seen inside the pyramid, the Kraken used to terrorize the Old People," said Sala, "until they used their magic to defeat it somehow. But now, thousands of years later, it has returned, to wreak havoc on the ocean once more."

Sala smiled.

"But that's enough about the Kraken for now," she said. "As long as you remain in the pyramid you'll be safe. Even the Kraken isn't strong enough to penetrate our prismarine walls."

"Has it tried?" Porkins asked.

"Not yet," said Sala. "My scouts have seen it destroying underwater ruins and smaller monuments, but it has, thankfully, left our home alone. Now come, let us show you to your room. You must be tired."

One of the villagers led Porkins down another corridor. Eventually they arrived in a large indoor courtyard. There were doorways and windows all along the walls, and villagers looked down on them from balconies.

"These are the living quarters," said the villager. "When we first arrived our builders hollowed out the walls, building these apartments. We have a few spare, for the rare occasions we get guests."

Porkins's apartment was a large room with a sloped ceiling (*we must be at the top of the pyramid,* Porkins realized), plush carpets and a window that looked out on to the ocean.

"Very few of our rooms have windows," the villager told him, "you're lucky."

I certainly am, thought Porkins. A gap had been carved in the prismarine wall and then filled in with glass blocks. Through the window Porkins could see schools of fish swimming by and dolphins in the distance. It was beautiful.

"Are you sure it's secure, old chap?" asked Porkins, feeling a bit nervous. "I'm not going to wake in the middle of the night to find the glass broken and water up to my ears?"

The villager laughed. "Well, it's survived for ten years," he said. "So you should be ok."

Porkins had some food (some cooked fish had been left out on a table for him), then he climbed into the bed.

I hope Dave and Carl are ok, he thought. But he was so tired that it wasn't long before he was drifting off.

When he woke the room was dark, the redstone lamps having automatically turned off. The only light was from the window; the light from the sea covering the room in a shimmery blue haze.

Porkins used a trotter to rub the sleep from his eyes, then strode over to the glass.

What a spiffing view, he thought to himself. He could see ruins and shipwrecks in the distance through the murk of the water, and columns of bubbles. But there was something missing...

All the fish are gone! he realized. When he'd gone to bed the ocean had been teeming with sea life, but now there was nothing.

He wondered if they'd gone to sleep. Did fish sleep? Porkins didn't know.

But then, in the distance, he saw something moving. It was so far away that he could only make out its faint shadow in the water, but it was alive, and it was *big*.

That's what scared away all the fish, Porkins realized.

The creature swam through the water, using its tentacles to propel itself forward at incredible speed. It smashed into a shipwreck, shattering it to pieces, wooden blocks rising up to the surface.

The Kraken, thought Porkins, ice cold fear running through him. *It's the Kraken.*

Next the Kraken smashed into a monument. Like the Aquatropolis pyramid it was made of prismarine blocks, but the Kraken ripped it apart with ease.

If it comes for the pyramid, we'll never be able to stop it, thought Porkins. *I don't care what Sala says.*

Once the monument was destroyed, the Kraken swam off, disappearing into the distance. Barely a minute passed before the ocean was teeming with life again: the fish, dolphins and turtles emerging from their hiding places.

The Kraken was gone—for now.

"Oh crumbs," Porkins whispered to himself. "I think we're in big trouble."

CHAPTER TEN

The Mysterious Island

Dave was finding it hard to stay awake. He'd been swimming for so long that the sun was beginning to go down.

If I don't find land soon, I'm finished, he thought miserably.

Then, just as his eyelids were beginning to droop, he finally saw land on the horizon. He swam faster, eager to get there, but as he got closer he was confused about what he was looking at. The land appeared to be a small island, but the ground seemed to be made of grayish soil and the trees... the trees were mushrooms. Giant mushrooms.

It's a mushroom biome! he realized. He'd heard about these biomes before, in the fairy stories his mother had told him as a child, but to see one in person was something else entirely.

Before long he reached the shore. It felt so good to be back on dry land that he just lay down for a while, enjoying the sun on his skin. But night was setting in—Dave had no idea what kind of monsters lived in mushroom biomes, and he had no desire to find out. He took some wooden planks from his bag and built himself a small house. He was about to put three beds down inside, when he realized that Porkins and Carl were no longer with him.

I hope they're ok, he thought. When the sun came up he'd have to look up the recipe for boats and go looking for them.

Dave climbed in under the covers and soon drifted to sleep. He dreamed of dragons—huge black dragons circling above him, in a world with an empty black sky. One of the dragons dropped something in front of Dave. He walked closer for a look and saw that it was an egg. A huge egg. The egg began to crack, then it burst open and skeletons poured out, thousands and thousands of skeletons, all with blank white eyes. *Herobrine's* eyes.

Dave awoke with a start. He was covered in sweat.

"What a horrible nightmare," he said to himself. He hoped that was all it was; his grandmother had told him once that dreams could be prophecies of things to come, messages that meant something. Though what an egg full of skeletons meant, Dave had no idea.

BANG BANG BANG!

Dave was confused for a moment. What was that noise? But then he realized: someone was knocking on the door.

"Er, who is it?" he asked.

"Mushroom Town Police," said a gruff voice. "You come out of there this instant, sonny boy. You're in a *lot* of trouble."

CHAPTER ELEVEN
Carl the Pirate

Carl hated to admit it, but he was starting to enjoy life as a pirate.

They had just completed their first raid on another ship—a trading ship full of villagers—and were now counting their booty.

"Argh," said one of the pirates, looking down at their haul, which was piled high on the deck, "that's a lot of gold!"

The trading ship had surrendered easily. Blackbeard and his crew were notorious, Carl was told, so as soon as the villagers had seen the skull and crossbones of his sail they pulled up anchor and handed all their gold, diamond and emeralds over without a fight.

"Being a pirate is easier than I thought it would be," Carl said to Captain Blackbeard as the other pirates divided up the spoils. "There wasn't even a battle."

"Arr," said Blackbeard sadly. "It's not the same as it was when I was a boy. Villagers have become too cowardly, too quick to surrender. In my father's day they used to put up a fight. That's why I brought us to this ocean: to fight the *Kraken*."

"I'm sorry, what?" said Carl.

"Us pirates have had it easy for too long," said Blackbeard, "so when I heard stories that the legendary monster had emerged from the depths once more, we set sail straight away. We're going to hunt the Kraken down, kill it, and prove that we're the greatest pirates on the seven seas!"

Carl's blood went cold. He'd heard legends of the *Kraken* when he was a little creeper. According to the stories, it was a squid so big that it could devour ships whole. *Don't swim too far out*, his mother had said to him when they went swimming in the underground caves of their home. *If you do the Kraken might get you!*

Carl was shaken from his thoughts by a shout from the crows nest: "SHIP!"

The crew all rushed over to the side of the deck and saw that, yes, there was a ship.

"Arr, looks like we're going to have even more booty today, lads!" said Blackbeard. "Man the cannons! Starboard turn!"

They unfurled their skull-and-crossbones sail and sped after the other ship. Carl could just about make out villagers on board—it looked like another trading vessel.

"They'll slow down and surrender when they realize who we are," growled Blackbeard. "They'll know that they can't escape from the Crimson Creeper!"

But it looked like the villagers were going to try. Even when the pirates were almost upon them, they didn't slow down.

"They're trying to run!" snarled Blackbeard. "That'll be their last mistake. Cannons!!"

Carl had originally assumed the cannons just fired TNT blocks, but as he watched some of the creepers climb inside them, he realized the horrible truth.

"Wait," said Carl to Blackbeard, "you use your crew as ammo?"

"Of course," said Blackbeard. "A creeper's purpose in life is to explode. What's wrong with that?"

Carl didn't know how to answer. He'd seen countless members of his friends and family blow themselves up over the years. That was what a creeper was supposed to *do*. And it had never affected him before.

Until I started hanging around with Dave and Porkins, he realized. Somehow, traveling with the villager and the pigman had changed him. The idea of blowing himself up now seemed horrible.

Dave and Porkins have made me weak, Carl thought, feeling ashamed. *I should be happy to see creepers blowing themselves up.*

But as he watched members of the crew climb into the cannons, he felt sick to his stomach.

"Can't you just fire TNT?" asked Carl. "You've got plenty of it on board."

"We use the TNT to propel the crew out of the cannons," said Blackbeard, "but firing TNT blocks is messy and unpredictable. Creepers are far better."

"But they're your crew!" said Carl.

Blackbeard gave Carl a funny look. "Where you're from, don't creepers explode themselves to kill their enemies?" he asked.

"They do," Carl admitted

"Then I don't see what the problem is," said Blackbeard. "Right, prepare the fuses!"

The creepers standing at the back of the cannons placed down TNT blocks and got their flint and steel ready.

"Godspeed, lads," Blackbeard said. "You do your crew proud!"

The Crimson Creeper was almost upon the other ship now. On the deck of the other ship Carl could see the terror in the villagers' eyes.

This isn't right, Carl thought. *None of this is right.*

"Fire!" yelled Blackbeard.

DOOF DOOF DOOF DOOF!!!

The cannons fired, sending the creepers inside them hurtling towards the villager ship.

BOOM BOOM BOOM BOOM!!!

The creepers hit the ship, exploding it into blocks. Carl was pleased to see the villagers jump into the water just in time.

The pirates all cheered.

"Come on, we have to help them," said Carl, looking at the villagers. "We can't just leave them in the water."

"Arr, ok, ok," sighed Blackbeard. "Bring the prisoners aboard and lock them in the cells!" he shouted to his men.

But before they could, the Crimson Creeper began to shake, the waves violently shaking them back and forth.

"What's going on, Captain?" said Bill desperately.

Then, from out of the depths, the Kraken rose up. Its tentacles first, then its gaping mouth, appearing from underneath the terrified villagers and the remains of their ship.

It's a gigantic squid! Carl realized, to his horror. It was a normal-looking squid, but with green skin instead of black and about a thousand times bigger.

The villagers screamed as they were swallowed up by the Kraken's mouth, and then they—and their ship—were gone. There was an almighty splash, and then the Kraken disappeared, returning beneath the waves.

Carl somehow got back to his feet. The crew all looked terrified, apart from their captain—Blackbeard was laughing.

"That's it, boys!" he shouted. "That's the mighty Kraken! It's real, and we're going to hunt it down!"

But if the crew were happy about this, it wasn't showing on their faces. Bill looked like he wanted to cry.

"Come on you landlubbers," said Blackbeard, "man your posts!"

Reluctantly the pirates slunk back to their assigned stations.

We're all going to die, Carl realized. *That madman is going to lead us to our doom.*

Pirate Ship credit: InfinityDood, Planetminecraft.com

CHAPTER TWELVE
Princess Alicia

It was dark in his jail cell, so Dave had no idea how long he'd been there. All he'd had to eat was a bowl of mushroom stew, pushed through a slot in the wall.

Finally, when he'd given up hope of ever seeing daylight again, the door opened.

"How long have I been in here?" Dave asked, his voice hoarse.

"Thirty minutes," said a voice.

"Oh," said Dave.

His eyes began to adjust to the light, and he saw a beautiful villager girl about his age, wearing an extravagant, poofy pink dress.

She's beautiful, he thought. He felt his cheeks begin to glow red.

"My father, the King, wants to know if you're responsible for the Kraken. Are you?"

"Er no," said Dave. "What's a Kraken?"

"See?" The girl said to someone. "I told you it wouldn't be him. Does he look like a witch to you?"

A police officer, one of the ones who'd captured Dave, appeared in the doorway.

"Begging your pardon, your majesty," he said, "but a witch wouldn't look like a witch either. They wears disguises, so they do."

The girl rolled her eyes.

"What's your name, boy?" she asked Dave.

"Dave," said Dave.

"*Dave,*" she said, rolling the word around in her mouth. "What a funny name. Dave, I am Alicia, Princess of Mushroom Town and heir to the mycelium throne. This here is PC Plod, the head of our police force."

"We've met," said Dave. "He threw me into this cell."

"PC Plod wants to know if you're a witch," said Princess Alicia. "And if you are, did you summon the Kraken?"

"Um, no and no," said Dave.

"That's good enough for me," said Alicia.

"But princess," said PC Plod, "he would say that!"

"You think I can't tell when a man is lying?" Alicia snapped.

"Er, no," said Plod. "Ok you," he said to Dave, "you're free to go."

Alicia ledDave out of the small stone police station. When they walked out the front door he had to put his hand up to shield his eyes from the sun.

He'd only had a brief look at the town when he'd been dragged to the police station, but now he could see it in all its glory. It was a small town made of small, squat houses, nestled between the stalks of giant mushrooms. On a hill overlooking the town was a small stone castle, barely bigger than a house.

"Welcome to Mushroom Town, Dave," said Princess Alicia. "We build in stone, as the sea air rots wood, and we like to say that our people are made from stone too. We are a hard people, a tough people, but even we have met our match against the might of the Kraken."

"What is this Kraken everyone keeps talking about?" Dave asked.

"You came from the sea, yet you haven't seen it?" said Alicia, sounding surprised. "You are lucky. It has been sinking ships for miles around. Our fishing boats have all been destroyed, and it has even terrorized the town." She pointed to some ruined houses next to the water. "It stretches its long tentacles across the land, smashing houses and snatching our mooshroom livestock."

Alicia led Dave towards the castle. As they walked through the town the townsfolk bowed as Alicia passed.

"So, you're like a princess?" Dave asked her.

"I'm not *like* a princess, I *am* a princess," Alicia snapped.

"Do towns normally have princesses?" asked Dave.

Alicia sighed. "If you must know, my great, great grandmother was the queen of a powerful nation, as were all her ancestors. But then there was a war and she had to flee. She set sail and came to this island, and we have lived here ever since. I know this island isn't much, but it is our home, and we are a proud people."

She began to lead Dave up some stone steps towards the castle.

"My father thinks we should leave," Alicia continued. "He thinks we should set sail and find somewhere else to live; somewhere far from the Kraken. But I think we should stay and fight. And I want you to help me convince him."

"Er, what?" said Dave.

"You're the only outsider in the villager," said Alicia. "You can pretend that you're a famous sailor, and tell him you can lead us to victory against the Kraken. You're the only one who can convince him."

"Listen," said Dave, "maybe your dad's right. If this Kraken is as bad as you say, maybe leaving is the best option."

Alicia stamped her foot.

"So you're a coward too?" she said.

"No!" said Dave. "I—"

"My family built this town, I will not abandon it," said Alicia. "And you're going to convince my father to fight. Got it?"

"Got it," said Dave.

They finally arrived at the castle. Alicia opened the door and walked in, followed by Dave. The entrance hall was barely bigger than Dave's old house had been. At the back was an enormously fat villager on a throne. He was munching down on a whole cooked chicken.

"Ah, hello daughter," the fat villager said, bits of chicken spraying from his mouth. "It's good to see you. Who's your friend?"

"This is Dave, father," she said. "He's a legendary sailor, and he knows how to defeat the Kraken. Dave, this is my father—King Dontos."

"Well met, Dave," said the king, "but my daughter knows my feelings on this matter. The Kraken is too powerful—we must flee. We wouldn't stand a chance against it."

Dave looked at Alicia. She was looking at him with pleading eyes.

Gosh, she is beautiful, he thought.

"King Dontos," said Dave, trying to sound more confident than he felt, "this is your home. Would the kings and queens who came before you have fled? If this is your kingdom, you should defend it. And I can help you."

The king looked hard at him, occasionally taking another bite of chicken. "Brave Dave, you have convinced me. What should we do?"

"Er..." said Dave.

"Dave was telling me we should build a big ship, with holes on the side for archers to fire arrows through," said Alicia. "He said we should tell the archers to fire into the Kraken's mouth, as that's its weak spot."

"Good lord," said the king, "you are clever, Dave."

"Um, I sure am," said Dave.

Afterwards, Alicia led Dave down to the docks. Most of the buildings there were in ruins, destroyed by the Kraken.

"How did you know about the shooting the Kraken in the mouth thing?" Dave asked Alicia.

"The castle has a big library," Alicia said. "They brought the books with them when they fled the old kingdom. My father never bothers to read the books, but I do. There's an account there of how the Old People defeated the Kraken. Apparently it's some kind of immortal being: it can be killed by a direct hit down its throat, but it can be summoned again and respawned. According to one of the books I read, the Old People created the Kraken with their magic, as a weapon during one of their wars. They sent it against their enemies' ships, and if it died they blew a magical horn to respawn it."

"Maybe that's how it's come back after so many years," said Dave. "Maybe someone found that horn and blew it."

"Exactly what I thought," said Alicia. "But who would do such a terrible thing?"

CHAPTER THIRTEEN
The Kraken Attacken

The villagers of Aquatropolis were preparing for war.

Their blacksmiths were busy building diamond armor and enchanting tridents, ready for an attack on the Kraken.

"Are you sure this is a good idea?" Porkins asked Sala, as they watched some of the villagers practice their attack moves in the big pool. "That Kraken is almost as big as this pyramid. You won't stand a chance."

"My scouts report that the Kraken rests sometimes," said Sala. "Perhaps it sleeps, it's hard to tell. We can catch it unaware and kill it. Its tentacles will be its weakest bit: we can slice them off, then the monster will be powerless."

It seemed like a good enough plan to Porkins, but he still couldn't help but worry. There were so many things that could go wrong.

When there was finally enough armor for them all, the villagers gathered by the side of the pool. They were a magnificent sight: dressed in diamond armor and wearing turtle shell helmets, each of them holding a trident and with potions of water breathing attached to their belts.

Nearly all the men and women of fighting age had volunteered to fight against the Kraken. The only ones staying behind were the elderly, the children and the council. And Porkins. The pigman had wanted to go, but had realized that with his sloppy swimming skills he'd just get in the way.

"Good luck, all of you," Sala told them. "May your tridents fly true. And remember—we're all counting on you."

The armored villagers dived into the pool. They trod water until they were all ready, then they dived down into the water, disappearing into the depths of the pyramid.

There was nothing for the rest of them to do but wait. Porkins went back to his bedroom, watching the villagers swimming into the distance through his window.

"I should have gone with them," he thought. He had already lost so many people: his fellow pigmen, who'd all been turned into zombies, Carl and Dave, who could be anywhere—if they were even still alive—and now the villagers who'd saved his life from the drowned were risking their lives without him.

He watched through the window until he could no longer see the villagers, then he went back down to the pool. Sala was resting her feet in the water.

"In my youth I would have gone with them," she said sadly to Porkins. "But age catches up with all of us, I'm afraid."

"I'm sure those chaps will be fine," Porkins said, although he didn't really believe it himself.

"When I and the rest of the council founded this place, we thought it would be a safe haven," said Sala. "I thought we could hide away from the rest of the world. I never dreamed that something like this could happen. That we'd be under attack from an ancient monster."

"It's a real pickle, alright," said Porkins.

Porkins sat down on the edge of the pool next to Sala, sliding his trotters into the water.

"What's that?" he said suddenly. Something was swimming up towards them.

SPLASH!

A villager burst out of the water. He splashed over to Porkins and Sala, grabbing on to the side of the pool. His armor was badly damaged, Porkins saw, and his turtle shell helmet was gone.

"It's coming!" the villager gasped, his eyes bulging madly. "It killed everyone! Everyone but me! The Kraken is coming!"

KRAKA-THOOM!!!!

The pyramid shook. Something big had just crashed into it, and Porkins had a good idea what it was.

"The Kraken is here!" Sala yelled. "Everyone, get ready to

protect the pyramid! Grab as many prismarine blocks as you can from the storage room, we may need to plug the gaps if it breaks through!"

Porkins followed the other villagers to a cellar full of chests, each one filled with blocks. He grabbed as many as he could, then ran back up to the main chamber.

THOOM!!!!

The pyramid shook violently as the Kraken smashed into it once more.

"Water's coming in through the council chamber walls!" someone yelled.

Porkins ran to the council chamber. Water was pouring through a gap in the wall, and he and some other villagers placed blocks down as quickly as they could, sealing the gap back up.

Before long, Porkins found himself running back and forth all over the upper floors of the pyramid, plugging up gaps. Every time the Kraken smashed into the pyramid, more gaps would open, and it became harder and harder to keep on top of them.

"We can't keep this up forever," Porkins said, when he found himself next to Sala, plugging up one of the walls in the apartment complex. "Do you have any wood? We could build some boats for the kids, in case the pyramid floods."

"Good idea," said Sala. "There should be some in the storage room."

So Porkins ran back to the room with the chests, searching through them until he found some wooden planks and some spades to use as oars. Porkins didn't know many crafting recipes, but he'd discovered how to build boats back when he lived in underground caves after first escaping the Nether.

He ran back up to the chamber with the pool, then started building boats and throwing them into the water.

"Little chaps and chapettes!" Porkins yelled. "Who wants to go for a lovely boat ride?"

Soon each of the kids was sat in their own boat in the pool.

"What's going to happen?" one of the children asked. "Is the pyramid going to break?"

"Of course not," said Porkins, trying to smile. "As long as we're in here we're perfectly safe.

GRA-THOOOM!!!!!

The Kraken smashed into the pyramid once more, but this time it broke through. For a moment Porkins looked up in horror at its huge gaping mouth and grasping tentacles, the children screaming in terror behind him. Then the water flooded in, washing over them and filling the pyramid.

Porkins was caught in the flood, the water carrying him along. He quickly grabbed a boat and got into it.

Porkins lost all sense of direction as he was washed this way and that. All around him were broken blocks swirling waters and chaos. He began to run out of air, and started to feel faint...

When he awoke, Porkins was floating in the sea in his boat. The sky above him was blue.

"I survived..." he gasped. He looked around: the sea was full of tiny prismarine blocks, floating on the waves—the last remains of the pyramid. But that wasn't all, thankfully. The children villagers were there too, floating in their wooden boats.

"Thank goodness," said Porkins.

Then he saw a sight that filled his heart with joy: a big ship was sailing towards them.

"Over here!" Porkins yelled. "I say, over here! We need assistance!"

The ship pulled up, and Porkins was surprised to see that its crew were all creepers.

A creeper with a black beard and a pirate hat stepped forward.

"You are now prisoners of the Crimson Creeper," he growled at Porkins and the kids.

But Porkins's attention was elsewhere. He *recognized* one of the creepers. The smallest one, who was looking guilty.

"Carl, old chap!" said Porkins happily. "You're alive!"

The creepers helped Porkins and the kids up onto the ship.

"It's so good to see you, old bean!" Porkins said, giving Carl a big hug. "I don't suppose Dave's here too?"

"Afraid not," said Carl sadly.

"Right," growled the creeper with the beard. "Throw them all in the cells!"

"But, Captain, they's only children!" said one of the other creepers.

"We're pirates," growled the bearded pirate. "We don't help people, we take them prisoners! Maybe we can ransom them back to their people."

"I... I'm afraid they're *orphans*," Porkins whispered, making sure the children didn't hear him. "Their home was destroyed by the Kraken."

"I know this pigman, Captain," said Carl. "He's a bit of a moron, but he's a good person."

"Quiet, all of you!" The captain growled. "We're only in this ocean to defeat the Kraken, and that's what we're going to do—no distractions! Now lock them all up."

Porkins was grabbed by two creepers and led towards a trapdoor. The children were led the same way, most of them crying.

"Sorry Porkins," Carl whispered to him. "I'll get you out, I promise."

CHAPTER FOURTEEN
Reunited

Alicia's ship was finally ready to set sail. She'd called it, appropriately, the *Golden Princess*.

"I got the design from a book," she told Dave. "It should be a lot tougher than our old fishing boats. The ones the Kraken destroyed."

She had selected a small crew of her town's best archers and warriors, and they were all onboard now, waiting to leave.

"Are you sure you won't change your mind, daughter?" the king called from the dock. He and the other townsfolk had gathered to see them off.

"Our people already left one kingdom behind," Alicia said. "I won't let us flee another. We will defend Mushroom Town—with our life if we have to."

The king's face went pale. "Be careful!" he begged.

And so they set sail. Dave stayed at the front of the boat, looking for any sign of Carl and Porkins. It seemed unlikely that they were still alive in the water, but he hadn't given up hope. Not yet.

"How will we find the Kraken?" Dave asked Alicia.

"Don't worry," Alicia said darkly, "it'll find us."

But the day went on, and there was no sign of the Kraken. It was only when the sun started going down that they saw something on the horizon coming towards them.

"Is that it?" asked Dave.

Alicia squinted. "No," she said, "it looks more like... a ship

As the ship came closer, they could see its black sail—a black sail with a skull on it.

"Pirates!" one of the villagers yelled. "Let's get out of here!"

"No," snapped Alicia. "We have a powerful ship, we can take on these rogues. These waters belong to my kingdom, and I'll arrest these pirates myself—or send them to the bottom of the ocean!"

So they sped towards the pirates, and the pirates towards them.

"Archers, prepare your bows!" yelled Alicia. "Everyone else, prepare your swords!"

From her pink dress she pulled out a diamond sword, glowing purple with enchantments.

As the pirate ship came closer, Dave saw they were creepers. That made him think of Carl.

I hope that little guy's ok, he thought sadly. *Wherever he is.*

*

"Full speed ahead!" yelled Blackbeard. "It looks like these landlubbers want a fight. Let's give it to them!"

Carl had his sword ready. As the other ship got nearer he saw it was crewed by villagers.

This isn't right, he thought. *There's a Kraken on the loose and we're wasting time killing each other.* Plus, he was having second thoughts about being a pirate. It had been fun when they'd just been stealing gold, but their last battle had ended with all those villagers getting swallowed up by the Kraken. This hadn't been what he'd signed up for.

The two ships pulled up alongside each other.

"Hand over your gold or prepare to be boarded!" Blackbeard yelled.

"We don't have any gold, you pirate scum!" a villager in a pink dress and a crown yelled back. "We're only out here hunting the Kraken—but we've got time to deal with you first!"

They're only after the Kraken, the same as us, thought Carl. *Why are we fighting?*

"Prepare the cannons!" Blackbeard yelled. Some of the creeper crew began climbing into the cannons.

"Prepare your arrows!" yelled the villager girl.

I've got to stop these idiots from killing each other, Carl realized. He took a deep breath then ran forward to the railing.

"WAIT!!!" he yelled. Both crews stopped and stared at him.

"Carl?" said a surprised voice. To his surprise, Carl saw that Dave was one of the crew on the villager ship.

"Dave, you're alive?" said Carl.

"Looks like it," grinned Dave. Then his face fell. "I don't suppose you've seen Porkins?"

"Um, actually he's one of our prisoners," said Carl.

"Carl!" Blackbeard snapped. "Stop chatting with the enemy! Are you with us or not?"

"Everyone just listen," said Carl. "We have a common enemy— the Kraken! Let's defeat it together. The ocean isn't safe for anyone while it lives."

"Never," snarled Blackbeard. "Pirates don't team up with landlubbers."

"And we don't team up with criminals," the girl in the pink dress said.

"Carl's right," Dave said. "If we fight, the only people we'll harm are ourselves. Whoever wins the battle will have a damaged ship and less crew, and will be easy prey for the Kraken."

"Come on guys," Carl said to the pirates, "you know it makes sense."

*

Porkins was trying to pick the lock of his cell with his curly tail. He'd read a story about a pigman doing this once, but he didn't know if it was actually possible. He had to try, though.

"Nearly there," he said to the kids, "don't worry little chaps, I'll have you free soon!"

Porkins and the villager children had all been locked in the same cell. It was very cramped, but Porkins hoped they wouldn't be there long.

Suddenly the hatch above swung open and a villager came

down the ladder. A villager Porkins recognized.

"Dave!" he said, amazed. "Oh no, you're not a prisoner too?"

"Hey Porkins, good to see you," Dave grinned. "And no, I'm not a prisoner. And neither are you guys anymore."

Dave explained that the villagers had made a deal with the pirates: Porkins and the villager children from Aquatropolis would be allowed to go free, and a princess from a mushroom biome island had agreed to take them on her ship. It was all very confusing for the children, but Porkins explained it to them as clearly as he could.

"Sorry for locking you up in a cell, Porkins," Carl said to him.

"Not to worry, old bean," said Porkins, "it's all sorted now. I'm just glad the three of us are together again!"

So Porkins, Dave and the villager children went to the Golden Princess ship, and Carl stayed with the pirates on the Crimson Creeper.

"At least until we've defeated the Kraken," Carl said to Dave and Porkins. "These pirates have been good to me—I owe them a debt."

So all that was left was for the two ships to wait—to wait until the Kraken emerged once more.

CHAPTER FIFTEEN
Drowned

Carl was having a crisis. He was overjoyed that Dave and Porkins had survived, but now he faced a dilemma: should he continue with them, on Dave's quest to defeat the ender dragon, or should he stay with the pirates?

Dave and Porkins were his friends, but being with Blackbeard's crew had reminded Carl of what it was like to hang around with other creepers, and part of him missed it. He had been with Dave and Porkins so long that the idea of blowing himself up seemed horrible. Maybe he needed to stay with the pirates, so he could remember what being a creeper was all about.

Carl had taken lookout duty tonight, so he had plenty of time to think, up in the crows nest. Across the water he could see the Golden Princess. Dave and Porkins were on there, he knew. He wondered if they were having as complicated thoughts as him.

Then, in the moonlight, Carl saw a small rowboat making its way over from the Golden Princess.

Who's that? he wondered

The row boat pulled up alongside the Crimson Creeper and Carl saw that it was Captain Blackbeard.

I wonder what he was doing over on the Golden Princess, Carl thought. He was about to call out to the captain when suddenly there was a huge explosion across the water. Half of the Golden Princess was destroyed, and the other half was on fire and sinking into the water.

Blackbeard had climbed back onto the deck of the Crimson Creeper. He was watching the Golden Princess burn with a big grin on his face.

"You did that, didn't you!" Carl yelled down at him. "Why?"

Blackbeard looked up at him, a look of anger flashing across his face.

The rest of the creeper crew were running up to the deck now, rubbing the sleep from their eyes.

"What happened?" asked Bill, looking in disbelief at the Golden Princess across the water.

"Captain Blackbeard snuck over and blew it up with TNT!" yelled Carl, climbing down from the crows nest.

"Liar!" spat Blackbeard. "He's the little coward who wouldn't even blow himself up. You're really going to believe him over me?"

"Why did you do it?" said Carl angrily. "They were going to help us defeat the Kraken!"

"We don't need their help!" yelled Blackbeard. "I didn't summon the Kraken so that those landlubbers could take all the glory!"

The creepers all looked at Blackbeard in shock. Blackbeard's face fell as he realized what he'd just said.

"You summoned the Kraken?!" said Carl.

"Arr, that I did," said Blackbeard, reluctantly.

"Why would you do something so dumb?" said Carl.

Blackbeard laughed. "When I was a little pirate, serving on me dad's ship, he would tell us all stories of the legend of the Kraken. Back in ancient times, when the Old People ruled, the Kraken terrorized ships and villages and towns along the coasts. Then one day, a legendary pirate rose up and defeated it, banishing it to the depths of the ocean with a legendary magic horn." He held up a horn encrusted with jewels. "When my men found this in a treasure chest, I knew immediately what it was: the legendary pirate's horn."

"So you blew a magic horn and freed the Kraken," said Carl. "Why?"

"So I could defeat it and become the most famous pirate in the world, of course!" said Blackbeard. He looked round at his crew. "We can still do it," he said. "Help me to defeat the monster and our names will live on in pirate history."

"People have died because of you!" said Carl.

"I'm a pirate, what do you expect?" growled Blackbeard. "We're all pirates. All my men are willing to lay down their lives, like real creepers—unlike you. You coward."

Blackbeard's words cut Carl deep.

Maybe I am a coward, he thought. *A creeper who won't even blow himself up.*

Blackbeard drew his sword—a gleaming golden blade—and walked towards Carl.

"And cowards have no place on this ship," Blackbeard said. He charged at Carl, swinging his golden sword, but Carl was too quick—rolling out of the way so that Blackbeard missed him. Blackbeard lost his balance and smashed into the railings, almost going over into the sea.

"Coward!" Blackbeard yelled at Carl.

"Captain, that's enough," said Bill. He'd drawn his sword and pointed it at Blackbeard.

"What are you doing, boy?" Blackbeard laughed.

"This has gone far enough," said Bill. "Members of our crew have died chasing the Kraken. And you were the one who summoned it! They died for nothing!"

"Creepers are supposed to die!" yelled Blackbeard. "That's what we do, we blow ourselves up!"

He looked round at the crew.

"Will none of you stand up for me?" said Blackbeard. "After all I've done for this crew."

"You've led them to their deaths just so you could be famous," said Carl. "I think you've done enough."

"So be it," said Blackbeard darkly. "You leave me no choice."

Blackbeard's body began hissing and flashing white.

"He's exploding himself!" one of the crew yelled.

Bill charged forward. Where the cabin boy found the bravery from, Carl had no idea, but he smashed Blackbeard with his shoulder, sending him flying over the railing into the ocean.

"Cowaaaaards!" Blackbeard yelled as he fell, then SPLOOSH!—he was gone.

A tiny explosion splashed up from the water. Captain

Blackbeard was dead. All that was left was his hat, which had fallen off his head onto the deck when he'd fallen.

Carl was about to make a sarcastic comment, but then he heard screaming in the distance, and remembered the Golden Princess was still on fire.

"Let's get in row boats and go save them!" he yelled. "Go go go!"

*

Dave was woken by an explosion. He opened his eyes and saw that half of his cabin was destroyed, and the other half was on fire.

He laid some sand blocks down, extinguishing the flames, then ran into the corridor. Some of the crew and the kids were trapped by the fire, so Dave laid more sand blocks down to free them, then led everyone up onto the deck.

The ship—or what was left of it—was sinking into the water.

"Is everyone alright?" Princess Alicia asked, as everyone gathered on the deck. "Is anyone missing?"

Thankfully it turned out that the part of the ship that had exploded had only been full of supplies, so no-one was harmed, but that didn't change the fact that they were sinking rapidly into the water.

And just when Dave thought it couldn't get worse, it did.

"Drowned!" someone yelled.

Drowned? thought Dave. *Who's drowned?* But then he realized what they were talking about: climbing up the ruins of the ship were water zombies.

"Archers, form up!" Alicia yelled. "Children, behind us!"

The archers stepped forward, readying their bows, and the villager kids from Aquatropolis ran out of the way to safety.

"FIRE!" Alicia yelled, and the archers unleashed a torrent of arrows, pushing the drowned back.

The drowned were now climbing up all the sides of the ship, so Dave and Porkins and the other remaining adult villagers unsheathed their swords and started slashing at them, sending them back into the water.

"There's too many of the blighters!" Porkins yelled. "We can't keep this up forever!"

Dave saw that he was right: the water was *full* of drowned—hundreds of them, all clambering towards the boat.

"Fall back!" Dave heard Alicia yell. He looked over and saw the archers retreating; the drowned had climbed on board the boat now—for every one of them the archers shot down, two more took its place.

On all sides of the boat, the drowned had climbed onto the deck. Alicia, Porkins, Dave, the crew and the children all retreated to the middle of the deck, surrounded on all sides.

"What now?" one of the crew asked.

Dave had no idea.

*

Porkins wasn't worried about his own life, he was only worried about the children.

Everything I do just gets them into more trouble, he thought desperately. He'd saved them from the Kraken at Aquatropolis, only to get captured by pirates. Now they were free from the pirates, only to get slain by drowned.

He gripped his sword tightly, prepared to fight the drowned to his last breath.

Then a scuffle broke out on deck. At first Porkins couldn't work out what it was; something was attacking the drowned. Then he saw green shapes fighting with swords and he realized what it was: the pirates had arrived to save them!

"Have at thee!" one of the pirates yelled, throwing a trident through a drowned's chest.

"Come on," Princess Alicia yelled, "it's time to fight back!"

The drowned didn't know which way to turn: they had the creeper pirates behind them and Porkins, Dave and the villagers in front.

The creepers and villagers fought hard. They were

outnumbered by the drowned, but the zombies were poor fighters—especially on land. Soon all the drowned were dead. They left a few tridents behind, and Dave and Porkins both grabbed one. There was a fishing rod too, and Porkins grabbed that.

They'd won the battle, but the ship was still sinking.

"Come on," said Carl, "we have boats."

The pirates had come over in row boats, and they'd brought spares. Everyone climbed into a boat, then they rowed back to the Crimson Creeper.

As they rowed across the water they watched as the flaming ruin of the Golden Princess disappeared into the water.

"Sorry about your boat," Porkins heard one of the pirates say to Princess Alicia. "Our Captain did that."

"What?!" snapped Alicia. "I'll have his head!"

"You're too late," said Carl. "His head's blown up, along with the rest of him."

CHAPTER SIXTEEN
Carl's Big Decision

With two crews packed aboard the Crimson Creeper, it was a bit cramped.

Dave suggested that they go back to Mushroom Town to drop the kids off, but, to his surprise, the kids wanted to stay.

"The Kraken destroyed our home," one of the kids said. "We want to see it get blowed up!"

So now all that was left to do was wait for the Kraken to return. This time, however, they didn't have to wait long. The sun was only just starting to rise when a shout rang out from the crow's nest:

"KRAKEN!"

Dave ran over to the side of the boat, and got his first look at Kraken.

"Holy smokes," he gasped.

It was the biggest mob he'd ever seen: a gigantic green beast the size of an island, with thick, grasping tentacles and a round gaping mouth rimmed with sharp teeth.

It rose from the water, its tentacles reaching up higher than a mountain, then it splashed back down into the ocean, the impact sending out waves that shook their ship.

"It's coming towards us underwater!" the creeper in the crows nest shouted.

The other creepers were running about in confusion.

"Should we man the cannons?" one asked.

"Who's the new captain?" asked another. "Who's gonna tell us what to do?"

Alicia was on deck now, shouting for the archers to prepare their bows once more. Dave wasn't much of an archer, but he grabbed a bow too. His sword wouldn't be much use against the Kraken. Porkins stood next to him, his own bow at the ready.

"Why can't we ever have an adventure that doesn't end in a big battle?" Porkins said, smiling.

"That would be too easy, wouldn't it," Dave grinned. "Where's Carl, by the way?"

*

The creepers were running around like headless chickens.

They need a leader, Carl thought. But how could he lead them? For all Blackbeard's faults, he'd been right about Carl: he *was* a coward. What kind of creeper couldn't even blow himself up?

"Everyone, man the cannons!"

It was Bill. Carl looked round in amazement. The cabin boy was shaking and nervous, but he was stepping up to take command.

"Who put you in charge?" one of the creepers sneered.

"No-one," Bill said, "but we need someone to lead!"

"Not you though," said the creeper. "You're just a cabin boy."

"ALRIGHT YOU LAZY LANDLUBBERS!!!" Bill shouted. "MAN THOSE CANNONS! LOOK SHARP!"

Everyone was looking at him in amazement.

"Wow, Bill," said Carl, "I didn't know you had it in you!"

"I didn't know either," said Bill, his cheeks glowing red. "Right everyone," he continued, "I'm not your captain, so I'm not going to order you to blow yourselves up. I don't have that right. But we *can* use TNT in the cannons instead. One TNT block to launch another. So get those cannons loaded, go go go!"

Carl watched in awe as the creepers ran around, following Bill's orders.

I thought that kid was just a little runt, Carl thought. *But he's a real creeper. Unlike me.*

The Kraken was almost upon them. Everyone had their part to play: the villagers with their bows and the creepers with the cannons. Even Porkins and Dave had their bows ready.

My legs are too short to use a bow, Carl thought miserably. *And all the cannons are taken. What use am I?*

And then he realized; he realized what he could do to help.

He climbed into one of the cannons.

CHAPTER SEVENTEEN
The Kraken Returns

Dave readied his bow. He could see the Kraken now, ploughing towards them just under the water.

"Remember, aim for its mouth if you can!" Alicia shouted. "That's its weak spot!"

The Kraken was coming nearer… nearer…

"Archers FIRE!" Alicia screamed. Arrows flew through the air, raining down on the Kraken's back.

"Cannons FIRE!" one of the creepers yelled.

DOOF! DOOF! DOOF!

TNT blocks went flying out of the cannons, exploding as they hit the Kraken. It roared in pain, then dived back into the water, disappearing into the depths. Everyone on the boats—creepers, villagers and pigman—all cheered.

"I dropped my flint and steel," said one of the creepers. "I couldn't light my TNT in time, sorry."

"Don't worry," said Alicia, "I'll think you'll get another chance. I don't think the Kraken's defeated yet."

*

Carl's heart was beating like crazy. He'd closed his eyes and braced himself to be fired out of the cannon, but—by some miracle—the creeper who was meant to light the fuse of his cannon had messed up.

"I dropped my flint and steel," he heard the creeper say. *"I couldn't light my TNT in time, sorry."*

Carl was in two minds whether to climb out. The Kraken would surely be coming back round for another attack, and he didn't think the creeper manning his cannon would make the same mistake twice.

"What should I do?" he muttered.

*

"I swear that cannon just spoke," Porkins said.

Dave gave him a funny look.

"I swear!" said Porkins. "Us pigmen have very good hearing—it's our big ears. There's someone inside it!"

Dave looked around. *Wait a minute,* he thought, *where's Carl?*

Suddenly he had a nasty feeling. He ran over to the cannon.

"Hey!" said the creeper manning it. "Don't look into the barrel, you'll get your head blown off!"

But Dave didn't hear him. He was too busy looking at what was inside the cannon: it was Carl.

"What are you doing?" said Dave. "Get out of there!"

Carl sighed.

"Blackbeard was an idiot," he said, "but he was right about one thing. I'm a creeper, my purpose is to explode. Ever since I realized my fuse doesn't work, after I tried to blow you up, I've been wondering what the point of me is. What's the point of a creeper who can't blow up?"

"What's the point of anyone?" Dave said. "Why do you need to do the same thing as every other creeper? It's your life, you can do what you like with it."

"And I want to blow myself up," said Carl.

"I don't think you really do," said Dave. "You just think you should."

"Listen," snapped Carl, "don't you want to defeat the Kraken?"

"I do," said Dave, "but not if it means losing one of my friends."

"You're not going to get out of the way of the cannon, are you?" said Carl.

"Nope," said Dave. "If you want to fire yourself out of it, you'll have to blow me up too."

"It's tempting," said Carl, grinning.

Dave reached into the cannon and helped pull Carl out.

*

I almost made a terrible mistake, thought Carl, as Dave helped him onto the deck. He was about to say thank you to Dave, when a cry went out:

"Look out chaps!" Porkins yelled. "It's coming back around!"

He was right, the Kraken had risen from the waves once more and was ploughing through the water towards them.

"Bill," Carl said, "you need to get the crew together and swing the ship around so we have a clear shot from the cannons."

"But I'm not the captain!" said Bill.

"You are now," said Carl, picking up Blackbeard's hat and handing it to him. "You defeated Blackbeard. This is yours now."

Bill looked down at the hat. Then a look of determination crossed his face, and he placed the hat onto his head.

"AVAST YE SCURVY DOGS!" he yelled. "ALL HANDS ON DECK!"

"AVAST YE SCURVY DOGS!"

The crew immediately jumped to their feet.

The creepers prepared the cannons and the villagers notched their bows. They fired as the Kraken came near, and it retreated into the water once more.

"This is no good, " said Princess Alicia, "we need to hit it in the mouth!"

"How can we?" asked one of the creepers. "It keeps its mouth in the water."

"If only we could get its attention somehow," said Alicia. "Get it to rise up out of the waves."

Then Carl had a brainwave. He ran below deck, straight to Blackbeard's old quarters. He started rummaging through Blackbeard's things until he saw a chest hidden away in the corner of the room with a sheet over it.

Aha, Carl thought. He opened the chest and immediately saw what he'd been looking for.

*

Dave and the others were getting ready to fend the Kraken off for the third time. The monster was charging towards them under the water, getting nearer by the second.

"We'll run out of TNT and arrows soon," said Princess Alicia. "We need to get it to show us its mouth!"

"I think I can help."

It was Carl. He'd come back on deck, and was holding an enormous horn. It looked very old, and was encrusted with jewels.

"Blackbeard used this to summon the Kraken," Carl said. "Maybe if we blow it, it'll get its attention."

"Well do it then!" snapped Alicia. "Hurry up!"

Carl put the horn to his lips and blew. A deep, terrible sound came out of it; so loud that everyone covered their ears.

"It's working!" Porkins yelled. "Look at the Kraken!"

The Kraken reared out of the water, attracted by the sound. Its huge, gaping mouth was wide open and facing them.

"FIRE EVERYTHING!" Alicia yelled.

TNT and arrows whizzed through the sky, hitting the Kraken right in the mouth. It roared in pain.

"Aim down its throat!" yelled Bill.

Finally, one of the TNT blocks went right down the Kraken's throat, disappearing from view.

From inside the Kraken came a muffled explosion, then smoke started pouring from its mouth. The Kraken screamed in pain, its tentacles flailing wildly, then it stopped moving, floating limply to the top of the water.

"It's a goner!" Porkins yelled happily.

POOF! The Kraken disappeared, just like any other mob. Hundreds of ink sacs floated to the surface.

Everyone was jumping up and down and hugging each other.

"We did it!" they said to each other. "We did it!"

Porkins gave Dave and Carl a hug.

"Well done, chaps!" he said. "Top work!"

CHAPTER EIGHTEEN
Aftermath

After picking up all the ink sacs, the crew set sail once again. Their first stop was Mushroom Town, where they dropped Princess Alicia and her people off. Most of the villager children from Aquatropolis decided to stay on the island, but some insisted on staying on the ship and becoming pirates. Bill—who the crew had made their official captain—agreed to take them on.

"Thank you for all your help," Princess Alicia said to Dave. "I'm sorry if I was a bit mean to you. You're a real hero."

She kissed him on the cheek, and Dave went bright red.

"Er, thank you," he muttered.

Then the Crimson Creeper set sail once more. Bill agreed to bring Dave, Porkins and Carl to the nearest land to drop them off.

"What will you do now?" Carl asked Bill. "Keep pirating?"

"Yeah," said Bill. "But we'll be nicer pirates from now on. Helping people, and only robbing bad guys. Oh, and no more blowing ourselves up."

"Sounds good," grinned Carl.

"You should come with us," Bill added. "You could be my first officer."

"Sorry," said Carl, "I'm gonna stick with Dave and Porkins for now. They may be idiots, but they're my idiots."

"Er, we're right here," said Dave.

Dave threw an ender eye into the sky; it hovered there for a moment then flew off into the distance.

"It went north," said Bill. "SET A COURSE FOR NORTH!"

The pirates prepared the rigging then set sail, heading off towards the horizon.

EPILOGUE

Dave lay on his back, looking up at the stars and listening to the lapping of the waves as the Crimson Creeper ploughed gently across the ocean. He was on the deck, having come up here for some peace and quiet. The only other people up here were the creeper who turned the wheel and the creeper keeping lookout in the crows nest, and they were keeping themselves to themselves.

Once we get back to dry land, we can continue with our adventure, he thought. He had all that he needed now: the ender eyes would lead him, Porkins and Carl to another stronghold, then they could go into the End and defeat the ender dragon.

Dave had no doubt that there would be more troubles ahead, but at least they had left Herobrine far behind them, and there had been no sign of Robo Steve since he teleported away after the battle in Snow Town.

All we have to do is keep out of trouble and follow the path the eyes show us, thought Dave.

For the first time in ages he wondered how his parents were doing. After the destruction of his village, his parents and the rest of his people had gone off to find a new home. He hoped that they were doing alright, but he had no way of checking.

"Ship ahoy!" yelled the creeper in the crows nest. Dave jumped up and ran to the side of the ship. Sure enough, there was another ship approaching theirs: a huge ship with a bright red sail.

The other creeper pirates were emerging from below deck now, wiping the sleep from their eyes. Porkins and Carl came up too.

"What's going on, old bean?" yawned Porkins, walking over to Dave.

"A ship," said Dave. "A big one."

The other ship pulled to a stop just before it hit theirs. It towered over them.

A villager appeared on deck, looking down at then. He was wearing a red baseball cap and a pair of sunglasses.

"Ahoy there!" Bill the creeper yelled up at him. "To what do we owe the pleasure?"

"We're looking for warriors," the villager yelled back. "The bravest warriors there are. Do you dudes have any warriors among you? We have prizes to win!"

"We're warriors!" said Porkins excitedly, putting his arms round Dave and Carl. "Me, Dave and Carl."

"What are you doing, pork brain?" hissed Carl.

"He said they have prizes!" said Porkins.

The villager in the baseball cap smiled. "Great," he said. "Come on board!"

A doorway opened in the side of the big ship and a gangway slid down to the deck of the Crimson Creeper, creating a bridge between them.

"Come on then," said the baseball cap villager.

"Porkins I don't think this is such a great idea," whispered Dave. "We have no idea what they want or who they are."

Dave stepped forward. "I'm afraid we've changed our mind," he said. "Sorry about that."

"That's a shame," said the villager with the baseball cap. "It's a great honor to compete in the Cool Dude Battle Royale. Are you sure you won't change your mind?"

"Sorry," said Dave.

"Then you leave us no choice," said baseball cap, his smile disappearing. "Our master needs warriors, and warriors he shall have. Seize them!"

Three huge stone golems ran out of the doorway, rushing across the gangplank.

They're wearing sunglasses! Dave had time to think, before the golems grabbed him, Porkins and Carl.

"Unhand them!" said Bill. "Pirates, attack!"

The creeper pirates drew their swords and swung them at the

golems, but the golems were too strong, batting the creepers away with their huge arms,

Dave tried to struggle free, but the golem's grip on him was too powerful.

Dave, Carl and Porkins were dragged into the belly of the big ship, the door closing behind them. For a moment they were in complete darkness, but then some redstone lights flickered on.

There were surrounded by villagers in baseball caps and sunglasses.

"Who are you weirdos?" asked Carl.

"We are the Cool Dudes," said the villager with the red baseball cap, coming down a ladder from above. "An ancient order of knights who throughout time have served the coolest dudes in history."

"Er, what?" said Dave.

"Welcome to our ship, the HMS Awesome. You will be our prisoners until we reach Cool Island."

"I hate to ask, old bean," said Porkins, "but what's going to happen to us when we get to Cool Island?"

The villager with the red baseball cap grinned.

"You and ninety seven others will be competing in the Cool Dude Battle Royale—one hundred competitors, one winner. It's the coolest tournament in the world."

"What will we be competing in?" asked Dave.

"Fighting," said red baseball cap. "To the death!"

BOOK 4

The Cool Dude Battle Royale

CHAPTER ONE
Cool Island

"This is another fine mess you've got me into," said Carl.

"I am sorry, chaps," said Porkins. "I need to know when to keep my mouth jolly well shut."

"How about *all* the time?" said Carl. "If it helps, I can sew your mouth shut for you. I'm very handy with a needle and thread."

"Don't be too hard on Porkins," said Dave. "I think they would have taken three prisoners whatever happened."

"Yes," said Carl, "but they might have taken three *different* prisoners. Not us!"

The three of them were locked up in jail cells in the bowels of the big ship. The villagers holding them prisoner called themselves the *Cool Dudes*.

The villager who seemed to be in charge, the one with the red baseball cap, had told Dave, Carl and Porkins that they were being entered into the *Cool Dude Battle Royale*—a one-hundred man battle to the death on a place called "Cool Island."

Dave had never heard of the "Cool Dudes" before, or their "Battle Royale", but he knew it was something he wanted no part of.

"Just keep your wits about you," Dave said. "As soon as we get a chance, we make our escape."

Annoyingly, the villagers had taken his rucksack, so building a portal was out of the question. And they'd taken his weapons and armor too.

"I seem to spend most of my life getting captured these days," sighed Carl. "I think I'm actually getting used to it."

Suddenly the ship began to wobble, then it slowly came to a stop.

"We must be here," said Dave.

"Oh goody," said Carl. "How exciting."

A door opened and three villagers in baseball caps entered, accompanied by an iron golem.

"Come with us," one of the villagers said. "And don't try anything."

They led Dave, Carl and Porkins out of the door and down a corridor. Finally they reached a ladder.

"Climb," said the villager.

Dave, Carl and Porkins climbed, Dave leading the way. When he got to the top he opened a trapdoor and climbed out onto the deck of the ship. His mouth dropped open in shock.

The ship was docked in a harbor, but the harbor wasn't what Dave was staring at. Beyond the harbor was a city—the biggest city Dave had ever seen. Actually, Dave realized, it was the *only* city he'd ever seen. It was covered in towers made from a hundred different materials, all lit up by neon lights. There were diamond towers, emerald towers, even *sponge* towers. And in the middle of the city was a tower twice as large as the others, made of solid gold. On the side of the tower, made from flashing redstone lights, was the word *COOL*.

Porkins and Carl were on deck now, also looking in amazement at the city.

The villager in the red baseball cap appeared behind them.

"I didn't introduce myself earlier," he said. "I'm Ron, personal assistant to Derek Cool."

"Who the heck is Derek Cool?" said Carl.

"The mayor of this city," said Ron. "The guy in charge of everything you see before you. Welcome... to Cool Island."

CHAPTER TWO
Cool City

Dave wasn't surprised at all to hear that the city on Cool Island was called Cool City. As he, Porkins and Carl were led through the streets, he saw that life in Cool City seemed to be one long party. DJs were playing music on the street, people were dancing, and everyone seemed to be in a good mood.

The villagers who lived in the city wore all sorts of extravagant clothes of many different colors, and a lot of them wore sunglasses—even though it was night.

The guards leading Dave and the others through the city all wore baseball caps and sunglasses—that seemed to be their uniform.

"Hey," a villager with dyed green hair said as they passed, "are you three dudes entering the tournament this year?"

"Yes they are," said Ron, who was leading the guards.

"Right on!" said the villager. "Can't wait to see you on TV!"

"So what's the deal with this tournament to the death thing?" Carl asked Ron.

"You'll find out more when we get to Cool Tower, creeper," said Ron.

As they got nearer to Cool Tower, most of the people in the streets wore clothing made of gold and emeralds. It didn't look very comfortable to Dave. The streets here were made of gold too—solid gold blocks.

"Where did all this gold come from?" Dave marveled. "I didn't know there was this much gold in the whole world!"

"Derek Cool's father was a brave explorer," said Ron. He came to this island years ago, without an emerald to his name, and discovered that the mountains were filled with gold. He set up a mine, made his fortune and built Gold City."

"Gold City?"

"That was what the city used to be called. But when Derek took over after his dad passed, he renamed it Cool City. He wanted it to be the coolest place on earth."

They finally reached Cool Tower. A villager in a bellboy outfit opened the door for them. As Dave walked into the lobby he was amazed to see that everything inside—from the front desk to the doors—was made of gold. The only thing that wasn't gold was the plush red carpet.

"Wow," said Carl. "Your mayor may be cool, but he doesn't have much taste."

"Silence!" snapped Ron. "Don't you dare talk about our mayor like that! You will keep a civil tongue when you meet Derek Cool, creeper, or you will pay for it later. Do I make myself clear?"

"Ok, ok," said Carl. "I was only joking."

"Oh yes," said Ron, "that's another thing. If the mayor makes a joke, you must laugh. Got it?"

"Even if it's not funny?" said Porkins.

"*Especially* if it's not funny!" said Ron. "I say this for your own sake. The mayor, for all his great qualities, is not exactly, um, keen on people disagreeing with him. Or not being nice to him. Or not laughing at his jokes. Oh, and if he asks you if he's cool—please, please please tell him he's cool."

"Is he not cool?" asked Carl.

Everyone in the lobby gasped. A waitress dropped a tray, glass shattering across the floor.

"The mayor is the coolest person who ever lived," Ron said nervously. "He is amazing and awesome and definitely—definitely, definitely, *definitely*—not a nerd. Got it?"

"Um, ok," said Carl.

He led Dave, Carl and Porkins towards an elevator. Dave was completely unsurprised to see that the elevator was made of gold too. Ron entered the elevator with them, leaving the baseball cap guards in the lobby.

"Remember," said Ron sternly as the elevator began to rise,

"be on your best behavior." He adjusted his red baseball cap, making sure it was straight.

"So Derek Cool, the mayor, his father founded this city?" asked Carl.

"That's correct," said Ron.

"Was his name Cool as well?"

Ron bristled. "No," he said. "Derek changed his family name after his father passed away."

"So his real surname isn't *Cool?*"

"No," snapped Ron.

"So what was it originally?" Carl asked.

"Wimpy."

Carl snorted. "Derek Wimpy! No wonder he changed it."

Ron turned on Carl, fury in his eyes. "If I were you, little creeper, I would watch my tongue. The mayor *hates* his old surname, so make sure you never mention it in his presence."

"Alright," said Carl. "But one more thing: when you captured us you told us you were an ancient order of knights who have served the coolest dudes in history. Is that true, or just some lie that Derek told you to say?"

Ron's cheeks went red. "It is not a *lie*, creeper. We are an order of knights. All of my Baseball Cap Boys are great warriors."

Carl laughed. "Baseball Cap Boys!" he said. "What a terrible name."

"Creeper!" Ron yelled. "The mayor himself gave us that name, so *watch your tongue!*"

"Aha!" said Carl. "So Derek set up your little group of knights. You're not an ancient order after all!"

Ron's face was bright red.

"Not technically," he said. "The... the mayor likes us to say that. He thinks it sounds... *cool.*"

Carl grinned. "The more I hear about this mayor of yours, the less cool he sounds."

"You try saying that to him," said Ron. "See what happens to you."

"Maybe I will," said Carl.

"Carl, calm down," said Dave. "Don't go causing any trouble."

"As if I would," said Carl.

PING!

The elevator came to a stop.

"We're here," said Ron. "Behave yourselves."

The elevator doors slid open.

CHAPTER THREE
Derek Cool

In front of Dave was a huge room. As far as he could tell, the room took up a whole floor of the tower, with windows looking out in every direction.

The carpet was a deep red and all the furniture was gold. A jukebox in the corner was playing some music. Dave could just about make out the lyrics:

Derek Cool, is the coolest of them all,
His teachers couldn't teach him, 'cus he's too cool for school.
If you don't recognize his brilliance then you are a fool,
Because he is the coolest, the coolest of them all!

Various cool-looking people were lounging around the room, playing video games, watching tv, or just lying on the furniture.

At the back of the room was a huge throne made of gold blocks, and on it sat the fattest villager Dave had ever seen. He was wearing a white baseball cap, sunglasses, and a golden tracksuit. And he was munching on a cooked chicken.

"Your coolness," Ron announced. "May I present the last three warriors for this year's tournament."

He pushed Dave, Carl and Porkins forward.

"Right on," said the fat villager. "Ron, I was worried you weren't gonna be able to get enough warriors this year."

"It was a bit of a struggle, but we managed it," said Ron. "Warriors, this is our mayor, Derek Cool. The coolest dude in the galaxy."

"That's right," said Derek. "No-one's cooler than me. Here, watch this!"

He staggered to his feet, then waddled over to the foot of the throne, where there was a red skateboard. Derek picked up the skateboard in his fat hand, then placed it on the ground.

"Are you sure this is wise, your coolness?" Ron asked.

Derek scowled. "What's the matter, Ron?" he said. "You don't think I'm *cool* enough to skateboard?"

"No, no, of course not," said Ron quickly.

"Good," said Derek. "Come on everyone!" he shouted. "Watch me do some awesome tricks!"

Everyone gathered round. From the bored looks on their faces, Dave guessed that this was the kind of thing Derek did a lot: showing off how *cool* he was.

Derek Cool placed one foot on the skateboard. It groaned from the strain.

"I feel sorry for that skateboard," whispered Carl.

"Ssh," said Dave.

Derek gingerly used his other foot to push the board forward. It began to slowly roll across the floor, somehow managing to hold his weight.

"Well done, Mr Mayor!" someone yelled.

"Wow, such speed!" yelled another.

Derek was skateboarding so slowly that he was barely moving, but all the cool hangers on were cheering him on as if this was the most brilliant thing they'd ever seen.

"Yeah, look at me!" Derek yelled. "Tell me how cool I am!"

"You're so cool!" someone said.

Derek was so distracted by all the praise that he lost control, and the board began to roll across the room at speed.

"Waaaaaaa!!!!" yelled Derek.

CRASSSH!!! David smashed into a golden sofa. He ended up on his back and the skateboard broke in two.

All the cool hangers on cheered.

"That was amazing!" said one.

"That was the coolest thing I've ever seen!" said another.

Ron came over and helped Derek to his feet. Unlike everyone else in the room, Ron looked embarrassed.

"Did I do good, Ron?" Derek asked. "Am I cool?"

"Very cool, sir," said Ron.

"Yeah!" said Derek. "I'm cool, I'm cool!"

DEREK COOL

Dave, Porkins and Carl could only watch in amazement as everyone gathered around Derek, telling him how cool he was.

"I say," said Porkins, "I hate to be harsh, but he acts like a big baby. He's a fully grown man!"

"He's a spoiled brat," said Carl. "Because he's rich, everyone tells him what he wants to hear."

Carl had it right, Dave thought. From the looks of things, Derek Cool had been surrounded by people telling him what he wanted to hear his entire life.

"What about you three?" Derek said, waddling over to them. "Did you think I looked cool?"

Dave gave Carl a nudge.

"Oh, sooooo cool," said Carl. "I once went to a snow biome

and I thought *that* was cool, but you're even cooler."

"What about you, piggy?" Derek said to Porkins.

"It was, er, a spiffing display," said Porkins. "Really top draw stuff."

"I agree," said Dave, "it was amazing."

Dave was tempted to tell Derek he'd looked like an idiot, but he knew it would only lead to trouble. He, Carl and Porkins had to keep their heads down for now and stay out of trouble, until they could figure out a way to escape.

"So you're warriors," said Derek. He looked down at Carl, who was half the size of a regular creeper. "You don't look much like warriors."

"Oh we are, your coolness," said Dave. "We're seasoned warriors. We've fought zombies, zombie pigmen, endermen, robots, all sorts."

"Don't forget the Kraken," said Carl.

"Oh yes," said Dave. "We defeated a kraken as well."

"Well you're about to face your greatest battle," Derek said, wiping the flecks of chicken from his mouth with his sleeve. "My tournament is the greatest tournament in the history of the world. Isn't that right, everyone?"

"Oh yes," all the hangers on replies. "It's so great!"

"Come with me, warriors," Derek said. He walked over to one side of the room and Dave, Carl and Porkins followed.

Derek brought them over to the windows that overlooked the city. The view up here was incredible, Dave thought. Cool Tower was so high that they could see the entire city stretching out before them; all the colorful towers made from different blocks. Far in the distance he could see the docks, which were filled with luxury ships, their white hulls glistening in the moonlight. The wooden ship that had brought them was there too.

"This whole city is mine," said Derek. "This is what you get for working hard. No-one ever gave me anything. I worked for every emerald that I have."

"I thought your father founded the city?" said Carl.

"I earned everything I have!" Derek snapped. "I renamed the

city *Cool City*—that was all me!"

"Wow," said Carl. "You renamed a city. What a hero."

"Thanks!" said Derek, completely missing Carl's sarcasm. "The people in this city are all my best friends, they all love me. And one of the reasons they love me is because every year I put on the greatest tournament the world has ever seen!"

He waddled over to the other side of the room, Dave and the others following him. When they got there, Dave's mouth dropped open in shock.

Stretching out into the distance was the rest of the island. There was no city on this side of the island, just a mishmash of different biomes: snow, mountains, desert and more. But that wasn't what Dave had been so shocked by. What shocked him was that all these biomes were surrounded by a wall. A wall so high that it was almost as tall as Cool Tower. The wall had separated out a huge square of the island, sealing it in.

"That's the arena," Derek said excitedly. "One-hundred warriors go in, and only one comes out. It's a Battle Royale!"

Dave was amazed at the size of the arena. But he was starting to get scared too.*Once we're trapped in there, there's no way out,* he thought. The wall seemed to be made of iron blocks, and there were guard towers along the top at regular intervals.

"So, one-hundred people all fight to the *death?*" said Carl. Even he sounded a bit worried.

"That's right!" said Derek. "We'll be filming you the whole time. It's the most popular TV show in Cool City, and *I* invented it!"

"What does the winner get?" asked Carl. "I mean, apart from the opportunity to not be dead."

Derek's face went serious. "The winner," he said, "gets a prize that money can't buy. Something so spectacular that it's hard to put into words. They get... a solid gold house!!!"

He pointed to a hilltop in the distance, on the edge of the city. On it were rows of golden houses.

"That's Winners Row," said Derek, "the most exclusive neighborhood in Cool City. Only tournament winners are allowed to live there. If you win, that'll be your new home."

"Listen," said Carl, "as great as a solid gold house sounds, I'm not sure me and my friends can take part in your tournament any more. I've had a bit of a cold recently, and I think Dave's coming down with something too. And just look at Porkins—his cheeks are blushing pink. Maybe you should find three other warriors."

"Ron," said Derek, fury in his eyes, "you said these were my last three warriors!"

"They... they are, your coolness," said Ron. "They all want to take part, I promise you. The creeper is only making a joke."

"I'm really not," said Carl.

"You sure he's joking?" Derek asked.

"Yes, your coolness," said Ron.

"Ha, good joke, creeper!" said Derek. He waddled back over and sat down on his throne. "What are your names, warriors? You first, creeper."

"I'm Carl," said Carl.

"Is that it?" snapped Derek. "You're not going to tell me what a spectacular warrior you are, and how you are honored to fight and die for me?"

"O-k," said Carl. "I'm Clubber Carl, the mightiest creeper who ever lived. Other creepers fear my name."

"And...?" said Derek.

"Oh, and it's a great honor to fight and die for you... your coolness."

Dave could see from Carl's face that the creeper was doing everything he could to stop himself from making a sarcastic comment.

"You next, villager," said Derek.

"Um, I'm Dave the Destroyer," said Dave. "I'm so tough that I eat an enderman for breakfast and a zombie for lunch."

"What about dinner?" one of the cool hangers on asked.

"Just a mushroom stew," said Dave. "I, er, love to fight, and I'll be honored to fight in this tournament for you, Mayor Cool."

"Good, good," said Derek, taking a cooked chicken from a platter a servant was holding and starting to eat it. "And die for me, if need be?"

"Oh, I'd love to," said Dave.

"Your turn, pigman," said Derek, mouth full of chicken.

"I am Porkins the Magnificent!" said Porkins. "The last of the pigmen and destroyer of rotters and scoundrels everywhere! And it would be an honor to fight and die for you, sire."

"*Sire,* I like that," grinned Derek. "Good, good, you three really are a trio of cool dudes. I can't wait to see you on TV tomorrow. Ron, take them to the warriors enclosure!"

"Come on you three," said Ron, leading them to the elevator. "You need to get some sleep. You've got a big day ahead of you tomorrow."

They got into the elevator, the doors closing behind them. It was just Dave, Carl, Porkins and Ron. As the elevator began to move down, Dave looked over at Carl and Porkins and saw that they were thinking the same thing as him:

This might be our last chance to escape.

Their weapons had all been confiscated, along with the rest of their belongings. Ron's sword hung in the scabbard on his belt, but he was busy paying attention to the numbers on the digital display as they went down.

It was now or never...

Dave gave Carl and Porkins a nod, and the three of them leapt forward, grabbing Ron.

"Unhand me!" he yelled.

"Carl, get his sword!" said Dave. The creeper slid round, pulling Ron's sword from the scabbard with his mouth, then chucking it to Dave. Dave caught it and pointed the blade at Ron.

"Don't move," said Dave.

Ron snarled, but he stayed still.

"Well done, chaps!" said Porkins. "We ruddy well did it!"

PING!

The elevator door opened. A huge gang of baseball cap wearing Cool Dudes were waiting for them, all of them holding swords.

"Oh crumbs," said Porkins.

CHAPTER FOUR
The Opening Ceremony

The Cool Dudes brought Dave, Carl and Porkins to a building next to the wall. As they approached the wall from below, Dave was once again staggered at how tall it was. The building looked like a little toy next to it, but as they got nearer Dave saw that the building was huge too: just nowhere near as huge as the wall. It was a dull building made of iron blocks, surrounded by wooden watchtowers, where Cool Dudes stood guard.

"This is the Warriors Enclosure," Ron told them. "This is where you'll stay until the opening ceremony tomorrow. And don't even *think* about trying to escape—we've got guards everywhere."

"We would never dream of it," said Carl.

"You think you're funny, don't you, creeper?" snapped Ron. "But you won't be laughing tomorrow. You're gonna be all alone in the arena, with ninety-nine other people trying to get you. How long do you think you'll last? I've got a bet on with the boys that you won't even last an hour."

"Then I'll do my best to make sure I die as quickly as possible," said Carl. "I'd hate to think of you losing a bet because of me. Judging by your clothes, you could do with all the money you can get."

"Just keep joking, creeper," said Ron. "I can't wait to see you on TV tomorrow."

Inside the building they were led down a corridor full of identical iron doors. Each door had a small window, and every so often Dave would see a face at a window as they passed. Most were villagers, but Dave occasionally saw a zombie or a skeleton, or other mobs he didn't recognize. The doors had numbers on them as well. Finally they reached the end of the corridor, where there were three open doors. The numbers on these were 98, 99 and 100.

"Get in," Ron told them.

"Can't we share a cell?" Porkins asked.

"No," said Ron. "The next time you three meet, it'll be in the arena." He grinned nastily. "Good luck—especially you, creeper."

This is it, thought Dave, *the very last chance to escape.* He swiveled round and tried to grab Ron's sword, but Ron was too quick, dodging backwards out of the way.

One of the guards pulled a weapon from his belt. It looked like a redstone torch to Dave, but the tip was blue instead of red. The villager thrust it forward into Dave's stomach, and he was zapped with electricity.

"Dave!" Porkins yelled.

Dave staggered backwards in a daze. The guards roughly pushed him into a cell, then slammed the door shut. Ron appeared at the glass, smiling at him.

Ron and the guards left. Dave ran to the door to try and open it, but it was locked tight. Across the corridor he could see Carl and Porkins, looking back at him through the windows of their own cells.

He smiled at Carl and Porkins, to try and assure them that everything was alright, but the doors were soundproofed, so they couldn't speak to each other. Eventually Dave went over and slumped down on the bed in the corner of his cell. The only other things in the room were a toilet and a screen on the wall—although the screen had no buttons and there was no remote, so Dave had no way of turning it on. There was also a strange round pad on the floor made of a shiny material that Dave didn't recognize.

It was a tricky situation, but Dave still had hope that he, Carl and Porkins could escape. *They still have to bring us to the arena,* he thought. *When they let us out of our cells, we'll have to try to break free again.*

As he lay down on the bed he started to wonder about the other 'warriors' competing in the tournament. Were they all taking part against their will, like him, Porkins and Carl, or had they volunteered?

Despite all his worries, Dave soon found himself drifting off to sleep. He dreamed of home, remembering his soft bed and his mother's cooking.

BWWAARRRMM!!!

Dave was woken by an alarm, coming from a speaker in the room's ceiling.

"Rise and shine, warriors," said Ron's voice over the speaker. "Breakfast time."

A few moments later a hatch opened in the bottom of Dave's door, and a plate with two eggs on it came through.

Dave greedily wolfed down the eggs. Then, to his surprise, the TV screen turned on.

"Welcome ladies and gentlemen," said an announcer on the TV, "to the fifth annual Cool Dude Battle Royale!"

Dave sat on his bed and watched the screen. A huge crowd was gathered around Cool Tower, everyone cheering and waving.

Then the footage switched to a balcony on the tower. Derek Cool stepped out onto it and the crowd went wild.

"Here's our magnificent leader," the announcer continued, "the coolest dude of them all... DEREK COOL!!!"

The crowd went crazy: people were whistling and cheering and throwing their hats in the air.

"DEREK!" the crowd chanted. "DEREK! DEREK! DEREK!"

Derek waved at the crowd, soaking up the applause.

I'd love to biff that smug face of his, thought Dave bitterly. *Biff him right on the nose!*

Derek put his hands up and the crowd fell silent.

"Yo yo yo!" he shouted. The crowd cheered.

"We love you Derek!" someone shouted.

"Welcome to the fifth Cool Dude Battle Royale!" said Derek. "Every year I let the greatest warriors on the planet duke it out, to see who is the World's Coolest Warrior!"

The crowd all cheered and whooped.

"As always, we've got one-hundred brave warriors," continued Derek, "all competing for the most coveted award on Cool Island...

a solid gold house!"

"Oooo!" said the crowd.

"So without further ado," said Derek, "let the tournament begin!"

Suddenly a hissing noise came from the floor. Dave jumped in shock, thinking it must be a creeper, but then he saw it was the round panel. It was pulsating with light and making strange noises.

"*Step onto the pad,*" said a robotic voice.

Dave looked at the pad, which was now sending up blasts of white smoke, the white light pulsating like a heartbeat.

"Er, no," said Dave. "I don't think I will."

"*Step onto the pad,*" repeated the voice. Then purple smoke starting pouring out of an air vent in the ceiling.

"*Poison gas is entering the room,*" said the robotic voice. "*Step onto the pad please. Step onto the pad or you will die.*"

Dave began to cough. The purple gas was filling his lungs, making it hard to breathe.

Looks like I don't have much choice, he thought, staggering towards the bright light of the pad. He stepped onto it.

FLOOSH!!!

There was a brief flash of white light, then Dave wasn't standing in his cell anymore—he was in the middle of a large, open grassy field. He could see mountains in the distance, and, beyond them, a huge wall.

Oh no, he thought, *I've teleported inside the arena!*

"Maggot!" a gruff voice roared. Dave turned and saw a huge villager, with muscles on his arms that were bigger than Dave's head.

"You have the honor of being Thag's first victim," growled the villager. "Prepare to die!"

"Oh dear," said Dave.

CHAPTER FIVE
Battle Royale!

Carl hated to admit it, but he was scared.

No, scratch that—he was terrified.

A moment ago he'd been in his cell, about to pass out from the poison gas, and then he'd stepped onto a glowing pad and found himself in the middle of a battle.

The pad had teleported him to an abandoned village full of wooden houses. For a moment he'd been the only one there, but then FLOOSH! FLOOSH! FLOOSH! FLOOSH!—a load of others teleported into the village as well, and the fighting had begun.

Now Carl was hidden inside a small house, watching the battle raging outside through a window.

It was absolute chaos. There was a villager with gray skin, firing a crossbow at people. Another villager with gray skin and a black cloak seemed to be some sort of wizard. He was surrounded by a gaggle of tiny flying creatures with blue-gray skin with swords, and every time he raised his hands spikes would rise from the ground, slicing at people.

A huge, muscled pigman was smashing everything he could see with his fists, roaring like a wild animal. Two villagers were fighting with swords, one in gold armor and the other in diamond, as a wither roamed around throwing explosive skulls. Meanwhile a skeleton with black bones was slicing at people with his sword.

Maybe they'll all wipe each other out and I'll be safe, thought Carl. It seemed like he, Porkins and Dave were the only ones who didn't want to take part in this stupid tournament: all these warriors seemed to be having a great time.

Carl watched as mob after mob and villager after villager was slain. The village was a ruin now, the houses blasted to bits and huge craters in the ground, but the fight continued. In the distance, over the top of some trees, he could just about make out the wall, and, beyond, it, the glistening golden tower where Derek Cool lived.

I bet that idiot is watching all this on TV and loving it, thought Carl bitterly. He'd noticed that in the middle of the village there was a pole with a camera on it, which kept moving around to follow the action. Whatever the pole and the camera were made of was very sturdy, as even with all the village getting destroyed around it, the camera was fine.

The battle in the village was starting to wind down now, with only three fighters left: the gray-skinned villager with the magic powers, the huge pigman, and an iron golem.

The villager summoned another swarm of the little flying creatures, sending them at the golem. The golem tried to swat them away, but he was so distracted that he didn't noticed the pigman running right at him until it was too late. POW! The pigman whacked the golem right in the face, and its head went flying off. Its huge iron body crashed to the floor.

Now it was just the big pigman and the gray-skinned villager. The villager summoned a row of spikes under the pigman, but the pigman was too quick, darting out of the way. The villager tried to summon the flying things back to protect him, but they were too slow—the pigman jumped into the air, then smashed the villager with a huge fist. The villager went flying backwards, smashing into the wooden wall of the house. Then POOF he was gone.

Only the huge pigman remained now. *Please let him leave,* Carl thought desperately as he watched through the window.

The pigman began to sniff.

"I smell you, creeper!" it roared. "I can smell you hiding! Come out, come out, wherever you are!"

Carl's blood went cold.

CHAPTER SIX
A Lovely Walk

Porkins was having a lovely walk in the forest.

The teleport pad had brought him to a biome full of tall spruce trees, and there wasn't another soul in sight.

This must be the arena, thought Porkins, remembering that he'd seen a huge wooded area when they'd seen the arena from above from the top of Cool Tower. If that was the case, he was in here with a lot of other people who wanted to kill him.

But, for now, he seemed to be safe.

He didn't have any materials, so he decided to make some. He started by punching a tree until he had wood, then built some basic wooden materials and a crafting table. He did a bit of mining, until he had enough materials to make himself a stone sword.

That'll have to do for now, he thought. He didn't think it was safe to do too much mining, as someone could easily sneak up behind him if he was hacking away with a pickaxe.

Next he needed food, so he wandered about until he found a group of rabbits.

"Sorry little chaps," said Porkins, "but a pigman's got to eat."

Before long Porkins had lots of rabbit, but he was reluctant to start a fire, as everyone would be able to see where he was, so he ate it raw.

I hope those other chaps are ok, Porkins thought sadly, thinking of Dave and Carl. The villager and the creeper had been the first friends Porkins had made since his people had been turned into zombies by Herobrine. When he'd first escaped the Nether he'd lived underground. For a while he'd started to think he would be alone forever, but then Dave had come along and changed all that. Porkins didn't really care about Dave's quest to defeat the ender dragon, but it mattered to Dave—and Dave was Porkins's friend, so he'd do everything he could to help him.

Night crept in, so Porkins built himself a little shelter under a tree, sealing up the entrance behind him. When he'd been mining earlier he'd found a couple of bits of coal, so he put a torch down. His little hole was small but snug, and he soon found himself drifting off to sleep.

In the morning Porkins dug himself out, then continued to walk through the woods. Before long he came across a small wooden box.

A treasure chest! he realized. He ran forward excited to see what was inside. But when he opened it, it was empty.

"Oh bother," he said.

"Freeze!" said a voice from above. "Put your hands in the air!"

Porkins looked up and saw someone in the trees, aiming a bow and arrow at him.

"You... you're a pigman!" said Porkins happily.

"I am," said the pigman in the trees, "and if you don't do everything I say, you're going to be dead."

CHAPTER SEVEN
Thag

Dave ran into some trees, the huge villager hot on his tail.

"Come back, maggot!" the villager roared. "Thag wants to eat you!"

The huge villager—Thag—was so big that the ground shook as he chased after Dave.

I need to hide! thought Dave desperately. He ran through the trees, weaving this way and that to try and lose Thag, but the big villager wasn't giving up.

"You can't run from Thag!" he shouted. "Thag bestest warrior there is!"

Then Dave saw something unexpected: a treasure chest up ahead. He was about to run straight past it, but then he had a thought: *Why would there be a treasure chest here?* The only reason that came to him was that the chest might contain a weapon. They had all been dumped into this arena without weapons, so it made sense that the people who'd designed the arena would leave some weapons lying around: it wouldn't be much fun to watch on TV unless the warriors had weapons.

Dave quickly flipped the lid of the chest open, and saw that he was almost right. It wasn't a weapon, but a full set of golden armor. The only trouble was, he had no time to put it on, with Thag still rushing towards him, so he just kept running.

A sword would have been nice, thought Dave miserably. *Or a trident.*

"I almost caught you!" Thag roared from behind. "I'm gonna catch you and eat you!"

Suddenly the forest ended and Dave just managed to stop himself from toppling over a cliff. He was at the edge of the island:

far below him waves were crashing against the rocks.

"Can't run from Thag!" the huge villager roared.

Dave stood in front of the cliff, waving his arms.

"Ok Thag, I give up!" he said. "Come and get me!"

Thag rushed at him, huge legs pumping, big mouth hanging open. Just before Thag reached him, Dave jumped out of the way, and Thag went bursting out of the forest and ran straight off the cliff.

"ARRRRGGGHHHH!!!!" he yelled, as he fell down, down, down to the water below. Then *ploop*, he was gone.

I hope he can't swim, thought Dave. Then an idea struck him: if he found Porkins and Carl, they could escape the island by sea. They could jump off a cliff with wooden boats, then sail away.

SPLOOSH!

Thag's head burst up from the water. He looked up at Dave with fury in his eyes

"Thag kill you for that!" he roared.

Thag began swimming towards the cliff, but then, suddenly, drowned zombies burst up from the water, grabbing at him with their rotten hands.

"Get off!" roared Thag. "Get off me!"

There were more drowned than Dave could count, all grabbing at Thag and trying to pull him under. The huge villager struggled for a bit, but then disappeared under the water, a look of terror on his face.

"Ok," said Dave, with a sigh. "Looks like we can't escape via the sea."

CHAPTER EIGHT
Carl Steps Up

What am I going to do? thought Carl.

The huge pigman was smashing the village apart with his fists.

"Oh, I will find you creeper," he said, "the longer you make me wait, the worse it'll be for you."

Carl had gone from window to window of the small house he was in, but he could see no way to escape. The village was surrounded by open fields on all sides, so if he made a run for it, the pigman would definitely see him.

There were discarded weapons on the ground outside, from the warriors who had fallen during the battle, but Carl was under no illusions: even with an enchanted diamond sword he'd stand no chance against the huge pigman.

But there was something else out there, Carl realised, something he might be able to use. The iron golem's headless body was still on the ground. Carl had no idea how iron golems worked, but maybe, he thought, just maybe, he might be able to control it.

I don't even need Dave and Porkins, Carl thought miserably. *I'm coming up with stupid plans all by myself.*

It was the only idea he had. The huge pigman had nearly smashed up every building in the village: it wouldn't be long before he smashed up the house that Carl was hiding in too.

Alright, thought Carl. *Here goes.*

He opened the door and ran out. Immediately the huge pigman turned, looking right at him from across the village.

"There you are!" he grinned. Then he started running towards Carl, his huge, muscled legs pounding away.

"Waaaa!" yelled Carl, running as fast as his little creeper legs would carry him. He reached the headless iron golem's body.

There was a hole where the head had been, so Carl climbed in legs first, so just his head was sticking out.

This was a stupid plan! Carl thought, watching as the huge pigman rushed towards him. But then something unexpected happened: he could feel the iron golem's body moving. *Am I controlling it?* he wondered.

He tried making the iron golem stand up, and it actually worked. He tried moving the iron golem's arms and that worked too.

"Aww yeah," said Carl. "This is what I'm talking about!"

He picked up a golden sword from the ground with the iron golem's hand, and a diamond shield. The pigman rushed at him, trying to punch him, but Carl blocked the blow with the shield.

He slashed at the pigman with his sword: one blow, two blows, three! Then the pigman fell to his knees, defeated.

Then *POOF*, he was gone.

"Wow!" said Carl. He looked down in awe at his new iron body. For the first time in his life, he felt powerful, like a warrior. He'd always been a small creeper, but now he could actually fight.

Right, thought Carl, *now to find Dave and Porkins and get out of here!*

CHAPTER NINE
Gammon

"Keep moving," said the pigman. "I've got my bow aimed right at you, so no funny business."

Porkins was walking through the forest, the pigman with the bow walking a short distance behind him.

"It's so jolly exciting to meet another pigman," said Porkins happily. "I thought I was the last one left."

"Less talking, more walking," said the other pigman.

"What's your name, old bean?" Porkins asked.

"If you must know, it's Gammon," said the pigman.

"Nice to meet you, Gammon," said Porkins. "I'm Porkins."

"Just shut up, will you?" snapped Gammon. "Do you want everyone to find us?"

"Good point," said Porkins. "Shutting up now."

Eventually they found a small cave. The sun was starting to go down, so Gammon said that they should spend the night there.

"I'm a very light sleeper," he warned Porkins, "so if you try anything, or try to escape, I'll know. And you'll get an arrow through the knee."

Gammon sat by the cave entrance, to make sure Porkins couldn't get past without alerting him.

"So, what's the plan, old bean?" Porkins asked. "Are we going to storm the wall and break out? I've got two friends in here who can help us as well."

"What do you think's going on here?" Gammon asked.

"We're teaming up," said Porkins happily. "Two pigmen together, making their escape."

"No," said Gammon. "I didn't spare your life so we could team up, I spared it so that I could use you as bait."

"Oh," said Porkins.

Gammon looked around the cave.

"I think we're safe from the cameras here," he said. "So I might as well tell you. I'm going to win this stupid tournament. Then, at the winner's ceremony, I'm going to fire an arrow right at that stupid fat villager, right between his sunglasses."

"Derek Cool, you mean?" said Porkins.

"Yeah," said Gammon.

"I'm not keen on the chap, either," said Porkins. "Did he force you to fight in the tournament too?"

"No, I volunteered," Gammon said. "But two years ago, a friend of mine was forced to take part. They came to our village, those thugs in their baseball caps, and demanded that five of us enter the tournament. My friend put himself forward.

"He fought well. He came second. But he lost nonetheless. Now he's gone, all so those rich idiots could have an entertaining TV show."

"I'm sorry," said Porkins.

"But I'm going to put an end to it this year," said Gammon, darkly. "I'm going to put an end to the Cool Dude Battle Royale, and Cool City and, finally, Derek Cool himself."

He went silent. Porkins didn't know what to say.

"So is everyone competing in this tournament forced to fight?" Porkins asked.

"No," said Gammon. "As far as I know, most of the warriors chose to be here. They want the honor and prestige that comes from winning, as well as that stupid golden house. But every year it gets harder and harder to find new fighters, so sometimes they have to force people to fight. It's all kept very hush-hush, though. As far as the idiots watching on TV know, all the fighters are volunteers here of their own free will."

"You know," said Porkins, "maybe you don't have to win the tournament to get your revenge on Derek Cool. If you, me and my friends all team up, I'm sure we can escape. Then we can teach all these rotters a lesson. We can give them a dash good hiding."

Gammon laughed.

"Some of the older pigmen in my village talk like you," he said. "With all their *jolly goods* and *old chaps*. They were born in the Nether."

"So everyone in your village is a pigman?" Porkins asked.

"Yeah. My grandparents and some of the other old timers wanted to leave the Nether. They wanted to see what life was like in this world, so they built a nether portal and left, never to return. As far as I know, we're the only pigman village in this world."

"You're probably the last pigmen left anywhere," said Porkins sadly.

Gammon gave him a strange look. "You keep saying that. What happened in the Nether? What happened to our people?"

Porkins sighed. "They were turned into zombies," he said. "They were betrayed by a sorcerer named Herobrine."

As he said the name *Herobrine*, a chill went down Porkins's spine.

"I'm sorry to hear that," said Gammon. "I've heard the name Herobrine before. People talk of him like he's something from a fairy story, though. I didn't know he was real."

"I'm afraid he is," said Porkins. "Me and my chums met him, not long ago. The rotter tried to drop us into some lava!"

"You met Herobrine and survived?" Gammon said, sounding impressed. "You must be tougher than you look."

Gammon lay on his back. "Get some sleep, Porkins," he said. "We're going to need it if we're going to survive this."

"So you're up for trying to work together?" Porkins said happily.

"Maybe," said Gammon. "Either way, we're going to want to be well rested. There are some nasty warriors in this area. Two others from my village volunteered for this year's tournament, and we don't want to bump into them."

"Two other pigmen?" said Porkins. "What fun!"

Gammon laughed. "You won't be saying that if you meet them. These two are nasty customers. Pogo is a huge, muscle-bound idiot. He's tough, but he's no genius. But Curly... we do not want to bump into him. He had a nasty reputation in the village. Some of the rumors people said about him... Anyway, let's hope someone else finishes them off."

Before long, Gammon was asleep. Porkins found his own eyelids starting to droop as well.

I hope Dave and Carl are ok, was his final thought. Then he drifted off to sleep.

CHAPTER TEN
I Can Smell You!

Dave was pleased to see that the gold armor was still there.

He pulled it out of the chest and put it on.

Wow, thought Dave, *I never thought I'd be wearing an outfit made from solid gold.*

So now he had armor, but still no weapon. He thought about making a wooden sword, but a wooden blade would be next to useless against fighters like Thag. And mining for stone would be too loud, and make him an easy target.

No, he decided to sneak around and look for more chests. That was the safest thing to do, he thought.

Dave was sneaking through the trees when he heard sounds

up ahead. The sound of fighting. He crept forward, trying to be as quiet as possible, until he could see a fight going on through a gap in the trees.

The fighting was taking place next to a small pool. Two fighters were facing off against a third. One of the two fighters was a villager, the other was an illager. Dave had never seen an illager before, but he knew what they were: gray-skinned villagers who hated ordinary villagers. But, to Dave's surprise, the villager and the illager had joined forces against the third fighter, who Dave couldn't see yet.

AN ILLAGER

"Come on," said the illager, who was a woman. "You think you're tough? Try taking us both on!"

The third fighter stepped forward. It was a pigman. A pigman with a wooden sword.

Dave could see the fear in the eyes of the villager and the illager.

Why are they so afraid of one pigman with a wooden sword? he wondered. The pigman wasn't even wearing armor.

The pigman grinned. It was a nasty, horrible grin that chilled Dave's soul.

"You two really should start running" said the pigman in a

bored voice. "And as for your friend, the one hiding in the woods, he'd better start running too."

Then the pigman turned and looked Dave right in the eye.

"You can't hide from me, little villager," the pigman grinned. "I can *smell* you."

Then, moving so quickly that Dave could barely see him, the pigman ran forward and attacked the villager and the illager with his sword, slicing back and forth again and again. Before they even knew what was happening, they were defeated. Then *POOF* and *POOF*—they were gone.

The villager turned and looked at Dave again, his grin wider than before.

"Come on little villager," he said. "At least give me a challenge. Run! *Run!*"

Dave didn't need telling twice. He ran. He ran as fast as his legs could carry him.

"I'm coming for you, little villager!" The pigman screamed. "Curly's coming for you!"

CHAPTER ELEVEN
Carl the Golem

Carl was already in love with his new iron golem body. It was amazing to be so high up for once, and he felt so *strong*.

As he left the ruined villages he walked past a load of empty treasure chests.

That must be where they all got their weapons from, he thought, thinking back to the fight in the village.

Carl didn't know which direction he should head, so he just decided to start walking. Occasionally he would pass one of the cameras on poles, and the camera would follow him.

I can't believe there are idiots watching this on TV, he thought bitterly. Carl had never had a TV before, but, he thought, there must be more interesting things to watch than a load of people fighting each other.

He had just started to walk through a snow biome, when three gray-skinned villagers popped out of the snow, pointing their swords at him.

"Afraid you've taken the wrong turn, golem," said one of them.

"I dunno if that is a golem," another one added, a confused look on his face. "Why's he got a creeper head?"

"I don't care," growled the third one. "Let's get him!"

They all charged at him. Carl lifted up his iron arms, blocking the blows, but their swords were diamond, and he could feel the iron suit taking damage.

If my suit gets destroyed, I'm toast, Carl thought. He pulled out his golden sword, swinging it in front of him.

"I don't want to hurt you idiots unless I have to," he told the gray-skinned villagers. "So if I were you, I'd get running."

"We're not going anywhere," one of the villagers growled. "Charge!"

The three of them charged towards him once more. Carl blocked one of the sword blows with his own sword, and the other two with his shield. He lifted his sword to block another blow, but this time his golden sword shattered to pieces.

"Gold looks nice, but don't make much of a weapon," the villager who'd broken his sword grinned.

The three gray-skinned villagers circled him, their swords raised. All Carl had now was his shield.

Wait, Carl thought. *This is ridiculous. I'm an iron golem now. I need to use my strength!*

He dropped his shield on the ground.

"Heh," grinned one of the villagers. "He's given up."

"The only thing that's given up," said Carl, "is your FACE!"

POW! He punched the gray-skinned villager right in the chin with his iron fist. The villager went flying backwards, smacking into a tree.

The other two villagers rushed towards Carl, but he was ready for them. POW! POW! He sent them both flying with his fists.

"Come on then," Carl yelled. "You want some more?"

"We'll get you later," one of the gray-skinned villagers scowled. "You just wait."

And they ran off.

"Yeah, you'd better run!" Carl yelled after them.

Then, suddenly, a loud fanfare of music blasted through the air.

"What on earth?" said Carl. He looked up, and was shocked to see a giant image of Derek Cool projected across the sky.

It's a hologram, Carl realized.

"Yo warriors!" The hologram said. Carl realized that the sound was coming from the cameras scattered about the arena. He hadn't noticed before, but they all had speakers.

"I'm pleased to announce that there are now only fifty warriors left in this year's tournament," continued Derek. "So, as always, the arena size will now shrink. Please get to a safe zone within ten minutes, or you're gonna get fried by my Electric Cool Gas! Danger zones will be marked by blue light. Keep it cool, and good luck!"

The hologram in the sky disappeared. Suddenly bulbs popped out of the top of the nearby camera poles. They lit up, surrounding the area with blue light.

"Looks like I'm in a danger zone," sighed Carl. "Just my luck."

CHAPTER TWELVE
Curly

Dave had just watched Derek's message playing in the sky. Curly, the pigman chasing him, had stopped to watch it too.

"Well, there's no blue light here," Curly shouted. He was standing across a field from Dave. The pigman had been chasing him for what seemed like forever, and had been slowly gaining on him. "Looks like it's your lucky day, villager!"

Curly started chasing him again, and Dave started running.

This is ridiculous, Dave thought. *I'm running away from a pigman with no armor and a wooden sword.*

But Dave had seen how quickly Curly had defeated the villager and the illager. They'd both had armor and iron weapons, and Curly had cut through them like butter.

The hill they were running across was quite high up, and Dave could see a lot of the arena, including the wall. Huge sections of the arena, the parts closest to the wall, were bathed in blue light.

The danger zones, Dave knew. From Derek Cool's announcement in the sky, Dave had gathered that the danger zones were going to be introduced stage by stage, to force the remaining warriors closer together and keep the fight interesting. Now that they were down to fifty warriors, the arena was being shrunk by half. The outer parts of the arena would be covered in *Electric Cool Gas,* whatever that was, so anyone left there would be killed.

Dave looked round. Curly was gaining on him, fast. Dave felt like his lungs were about to burst from running, but the pigman didn't look tired at all.

"I'm gonna get you!" Curly yelled. "We're gonna have so much fun, you and I!"

Suddenly Dave realized what he had to do. There was only one place he could go where Curly wouldn't follow him.

The danger zone.

Dave estimated that there must still be around eight minutes left until the gas filled the danger zones. If Dave ran in there, he could escape Curly, then later make his escape from the gas. It wasn't much of a plan, but he had to try.

He ran down the hill, heading towards some nearby woods which were covered in blue light. He ran and ran, trying to ignore the sound of Curly behind him, getting closer and closer.

"Gotta keep running," Dave panted, trying to spur himself on. "Gotta keep running.

Finally Dave reached the woods. He ran in, and instantly everything around him was blue. He ran and ran, until he could no longer hear Curly running behind him. He turned round. The pigman was watching him from the edge of the danger zone, where the blue light ended.

"That's a smart plan, villager," yelled Curly, "escaping from me in the danger zone. The only trouble is, you'll have to come out eventually. And I'll be right here waiting for you."

Curly sat down on a rock.

Suddenly a voice boomed out from the speakers:

"Five minutes until danger zone activation."

What am I going to do? wondered Dave. In five minutes deadly gas would come pouring into the blue area, and he'd have to leave and get cut to bits by Curly.

For a moment Dave considered building himself a shelter from dirt, but somehow he knew it wouldn't work. The makers of this tournament had to have thought of that. Maybe the gas could pass through blocks.

Maybe I could escape underground? he thought. He knew that it would probably be impossible to dig under the wall, but perhaps he could dig underneath Curly and get back into the arena. But by the time he'd got some wood, created tools and dug deep enough, he'd be out of time.

I'm going to have to fight him, Dave realized. He didn't have a weapon, but he had armor. He could wrestle Curly for his sword, then maybe he might stand a chance.

Dave decided that he at least needed a wooden sword, so he quickly punched a tree for some blocks, built himself a crafting table then made a wooden sword.

Now we both have wooden swords, Dave thought. *And I'm the only one with armor, so I've got to at least stand a chance.*

"*One minute until danger zone activation.*"

Curly was still smiling at Dave from his rock.

"Almost time, villager," he shouted. "I can't wait!"

Suddenly Dave heard a hissing noise. He looked over and saw that the noise was coming from one of the camera poles.

That's where the gas is going to come from, he realized. In less than a minute, all the camera poles in the danger zone would be pumping out poison gas. It was now or never. He gripped his wooden sword tightly.

FSSSSHHHHHHH!!!!!!

Gas starting pouring out from the camera poles. It was thick, purple gas, crackling with bolts of electricity. Dave began to run away from it, right towards Curly, who was waiting just outside the blue light of the danger zone.

"Ha, come on!" Curly shouted. "Let's do this!"

Dave ran out of the blue light, swinging his wooden sword at Curly, but the pigman was too quick for him: he effortlessly stepped out of the way and Dave lost his balance, falling to the floor. Dave dropped his blade. He tried to grab it again, but Curly trod on his fingers.

"Arrgh!" Dave yelled.

Curly stood over Dave, pointing his wooden blade at him.

"Any last words, villager?" he grinned.

This is it, thought Dave. *This is the end.* The feeling of hopelessness was so great that he forgot to feel scared any more. He wasn't going to give Curly the satisfaction.

"My name's not 'villager'," said Dave, "it's Dave."

"Dave," chuckled Curly. "Well *Dave*, this is where it ends for you, I'm afraid. All scared and alone."

"I'm not scared," said Dave.

"And he's not alone, either," said a voice. Dave looked up and saw a huge iron golem standing over him. But there was something strange about the golem: instead of an iron golem's head, it had a *creeper's* head instead.

"Carl?" said Dave, feeling very confused.

"That's me," said Carl.

Dave looked back at Curly. There was fear in the pigman's eyes now, he was pleased to see.

"Two on one," snarled Curly. "Well, at least it'll be a fair fight."

"How about four on one, you rascallion?"

Dave turned and saw Porkins, standing next to another pigman. They both had bows aimed at Curly.

"Gammon!" said Curly with a grin. "Looks like you found a friend. Another pigman, no less. You realize that teaming up is pointless, don't you? There can only be one winner. And that's going to be *me*."

Curly rushed forward. Carl tried to grab him with his long iron golem arms, but the pigman was too quick. Porkins and the other pigman fired arrows, but Curly dodged them. He jumped up in the air, swinging his sword back ready to attack the other pigman. Dave was still on the ground, but he reached out, grabbing Curly's foot. Curly fell to the ground with a thud.

"I'll kill you!" Curly yelled, jumping up and lunging at Dave with his sword.

"No you won't," said Carl, and he punched Curly with a huge iron fist. Curly went flying, right into the danger zone.

It was the first time Dave had got a proper look at the danger zone since he'd run out of it. Somehow the gas knew exactly where to stop; the whole of the blue area was filled with gas, but none of it was spilling into the safe area, almost like it was kept in place by some kind of invisible wall. Curly landed in the middle of the gas. For a second it looked like he was ok. He stood up and turned to face Dave and the others once more, sword in hand. But then the gas around him started sparking and flashing, and suddenly Curly was being zapped full of electricity.

"ARRRRRGGGHHH!!!!!" he yelled, and then *POOF*, he was gone.

"We did it," Dave said, breathing a sigh of relief. He looked over at the others. "Who are you?" he asked the other pigman. "And Carl... why are you wearing an iron golem?"

CHAPTER THIRTEEN
What Now?

They spent the night in a hole that Gammon dug for them. He sealed the entrance and put a torch down.

"Going underground like this is the only way we can escape the cameras," he told them.

"Talking of going underground, I've been thinking," said Porkins. "Can't we just dig under the wall?"

Gammon shook his head. "The wall goes right down to bedrock. And if you tried to dig through it, you'd get a zillion volts of electricity for your troubles."

"So what's the plan then?" Dave asked. He was a bit reluctant about letting Gammon join their group, but Porkins trusted the pigman, so that was good enough for him.

"Before I met Porkins, my plan was to win the tournament," Gammon told them. "At the winner's ceremony I was going to assassinate Derek Cool, then the other rebels were going to storm the city and take over."

"Other rebels?" asked Carl. The creeper had taken off his iron golem suit and left it sitting in the corner.

"Yes," said Gammon. "I'm not the only one unhappy with Derek Cool's rule and his stupid tournament. Many, both in Cool City and towns and villages nearby, want to see him gone. He has ruined this once prosperous mining city, and year after year more people are forced to fight in this contest, all so Derek can watch it on TV. Most of the people in Cool City hate the show and think it's barbaric. But Derek and his Baseball Cap Boys force people to watch."

"So what now?" Carl asked.

"I don't know," said Gammon. "The other rebels are in hiding across Cool City, but I've no way of getting a signal to them."

"Yes you do," said Dave. "We're on TV, remember? If everyone is watching, and as many people hate Derek Cool as you say, we can send out a message that they all hear. I bet all the rebels are watching the show too. All you have to do is get out there and tell everyone to rise up. Say it quickly so that the people producing the show have no time to cut you off. I assume the show goes out live?"

"It does," said Gammon. "But I'm not much of a public speaker."

"Well, old chap," said Porkins. "Now seems like a good time to start."

"I'll do it," said Gammon, smiling. "I'll do it tomorrow once the sun comes up, to make sure as many people are watching as possible."

"Sounds good," said Dave. "Now let's get some sleep. It's gonna be a big day tomorrow."

Just then they heard a musical fanfare playing outside. It was so loud that even underground they could hear it clearly.

"Oh no," said Gammon, the color draining from his cheeks.

"Hello warriors!" they heard Derek Cool's voice say, projected across the arena. "I've got cool news—if you're still alive, you're one of the last twenty five warriors left. The arena will be shrinking in five minutes. Danger zones will be marked with blue light. Good luck!"

Even though they were underground, suddenly everything turned blue.

"I'm in a danger zone again!" wailed Carl. "Why can't I ever catch a break?!"

CHAPTER FOURTEEN
Metal in the Moonlight

Dave and Gammon climbed a tree, to find out which direction they had to go to get out of the danger zone. It was still dark, as it was night time, but everything around them was lit up with blue light.

When they reached the top of the tree, Dave could see the whole arena. It was one giant square, surrounded by the huge iron wall. The area nearest to the wall, the first danger zone, was full of the strange purple gas. The area they were in, the second danger zone, was all blue. In the middle of the arena was a small square area—the last remaining safe zone. It was lit up by lights on the top of its camera poles.

Twenty one other warriors are going to be heading that way as well, Dave thought glumly. The ones who were left would have to be pretty tough, he reasoned, or they wouldn't have survived this long.

Four minutes until the arena shrinks!" said the voice from the speaker. Gammon and Dave quickly climbed down the tree.

"This way," Gammon said. They all ran behind him, rushing through the trees.

Finally they could see where the blue light ended up ahead. They ran out into an open field, but they were completely out in the open, with no shelter.

"We need to find somewhere to hide, or we'll be sitting ducks," said Gammon. "Come on."

They ran across the field, until they came to a small grove of trees.

"This will have to do," said Gammon, "I think I can hear someone coming."

They hid between the trees. They were just in time, as three people ran out from the danger zone at just that moment.

"I've seen those gray-skinned villagers before," whispered Carl. "We can easily take them."

"They're called illagers," said Dave.

"Villagers, illagers, whatever," said Carl. "Last time I fought them I sent them running. Let's go and beat them up."

"Wait," said Gammon, "I can hear someone else coming as well."

Another figure stepped out from the danger zone. Dave's heart caught in his chest.

It's Steve! he thought. Then he realized it wasn't Steve after all. Its skin was metallic, gleaming in the moonlight.

"Oh gosh," said Porkins. Then he said what they were all thinking: "It's Robo-Steve!"

CHAPTER FIFTEEN
Critical Error

The last time Dave had seen Robo-Steve had been back in Snow Town. Robo-Steve had been created by Ripley, a villager who wanted to frame Steve for crimes he didn't commit. Robo-Steve had killed Ripley and blown up the town, before teleporting away.

How Robo-Steve had ended up here, in the Cool Dude Battle Royale, Dave had no idea. He guessed that the robot must have been picked up by Ron and his men when they were roaming the land looking for more warriors to compete. They must have patched the robot up as well, because he had new eyes: glowing green eyes to replace the red eyes that Porkins's arrows had destroyed.

The three illagers approached Robo-Steve, their swords drawn. *They have no idea how much danger they're in*, thought Dave.

"Hey buddy," said one of the illagers. "Looks like you're all on your own. We're friendly, you can trust us."

"*Voice analysis complete,*" said Robo-Steve. "*You are lying. You are not friendly. You mean me harm, and must be destroyed.*"

Moving at lightning speed, Robo-Steve ran forward. He had a diamond sword, and cut through the illagers so quickly that they didn't even have time to raise their own blades in defense. *POOF POOF POOF!* They were gone.

"Robo-Steve?" whispered Gammon. "Does that have anything to do do with Steve? As in Steve the Hero?"

"It's a long story," said Dave.

Suddenly they could hear the sound of fighting coming from somewhere nearby. Robo-Steve turned his head, and began walking towards the sound.

"Looks like the final battle is breaking out," said Gammon. "When it reaches this stage in the tournament, everyone is so close together that it becomes one big chaotic fight."

"Danger zone two now active!" came Derek's voice from the speakers. The blue light area began filling with the electric gas.

"How small does the arena get?" asked Carl. "Or is this it?"

"It shrinks again when there are ten warriors left," said Gammon. "And judging by how ferocious that battle over there sounds, that won't be long."

They crept forward, moving across the field towards the sound of the battle. Finally they reached the edge of a small valley, where down below a battle was taking place. No-one was teamed up anymore, everyone was fighting everyone else. There were villagers, illagers, a couple of zombies and one skeleton, and in the middle of it all was Robo-Steve, swinging his diamond sword at anyone he could hit.

"Let's just let them finish each other off," said Gammon.

"Maybe you should make your speech soon," said Dave. "To the camera. To tell the rebels outside to start rebelling. If they don't take down Derek Cool, we'll never get out of here."

"All in good time," said Gammon. "If I start shouting at the cameras now, I'll make myself a target. Let's wait until it's just us four left."

"I guess that makes sense," said Dave.

"Ten warriors are left!" Derek Cool's voice blared from the speakers. "The arena is shrinking!"

The field they had just come from went blue, but, Dave was thankful to see, the area they were in was a safe zone. But the remaining arena was tiny now: he could see it all from where they were hiding. And he could see all the warriors too: he, Porkins, Carl and Gammon were up here, while Robo-Steve and five remaining warriors were battling down in the valley below.

This really is the endgame now, Dave thought to himself.

Finally, Robo-Steve delivered a flurry of blows, defeating the last of the other warriors. Then he stood alone in the valley.

"It's just him and us now," said Porkins. "We can take him. We've beaten the rotter before."

"Agreed," said Dave. "Everyone, attack!"

Dave led the charge, followed by Carl in his iron golem armor and Porkins and Gammon with their bows. Robo-Steve turned to face them, his diamond sword at the ready.

"*You!*" said Robo-Steve. "*You bested me last time, but this time you will be destroyed!*"

Robo-Steve raised his diamond sword, but before he got a chance to use it, an arrow from Gammon's bow hit him in the chest. Then one from Porkins's bow hit him in the forehead.

"*Critical error!*" said Robo-Steve.

"Oh do shut up," said Carl. He lifted Robo-Steve into the air, then chucked him into the purple gas surrounding them.

Zillions of volts of electricity zapped through Robo-Steve's body.

"*Critical Errooooooor!!!!*" he yelled.

Then he collapsed to the floor.

"Is he... is he finished?" asked Porkins.

"I think so," said Dave.

But he was wrong. Suddenly Robo-Steve's body started flashing with yellow electricity, and he rose to his feet. Then he began floating in the air, his eyes bursting with white light.

"*Power levels at one-thousand percent!*" cried Robo-Steve.

"Uh oh," said Carl, "that stupid gas has made him even *more* powerful.

"Weapons ready," said Dave.

But something was happening to Robo-Steve. Rather than trying to attack them, he looked like he was confused.

"*Memory banks corrupted,*" he said. "*Identity crisis detected. Who am I? What is my purpose? What is my prime directive?*"

"Ok, that's enough," said Gammon. He stepped forward and pulled back his bow, firing an arrow right into Robo-Steve's chest.

"*Error!*" cried Robo-Steve, then he fell down, landing smack on the ground. His body crackled and jerked with electricity for a moment, and then was still.

Gammon turned to Dave, Porkins and Carl.

"It's just us four now," he said.

"Now what do we do?" said Dave. "Maybe it's time for you to give your speech? If everyone's watching us on TV you can tell the people to rise up. To fight Derek Cool's regime."

"Yes," said Gammon. "I guess now's as good a time as any." He sighed deeply. "Let's put down our weapons and stand in front of that camera, to show that we're not prepared to fight in this foolish tournament any more."

They all put down their swords, shields and bows, and followed Gammon. He stood in front of a camera, which swiveled to follow his every move.

"Right," said Gammon, "here goes."

Dave noticed that Gammon was still holding his bow. He was the only one of them still armed. He was about to say something to the pigman, when Gammon turned, aiming the bow and him, Porkins and Carl.

Gammon grinned.

"Gammon, old chap, what's going on?" said Porkins.

"This is a double cross," Gammon said. "And you're going to die.

CHAPTER SIXTEEN
A Trio of Cool Dudes

Dave was confused.

"What about all that stuff you said about rebelling against Derek Cool?" he asked Gammon.

"I lied, I'm afraid," said Gammon, grinning. "I don't want to get revenge on Derek Cool. I don't want revenge on anyone. I just want to win."

"But what about your friend who was forced to fight in the tournament?" said Porkins. "The one who was killed?"

"Oh him?" said Gammon. "He was no friend of mine, just a fool. I watched him on TV. All through the tournament he kept to himself, never made any allies. So when it came to the end, when he was one of the last two, it was just him and the strongest warrior left. He stood no chance. Curly was the same. Too stupid to know that in this game you need allies.

"I knew that I had to team up with others, so that they could help me whittle down the other warriors. And you three have helped me do just that. If I was on my own against Curly or that robot, I wouldn't have stood a chance. But thanks to you, I'm now in the final four. And soon I'll be in the final *one*."

"You dastardly fiend!" said Porkins. "Were you even telling the truth about coming from a pigman village?"

"Oh that's all true," said Gammon, "though most of the pigmen there are idiots, just like you. Since I was old enough, all I ever wanted was to escape and make my fortune. And now I'll be rich beyond my wildest dreams, living in a solid gold house."

"And the rebels that were going to help us?" said Carl. "I suppose you made them up too?"

"Well it's true that there are plenty of rebels who want to see

Derek Cool gone," said Gammon. "But I'm not one of them."

He pulled back his bow, taking aim.

"Now," he said, "which one of you wants to die first?"

"*DESTROY!*"

Robo-Steve, it seemed, was not quite dead. He reached up and grabbed Gammon's leg.

"Get off!" said Gammon, shaking his leg free. He was only distracted a moment, but it was all the time that Dave, Carl and Porkins needed. They charged at Gammon together.

"Stop, or I'll shoot!" yelled Gammon, raising his bow once more, but he was too late—Carl punched him with an iron fist, sending him flying into the wall of purple gas.

"Waaaaagghhh!!!!" Gammon screamed. And then *POOF,* he was gone.

"What a shame," said Porkins, "he seemed like such a nice chap."

"Well, now there's just three of us," said Dave. He looked into one of the TV cameras. "You might as well end the tournament. We're not going to kill each other. We're friends."

For a moment there was no response, then Derek Cool's voice blasted out from the speakers:

"Congratulations," he said, "you three are the last warriors left alive. You truly are a trio of cool dudes! Now, the arena is going to start shrinking, and will only stop when there's only one of you left. Good luck!"

To Dave's horror, the gas began to spread, moving towards them and making the arena smaller by the second.

"Now what?" said Carl.

Dave had no idea.

CHAPTER SEVENTEEN
The Purple Pearl

"I say," said Porkins. "What if Gammon was right? What if there are people out there watching who hate this Derek Cool chap as much as we do? Maybe they can help us."

"Maybe," said Dave. "But even if they did, I doubt they'd have time to do anything about it. Still, we can try and make sure that no-one else is forced to compete in this ridiculous tournament."

He turned to one of the cameras.

"Everyone listen!" shouted Dave. "Your leaders are lying to you! Not everyone who takes part in the tournament is a volunteer—we were forced to enter! It's too late for us, but you need to stop Derek Cool before he does it again next year. Next time *you* might be forced to compete, or someone you know. This tournament isn't cool, it's stupid. Oh, and Derek Cool isn't cool either. He's just a big cruel baby who's desperate for people to love him. You don't have to live like this—rise up and get rid of him."

"Wow," grinned Carl. "That was quite a speech. Derek Wimpy will not be happy."

Suddenly the speakers around the arena burst into life, and Derek Cool's voice blasted out:

"I *am* cool!" he roared. "I am, I am, I am!"

"No you're not," said Dave. "Everyone around you pretends to like you because they want your money. You're not cool at all. In fact, you're a nerd!"

"I AM NOT A NERD!!!" roared Derek. "And soon, you'll all be killed by my gas! So who's the nerd now?!"

"Still you," said Carl.

"KILL THEM!" roared Derek. "PUMP IN MORE GAS! KILL

THEM!"

Then his microphone cut off.

"Looks like someone smart took the microphone away from him," Carl said.

Dave, Carl and Porkins huddled together, as the gas crept closer and closer.

"Sorry I got us into this mess, chaps," said Porkins. "If I hadn't volunteered the three of us back on the pirate ship..."

"Don't worry about it," said Carl. "I'm just glad we got to tell Derek Cool what we really thought of him."

Just then Dave spotted something emerging from the gas. Something crawling along the floor...

"It's Robo-Steve!" he exclaimed. "He's still alive!"

The Robot was pulling its ruined metal body across the ground.

"*Des... troy...*" it said weakly, "*Des... troy...*"

"I don't think you're going to be destroying anything, old bean," said Porkins. He raised his bow. "Dave, old chap, shall I finish him off?"

Dave was about to say *yes*, but then a thought struck him.

"Robo-Steve's teleport," he said, "do you think it still works?"

"Maybe," said Carl, "but we don't know how to control it. It could bring us anywhere."

"Anywhere but here," Dave said.

"Good point," said Carl, with a grin.

Dave dived down and stuck his hands inside of Robo-Steve's shattered metal torso.

"I don't even know what I'm looking for," he said. "This was a stupid idea."

"Maybe the teleport thingie is a bit like an ender pearl," said Porkins. "That's the only other thing I can think of that lets you teleport."

"Good idea," said Dave.

Dave kept rummaging around inside Robo-Steve, looking for

something round like a pearl.

"*My brain functions... the electricity has damaged them...*" said Robo-Steve.

"Oh be quiet," said Dave, "haven't you caused enough trouble for one day?"

Finally he found something. Something *round.*

Dave pulled the round thing out of Robo-Steve's chest. It looked just like an ender pearl, apart from it was purple, and had a little button on the top.

"Ripley must have modified an ender pearl and used it to give Robo-Steve teleporting powers," said Dave. "That's fascinating."

"Yeah, that's great," said Carl, "but don't forget we're about to get killed by electric gas. Can it teleport us out of here or what?"

"Maybe if we press the button, it will activate the teleport," said Dave. "Both of you, touch the pearl with me."

Porkins and Carl both reached forward to touch the ender pearl.

"*Please...*" gasped Robo-Steve. "*Take me with you...*"

"Maybe we should," said Dave to the others.

"Dave, he's a killer robot," said Carl. "No way."

Dave nodded. Carl was right: no matter how weak he was, they couldn't trust Robo-Steve, after all the things he'd done.

"*I've... changed...*" said Robo-Steve. "*The electricity... has altered my electronic brain...*"

"The poor chap does seem like the electricity has changed him a bit," said Porkins. "Maybe we should..."

"No!" said Carl. "Come on, enough feeling sorry for robots— we need to get out of here."

Carl was right, Dave saw. They gas was almost upon them now. In less than a minute it would be surrounding them, and they'd be electrocuted.

"Ok," said Dave. "Let's go."

He took one last look at the wretched, broken Robo-Steve, then pressed the button on the purple ender pearl.

CHAPTER EIGHTEEN
Totally Cool!

There was a flash of purple, then Dave, Carl and Porkins found themselves in the middle of a busy street. They were surrounded by an angry crowd, and they only had to look up and see the golden tower in front of them to realize where they were.

"We're back in Cool City," said Dave. "It worked!" He popped the purple ender pearl into his pocket.

"And it looks like our message got across," said Carl. "These are protesters."

Dave saw that Carl was right. The crowd were protesting, surrounding the golden Cool Tower.

"Derek Cool must resign as mayor!" someone in the crowd yelled.

"Down with Derek Cool!" shouted another. "Open the doors and let us in!"

Ron, wearing his red baseball cap as always, was leaning out of a window. "Go back to your homes!" he shouted. "The mayor demands that you all go home!"

Just then, people in the crowd began to recognize Dave and his friends.

"It's Dave!" said someone.

"And Carl and Porker!" said someone else.

"Actually, it's Porkins," said Porkins.

Everyone started telling Dave, Porkins and Carl how great they thought they were, and how they had been rooting for them to win the contest on TV.

"How did you escape the arena?" someone asked. Obviously the crowd had started protesting before they saw how Dave had teleported them out of there with the modified ender pearl.

"We escaped so we could take down Derek Cool," said Carl. "Now out of my way—let's see if some iron golem muscle can take down these doors!"

The crowd parted to let Carl through. He stomped forward, his big iron feet clanging across the gold block road.

"Stay back, creeper!" Ron shouted at him as Carl approached. "I have archers trained on you—if you take another step forward, they'll shoot you down!"

"They can try," said Carl. He tucked his head inside the iron golem's body like a tortoise, then started charging towards the golden doors. The archers shot arrows at him, but they just bounced off his iron armor, and his little creeper head was safely hidden.

The headless iron golem started pounding the doors.

"I hope I'm hitting the right bit!" said Carl. "I can't see a thing!"

SMASH! The doors broke. The crowd all cheered and ran inside of the building.

"Retreat!" Ron yelled to his men. "Retreat!"

"Try not to hurt anyone," Dave told the crowd, as he, Porkins and Carl led the crowd into the lobby. "There's been too much violence already."

The elevator had been broken (probably by Ron and his men, Dave thought) so they charged up the stairs. Occasionally one of the Baseball Cap Boys would appear and try and stop them, but when they saw how big the crowd was they always surrendered. It took forever, but finally they reached the top floor. The door to Derek Cool's throne room was blocked off by iron blocks, and Ron stood in front of it, with the last of his men. All of them were wearing diamond armor, their baseball caps forgotten. When they drew their swords, they were diamond too.

"Surrender, Ron," said Dave. "It's over. Derek Cool's reign is finished."

"I promised Derek's father that I would protect his son," said Ron, "and I always keep my promises. Derek is an idiot, but his father was my closest friend. I won't abandon his son in his hour of need."

"I promise you that no harm will come to Derek," said Dave. "Or any of you, if you surrender."

"Not gonna happen," said Ron.

"I surrender!" said one of Ron's men, dropping his sword and putting his hands up. "I don't want to die for Derek the idiot."

"Me too!" said another one.

Then all Ron's men started surrendering, until there was only Ron left.

"Cowards," spat Ron.

"Come on Ron," said Derek. "Both you and Derek will be safe. I promise."

Ron gritted his teeth, then finally he dropped his sword.

"I surrender," he said.

When they broke into the throne room, Derek Cool was hiding behind a sofa.

"Please don't hurt me!" he blubbed. "I didn't mean it! I didn't know Ron was forcing people to fight who didn't want to! I only wanted to be cool!"

The crowd took Derek, Ron and their men away to be locked up, awaiting trial. There was a huge party in the streets, and everyone couldn't stop thanking Dave and his friends.

"You've saved our city," said one villager, "thank you so much!"

The villagers of Cool City wanted Dave, Porkins and Carl to stay, but Dave and his friends were keen to get going.

"We're on our own quest," Dave told them, "and we need to get back on the road."

Dave, Carl and Porkins had their belongings returned to them (Dave was pleased to see that his two books were safe) and the villagers gave them a load of diamond to bring with them. They wanted to give them gold as well, but Dave pointed out that diamond made much better armor and weapons, which was more important to them on the road.

The villagers gave them a ship as well, a small vessel that could be crewed by three people.

"Good luck!" Dave told the villagers as they set sail. "And no more battle royales!"

"Never again!" shouted a villager. And several other villagers shouted the same thing.

So Dave, Carl and Porkins set sail across the ocean once more, the villagers waving them off. Soon Cool City was far behind them, with just endless water in every direction. The sun had almost set, and the stars were twinkling in the sky.

"Which way shall we sail, captain?" Porkins asked Dave.

Dave took out an eye of ender from his bag and threw it into the sky. It hovered in place for a moment, then flew off into the distance.

"Straight ahead," said Dave with a grin. "Let's go find the ender dragon."

EPILOGUE

Paul Bunker had been sailing to Cool City for over thirty years. When he'd first started coming there it had been a young city, still being built. It had been called *Gold City* back then, and Paul had always preferred that name.

Paul was a simple villager, and hated the bright lights and flashy goings on of Cool City, but as a trader he often found himself going there. There was simply too much money to be made. The people of Cool city had no farms of their own, so Paul would sail over with a ship full of food to sell. By the time he left Cool City his ship was normally full to the brim with emeralds and gold.

There had been some commotion in the city in recent days. People had been talking about a revolution, and that the mayor had been overthrown, but Paul wasn't really interested. All he wanted to do was sell his wares and make some money. He had been at sea for too long, and was anxious to get back to his wife back in Villagertropolis.

It was going to be a long voyage home, so Paul decided to have one final meal of beetroot soup at the local cafe before heading to his ship and joining his men.

He was just about to take a spoonful of soup when a figure in a cloak sat down opposite him.

"Can I help you?" asked Paul. The cloak was covering the figure's face, so he couldn't see who it was.

"You have a ship," said the stranger. It wasn't a question. "I would like you to take me back to the mainland. Anywhere will do. I can work to pay for my keep."

There was something odd about the stranger's voice that Paul couldn't quite put his finger on.

"Who are you?" Paul asked.

"I was brought here against my will," said the stranger. "I was a mindless fool, but I think differently now. I think clearly. Something has changed inside of me."

"Right..." said Paul. "But I'm going to need a name, I'm afraid."

The figure pulled back his hood. Paul was shocked to see that his face was made of metal. His eyes glowed green.

"My name is... Robo-Steve."

Paul laughed. "You're a robot! That's pretty cool. But *Robo-Steve,* what kind of name is that?"

"It is... my name," said the stranger, sounding unsure. "You didn't see me on TV?"

"Mister, I don't really watch much television," said Paul. "It rots the brain. Look, you can join my crew, but you're gonna need a better name. *Robo-Steve* just sounds weird."

"What name do you suggest?" asked the stranger.

"How about Robo?" said Paul. "Or just Steve?"

"Not Steve," said the stranger, a note of bitterness in his voice.

"Well, it's a long voyage, so you'll have plenty of time to come up with something," said Paul. "Come on, let's get to the ship."

BOOK 5

Invasion

CHAPTER ONE
Land Ahoy!

"Land ahoy!" Porkins shouted. "I say, chaps, I can see land!"

Dave and Carl ran out from their cabins to look. Carl was wearing his huge iron golem suit.

Porkins was right, Dave was pleased to see—there were lush green hills in the distance and a golden beach. It was the first land they'd seen since leaving Cool Island three days earlier.

"At last," said Carl. "I've had enough of the ocean to last me a lifetime."

"Does it look like an island?" Dave asked Porkins, coming over to join him at the ship's controls.

"I don't think so," said Porkins. "I think we're finally back to the mainland."

Dave breathed a sigh of relief. Like Carl, he was fed up of being at sea. He wanted to get back to solid ground and resume his journey to find an ender portal.

It wasn't long before they reached the beach. Porkins dropped the anchor, then they swam to the shore.

"Land!" said Carl happily, rolling in the sand in his iron golem armor.

"Are you going to throw an ender eye?" Porkins asked Dave. "To see which way we should go?"

"I'll wait until we're a bit further inland," said Dave. "I don't want to waste them more than I have to."

So Dave, Porkins and Carl made their way across the beach, walking towards the green hills and trees that lay beyond.

"I say, what about the ship?" said Porkins, looking back at the ocean. Their small ship, the one the people of Cool Island had given them, was bobbing on the waves.

"Leave it," said Carl. "We don't need it anymore."

"I guess not," said Porkins.

They soon found themselves walking across a large plains biome. Sheep and rabbits were grazing on the grass and there were flowers everywhere. Porkins kept stopping to pick them.

"What do you need flowers for?" Carl asked. "Flowers are stupid."

"Flowers are good for dyes," said Porkins.

Carl rolled his eyes. "We're meant to be going to kill a dragon, not making pretty dresses."

"I always fancied some pink leather armor," said Porkins. "I think it would look rather fetching."

"You're pink already!" said Carl, in disbelief.

"Come on Carl, let Porkins pick flowers in peace," said Dave. "Talking of armor, we got so much diamond from Cool City that we ought to build some. Weapons too. You sure you wouldn't rather have new diamond armor, Porkins? It's stronger than leather, according to my crafting book."

"I guess so," said Porkins. "But I'll make myself some pink leather armor as well. For special occasions."

They soon came across some cows. Carl used his new iron golem strength to slay them, then Dave cooked the raw beef into steak and Porkins took the leather to make his armor. By the time Dave had finished cooking, Porkins was dressed head to toe in pink armor.

"Pretty snazzy, huh chaps?" said Porkins.

"You look like a giant sausage," said Carl.

They sat down and ate, then, because the sun was starting to go down, Dave made them a small house with three beds.

"Goodnight chaps," said Porkins, as they snuggled down into their beds.

"Goodnight, Porkins," said Dave.

For the first time in a long time, Dave was starting to feel good about their adventure. For too long they'd been distracted from their main quest, caught up in other adventures. But now, finally, they were on their way. All they had to do was keep on following the eyes of ender, and soon they'd find another stronghold. Then they could go to the End and slay the ender dragon, and Dave would be the hero he'd always dreamed of being.

Dave also began to wonder how Steve was getting on. Steve had been on a quest to slay the ender dragon as well, but Dave knew that Steve was easily distracted. Hopefully Steve had found something else to interest him, and had forgotten all about it. Dave's relationship with Steve was complicated: he'd started out hating him, but now... now he wasn't so sure.

Finally, Dave drifted off to sleep.

The next morning, Dave, Porkins and Carl destroyed the little house, putting the tiny blocks back in Dave's rucksack.

"Right," said Dave, "let's see what direction we need to go."

He took out an eye of ender and threw it into the sky. For a moment it hovered in place, then it zoomed off into the distance.

"This way then," said Dave, then he, Porkins and Carl followed the path the eye had taken.

They had only been walking an hour or so when they started to hear sounds coming from up ahead.

"What is that?" said Porkins. "I recognize the sound, but I can't ruddy well put my finger on it."

"It sounds like... digging," said Dave. "But I don't think it's just one person digging. I think it's lots."

They kept walking. As they got nearer it was clear that Dave was right: it was digging. But it sounded like *hundreds* of people digging.

Eventually they came over a hill and finally caught sight of the diggers. In front of them was a huge pit, as big as a small town, and hundreds of diggers were using pickaxes to chip away at it. As they got closer, Dave saw the pit already went down to bedrock: the diggers were just making it wider.

"They must be mining for emerald or gold," said Carl. "Maybe there's a mining town nearby."

"Shall we go and introduce ourselves?" Porkins asked Dave. "Maybe we can do some trading with them."

But something didn't seem right to Dave. On the face of it, it just looked like a normal mine, but there was something wrong.

Suddenly he realized what it was. Not all of the figures in the mine were villagers; some were pigmen. *Zombie* pigmen. And they weren't mining, they were guarding the villagers.

"Look," he whispered to Carl and Porkins, pointing at the pigmen.

"Zombie pigmen!" exclaimed Porkins. "But what are they doing outside of the Nether?"

"I don't know and I don't want to know," said Carl. "Come on, let's take another route."

"No," said Dave, "we can't just leave those villagers. It looks they're being forced to mine against their will."

"I thought you wanted to find this stupid dragon and be a hero?" said Carl.

"I do," said Dave, "but part of being a hero is helping people in need. And those villagers need our help."

CHAPTER TWO
The Mine

By Dave's count, there were twenty zombie pigmen and over one-hundred villagers. The zombie pigmen were armed though, with gold swords.

"This will be an easy fight," said Carl. "Zombies are just mindless idiots. We'll just go in and bish, bash, bosh! They'll be defeated in no time."

"Those *mindless idiots* used to be my people," said Porkins sadly.

"Oh... Sorry Porkins," said Carl.

"But you're right though, old bean," said Porkins. "They're nothing but zombies now. I wish that wasn't the case, but it is. And we must defeat them to save those villager chaps."

"Ok," said Dave, "Porkins, you use your bow to take out the ones furthest away—the six down near the bottom of the pit. Carl, you quickly charge around and take out the eight at the top of the pit, and I'll take out the last six. They're all gathered together around the middle of the pit, so I should be able to dispose of them quickly. We'll all attack together, to take them by surprise, so get in position and wait for my signal."

"What's the signal?" asked Carl.

"Um, I'll yell 'Now!'"

"Fair enough," said Carl.

"You sure you don't want some better armor?" Dave asked Porkins.

"Actually I think leather armor is better for my archery," said Porkins, "I can move easier in it than I can in diamond."

"Fair enough," said Dave.

Dave, Porkins and Carl all sneaked around the pit, getting into position. When Dave saw they were all ready, he took a deep breath, then yelled: "NOW!"

Porkins fired arrows at the zombie pigmen at the bottom of the pit, slaying them before they had a chance to realize what was happening. Carl used his huge iron arms to send the zombie pigmen around the top of the pit flying. Dave ran forward and slashed at the remaining pigmen. Once he'd attacked one, the rest came running at him, and he soon defeated them all.

The battle was over so quickly that the mining villagers were confused.

"What happened?" one asked.

"We saved your butts," said Carl, chambering down the pit to join Dave and Porkins.

"It's a creeper!" one of the villagers yelled. "A creeper... in an iron golem suit?!"

"Relax," said Dave, "he's a friend. We all are. We came to rescue you."

"Thanks," said a female villager in a white coat. "I'm Sally, by the way."

"Nice to meet you, Sally," said Dave. "What was going on here? Why were the pigmen making you mine?"

"*Zombie* pigmen," said Porkins. "Those chaps weren't pigmen anymore."

"Sorry Porkins," said Dave, "Good point."

"Where have you been?" Sally asked Dave. "I thought all villagers were being forced to dig these mines. When the pigmen invaded, we sent messages from village to village, and they'd all been invaded too."

"Invaded by pigmen?" asked Dave. "What's going on?"

Sally sighed. "I don't know where you've been, but a week ago nether portals started popping up in every village and town. I even heard reports that one appeared as far away as Villagertropolis. Zombie pigmen poured out of the portals and took over. Now they're forcing us to dig holes; they're looking for something called a *stronghold*. Apparently they're these really old structures that the Old People built underground."

Dave's blood went cold. Herobrine had been looking for a stronghold. Could this be anything to do with him?

"Wait a minute," said Carl, "this doesn't make sense. How could the zombie pigmen give you orders? They can't even speak!"

"The pigmen are not alone," said Sally. "They seem to be controlled by witches. From what I've heard, there's one witch in every village, controlling the pigmen. Ours is called Dotty. She gives us the orders, and the pigmen make sure we do what we're told."

"Dotty!" said Porkins. "That's the dastardly witch who gave us the sleeping potion in our food. The one who brought us to Herobrine."

"You've seen Emperor Herobrine?" said Sally, sounding amazed. "I thought he was just a myth that the witches made up to keep us under control."

"Wait, why did you call him *Emperor* Herobrine?" asked Dave.

"Because that's what the witches call him," said Sally. "They say that he's their boss. That he's now the ruler of the world, and we have to do what he says."

"We go away for a week and the world gets taken over by Herobrine," said Carl. "Can't people take care of themselves?"

"Wait," said another villager. "A villager, a pigman and a creeper... you're not Dave, are you?"

"I am," said Dave.

"Oh dear," said the villager. "That's another thing that Herobrine is making us do: as well as digging for strongholds, we've been told to be on the lookout for a villager named Dave, who hangs out with a tiny creeper and a pigman."

"Do I look tiny to you?" asked Carl, flexing his iron muscles.

"And what are you meant to do if you find me?" asked Dave.

"Capture you," said the villager. "I don't know what you've

done, Dave, but apparently Emperor Herobrine wants you alive."

"And are you going to bring me to him?" Dave asked.

The villager looked at Carl, then at Dave and Porkins with their weapons.

"Of course not," he said, smiling. But there was something about that smile that Dave didn't trust.

"What Adam is trying to say," said Sally, "is that we're very grateful to you for saving us."

Adam scoffed. "They haven't really saved us. There are still hundreds of pigmen back at the village."

"We can defeat those cads as well," said Porkins. "Dave, Carl and I are mighty warriors. We won the Cool Dude Battle Royale!"

"Never heard of it," said Adam. "Thanks for your help, but you should go. We'll have enough explaining to do when we return to the village without our zombie pigmen guards. If you come with us, there'll be no end of trouble."

"Adam," said Sally, "these three are warriors—they could help us! Even Emperor Herobrine is scared of Dave. They could help us defeat him and his pigmen once and for all."

"Are you mad?" said Adam. "Herobrine has taken over every village and town in the area. For all we know, he might have conquered the entire world. What use are these three going to be?"

"We've defeated Herobrine once and we can ruddy well do it again," said Porkins.

Porkins was stretching the truth a bit, Dave thought to himself. They hadn't really defeated Herobrine the last time they met, they'd merely escaped from him.

"Will you help us then?" Sally asked Dave. "Will you help us take back our village?"

Dave looked round. Some of the villagers looked as excited as Sally, but others looked worried, and some, like Adam, looked annoyed.

They're scared that I'll let them down, thought Dave. It was all very well marching into a village and defeating a load of zombie pigmen, but if Herobrine's army was as big as it sounded, it would only be a temporary measure. Soon Herobrine would send more troops, and take the village back again.

"Can you sneak us into your village?" Dave asked. "If we can have a look round, maybe we can figure out a plan."

"Great!" said Sally excitedly.

Adam gave Carl and Porkins a disapproving look. "And how do you intend to sneak them in?" he said. "A creeper and a pig?"

"I'm a pig*man*, thank you," said Porkins.

"Do you have iron golems in your village?" Dave asked. "If we painted Carl's face gray, he could pretend to be one of them."

"I'm afraid we don't," said Sally. "The pigmen slew them all when they took over."

"Well, at least Porkins can pretend to be a zombie pigman," said Dave.

"What what what?" said Porkins, a look of shock on his face.

"All we have to do is put a bit of gray dye on your face in the right places," said Dave. "Maybe a bit of green too."

"Good job you picked all those flowers," grinned Carl.

"How can we hide Carl?" Dave asked Sally.

Sally took a long hard look at Carl.

"Well, you'll have to take off the iron golem armor," she said. "There's no way we can sneak you in in that thing."

"No way!" said Carl. "I'm not losing my iron golem suit."

"We can hide it somewhere near the village," Dave reassured him. "You can get it back later, Carl."

"Hmmph," said Carl.

"I've got it!" said Sally excitedly. "We can disguise you as a pig!"

"What?" said Carl. Now it was his turn to look shocked.

"Our village is full of pigs," said Sally, "we've been pig farmers for generations. No-one will look twice at you if you're covered in pink dye with an apple for a nose."

Porkins chuckled. "I say Carl, I think you'd look rather cute."

"Shut your mouth," said Carl. He didn't look very happy.

"Then that's settled then," said Dave. Porkins will disguise himself as a zombie pigman, Carl will disguise himself as a pig, and we'll go undercover in your village to see what's going on. But who should I say I am?"

"I'll tell everyone you're my long-lost cousin," said Sally. "Although we'd better not call you Dave, as everyone is looking for a Dave. How about... Ian?"

"Ok, Ian it is," said Dave.

CHAPTER THREE
Greenleaf

Dave, Porkins, Carl and the villagers all began their long trek back to the village.

"Our village is called Greenleaf," Sally told Dave as they walked. "We're only a small community, but we're proud pig farmers. We sell most of our pigs to Villagertropolis and the big towns. Or at least we did, before the zombie pigmen came. Now everyone is forced to work in the pits."

"Pits?" said Dave. "There are more than one?"

"Yes," said Sally. "There are four in total. Dotty the witch told us where to dig them. Apparently all the other settlements taken over by the pigmen are digging pits as well."

Herobrine really is desperate to find a stronghold, Dave thought to himself. *But why?* The only theory he'd come up with so far was that Herobrine must want to tame the ender dragon, to use it for his evil deeds. But that seemed too simple. From what Dave had seen of Herobrine, he was powerful enough already, without a dragon.

They came through some trees and finally they could see Greenleaf. It was only a small village, as Sally had said, and it was on the top of a small hill.

"Right," said Sally. "Porkins, Carl, you two ought to get in disguise."

Adam marched over.

"I've been talking with some of the others," he said, "and we've agreed that this is a stupid idea. Dave and his friends will get found out, and then we'll all be in trouble. Nothing good can come of this, mark my words."

"Do you really want to be digging mines for the rest of your life?" Sally asked him. "This could be our chance to fight back."

Adam said nothing, but he muttered something angrily under his breath.

"Attention everyone!" Sally said, talking to the rest of the villagers. "As you know, Dave and his friends are going to enter the village in secret, so please don't accidentally give them away. And don't tell anyone else about this either—we want to keep Dave's presence here as secret as possible for now, to stop the zombie pigmen from finding out."

"It's not the zombie pigmen I'm worried about," said Adam. "They just do as they're told. It's Dotty we need to watch. If she suspects anything, she'll contact her boss. And then we'll have Herobrine to deal with."

"Well, let's make sure that doesn't happen," said Sally. She turned to Carl and Porkins. "Right you two, let's get you in disguise."

"Oh crumbs," said Porkins.

"Oh dear," said Carl.

"Oh, stop complaining," said Dave, grinning. "I'm sure you'll both look lovely."

Sally and a few of the villagers got to work on Porkins and Carl, using Porkins's flowers to make the appropriate dyes for their skin. It took all Dave's willpower not to burst out laughing.

When they were finished, it was quite a sight to behold. Porkins looked just like a real zombie pigman, with the makeup making it look like he had rotten flesh and exposed bone.

"I bet I look frightfully ugly," sighed Porkins.

"Um, no... you look... fine," said Dave.

But when the villagers finished applying Carl's makeup, Dave couldn't stop himself from laughing.

"Yeah, yeah, laugh it up," said Carl, unhappily.

"I'm sorry," said Dave, wiping tears of laughter from his eyes. "It's just you look so... so... so much like a pig."

The villagers had done a great job. All of Carl's skin was

covered in pink dye, he had bits of bacon for ears and an apple for his nose, all tied on with string. The apple had been smothered with pink dye, with two black spots on it to look like nostrils.

"You'll fit right in with all our little piggies," said Sally, trying to be nice. "You look very cute."

"Bah!" said Carl.

"I say, Dave," said Porkins, "I've just realized—Dotty knows who you are. You'll need a disguise too."

"Oh dear," said Dave, "I never thought about that."

"Here," said Carl, "let me help."

He dipped his hand into some red dye, then wiped over the lower half of Dave's face.

"There you go," said Carl, "a lovely red beard."

"Uh, thanks," said Dave.

When everyone was ready, they continued the journey back to the village. The village was made up of small wooden houses; it reminded Dave of his own village, before Steve had blown it up with TNT, and it made him a bit homesick.

As they reached the first of the wooden buildings, two zombie pigmen came to meet them.

"Rrurk rrurk!" said one of the pigmen.

"Rrurk roik!" said the other.

"Hello," Sally said cheerily. "We're back for the day. No sign of a stronghold yet, I'm afraid."

"Can they understand what you're saying?" Dave whispered.

"I don't think so," Sally whispered. "Though they're not quite as dumb as they look. I think they know something's wrong."

They was a swishing sound, then a witch swooped down on elytra wings and landed in front of them.

It was Dotty.

"What happened to your pigman guards?" she asked Sally. "And who is this?" she said, looking at Dave.

"There was an ambush," said Sally. "A bunch of skeletons attacked us. The pigmen bravely stepped in to save us, but all of them were killed except one." She turned to Porkins.

"Um, rurk rurk!" said Porkins, doing his best zombie pigman impression.

Dotty gave him a suspicious look. Then she turned to Dave.

"Who are you, villager?" she asked.

"This is my cousin, D—Ian," said Sally.

"De-Ian?" said Dotty.

"Yes," said Sally, "De-Ian... Dean. His name is Dean."

"Ok," said Dotty. "Tell me, Dean, where do you come from? And to what do we owe the pleasure of your company?"

"I'm... a humble pig farmer from the mountains, Dave said, trying to remember the fake story that Sally had made up for him. "But all my pigs were eaten by zombies, so I decided to come and live in Greenleaf, with my cousin, as I knew that they farm pigs here too." He turned to Carl. "This is the last pig I have left. The only one that survived."

"Oink oink," said Carl.

"Well if you're going to stay here, you'd better be prepared to dig," said Dotty. "Emperor Herobrine doesn't want any slackers in his empire. You work hard, you get to live."

"That's very generous," said Dave.

Dotty gave him a suspicious look, trying to work out if he was being rude or not.

"Just watch yourself, Dean," she said. "And remember, I'm in charge around here."

And with that, Dotty walked off. Dave watched her head into a building made of dark reddish brown bricks.

Nether brick, Dave realized. The nether brick building was the only building in the village not made of wood.

"That's where the nether portal is," Sally whispered. "Once the pigmen took over the village they built that building around the portal. The witch lives in there, and it's where the pigmen sleep too."

"*Zombie* pigmen," Porkins reminded her.

"Sorry," said Sally. "No villagers are allowed in there. Well, apart from the witch. If we go near it, the pigmen chase us off. I mean *zombie* pigmen, sorry."

"Porkins, you sleep in there for now," said Dave. "You can see what it's like inside, and how easy it would be to get to the portal. Also, find out if Dotty has a way of communicating with Herobrine. The last thing we want is to start a revolution and have him arrive."

"He'll find out eventually, no matter what you do," snapped Adam. "Freeing our village from the pigmen won't do much good if Herobrine can just send more to replace them."

"That's why we have to see what kind of operation Herobrine is running," said Dave. "We have to get inside the Nether."

"We could just build another nether portal," said Carl.

"Good point," said Dave. "Porkins, how do multiple nether portals work—if we built one outside the village, would it bring us to the same portal in the nether as the village one, or would it create a new portal?"

"I think having portals on this side that close to each other, the portal would bring you to the same portal on the nether side as the original portal."

"This is making my head hurt," said Carl. "Nether portals are too complicated."

"Let's give it some thought, anyway," said Dave. "For now, let's assess what the situation is, and go from there."

"Do I have to stay dressed like a pig?" asked Carl.

"Yes," said Dave.

"Bah," said Carl.

"Don't you mean 'oink'?" said Sally, with a giggle.

Carl did not look happy.

CHAPTER FOUR
The Secret Base

Porkins had never been very good at pretending. When he'd been a baby pigman, back in the Nether, his friends had often put on plays. Whenever Porkins had been cast in a part, everyone told him what a terrible actor he was.

Nonetheless, Porkins was giving pretending to be a zombie his best shot.

"Rrurk!" he grunted as he walked past some zombie pigmen.

"Rrurk!" they grunted back.

Those poor chaps, thought Porkins, looking at the zombie pigmen. They were just mindless creatures now, with no will of their own.

Doing his best zombie walk, Porkins headed towards the nether brick building in the center of town. It was a large building, much larger than the wooden houses that surrounded it, and there were about ten zombie pigmen outside standing guard.

"Rrurk rrurk!" Porkins said to the zombie pigmen, as he walked towards the entrance.

For a second Porkins worried that the zombie pigmen would stop him, but they didn't, so he just walked straight through.

Inside the lobby of the building, zombie pigmen were wandering about aimlessly or just standing still. There were torches on the walls and several iron doors with switches. Some of the pigmen were asleep on the ground.

They just do nothing until they're given orders, thought Porkins. *They're little more than robots.*

Suddenly one of the iron doors sprang open and Dotty the witch marched across the room.

"Out my way!" she said, shoving Porkins.

"Er, rrurk rrurk!" said Porkins.

Dotty pressed a switch and disappeared through another iron door. It changed shut behind her.

Porkins decided to have a snoop round the room that Dotty had just left. None of the other pigmen were paying attention to him, so he just pressed the switch, then walked through the door.

He walked down a corridor lit by torches, then at the end of it he found himself in a room with a nether portal in the middle. Scattered around the room were tables with scraps of parchment on them.

Porkins thought about just going through the nether portal, but he imagined that on the other side there would be more zombie pigmen guards, and maybe some witches. But then a thought struck him—he was disguised as a zombie pigman; he could go where he wanted. If any of the witches found him, they'd just think he'd wandered into the wrong area.

Ok, thought Porkins. *Here goes.*

He stepped forward into the portal. It shimmered for a second, and then he was inside a corridor made of iron blocks.

Is this the Nether? he wondered. But before he could investigate further, two zombie pigman marched up to him angrily, swinging their golden swords. Porkins ran back inside the portal.

When he emerged back on the other side, he rushed down the nether brick corridor towards the door, but before he could get there, Dotty opened it.

"What are you doing in here?" she snapped. "These doors are meant to keep you idiots out. Come on, back you go."

She grabbed him roughly and pushed him out into the lobby area. The door slammed shut behind her.

So the witches have built some kind of iron structure in the Nether, Porkins thought. *I must tell Dave and the other chaps.*

Suddenly the door swung open again.

"Actually," said Dotty, grabbing Porkins and guiding him back into the portal room, "you can make yourself useful. I need you to deliver my status report to Isabella."

She handed him a piece of paper.

"You got that, idiot?" Dotty asked him. "Bring this... to Isabella."

"Roink roink!" said Porkins.

"Yes, yes," said Dotty impatiently, and she shoved him into the portal. There was a brief shimmer and then he was back inside the iron corridor once more. The two zombie pigman guards marched up to him again, but he waved his piece of paper at them.

"Rrrurk!" said Porkins.

That seemed to satisfy the guards, and they stood down and let him pass.

Porkins walked forward into the corridor. Running down it were two powered rails, and there was a large chest with the word 'minecarts' above it.

One track must run left and the other right, thought Porkins.

There were more signs too, with arrows next to them. There were signs that pointed to things such as 'Barracks' and 'Armory', but also signs with place names on then, each with an arrow pointing either left or right. Pointing right there were two signs with red writing on them: 'Headquarters' and 'Emperor Herobrine'.

Herobrine. Even the name was enough to make Porkins's heart stop in his chest. Herobrine had betrayed the pigmen and turned them into zombies. There was no-one Porkins hated more in the world, and if he took a minecart to the right, he could go see him.

And then what, you silly chap? thought Porkins to himself. Herobrine would probably be incredibly well guarded, and even if Porkins got past the guards he'd have to face Herobrine. He'd seen how powerful Herobrine was: he wouldn't stand a chance.

Porkins unfolded the piece of paper that Dotty had given him and had a look. The contents were fairly boring, it was basically a summary of how many mines had been set up around the village, how big they were, and if there had been any sign of Dave the villager or a stronghold.

Porkins decided the best thing to do was just deliver the piece of paper. He assumed that 'Headquarters' was where this Isabella would be, whoever she was. He opened the chest and pulled out a tiny minecart. When he laid it down on the tracks it grew to full size, so he hopped inside and it zoomed off.

"Waaaa!" yelled Porkins. He'd never ridden in a minecart before, and was amazed at how fast it was. He sped down the iron corridor, rushing past nether portal after nether portal, all guarded by pigmen. The nether portals had signs above them: 'Tree Town', 'Sheepburg', 'Villagertropolis', and many more. The pigmen had built a huge network to help them travel easily from place to place, Porkins realized. No wonder they'd taken over so quickly.

Suddenly the corridor ended, and the rail track sped Porkins across a huge iron bridge in the middle of the nether. Below he could see a sea of lava, stretching out in every direction, and high above him he could see the cavernous netherrack ceiling. He also got his first proper look at the iron building: it was a huge rectangle, with tunnels and bridges leading off to other huge rectangles.

With their minecarts they'll be able to travel anywhere they want in minutes, Porkins thought. He knew that distance in the Nether was different from distance in the overworld. A short minecart journey in the Nether could be a journey of miles in the overworld.

In the distance he could see several half-finished buildings, with pigmen working on them. It looked like Herobrine and the witches were trying to cover the whole of the Nether with their portals.

The bridge Porkins was on was leading towards another huge iron building. Standing around the entrance were more zombie pigmen guards. Porkins's cart zipped through the entrance, and he found himself traveling down another corridor. He sped past more portals, each with names on signs above them.

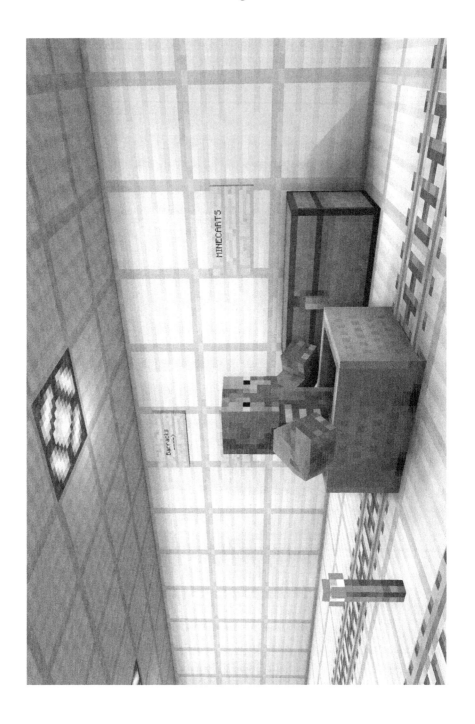

Suddenly Porkins's cart hit a block, coming to a stop. He was in a room with several minecart tracks leading off in different directions. One was labeled 'To Emperor Herobrine: Senior Witches Only!'. Porkins again had to resist the urge to go straight there.

I'll be back for you, Herobrine old chap, he thought. *You mark my words!*

Instead he placed his cart on the route labeled 'To Headquarters', and sped off once more. His cart traveled down another iron corridor, but that soon ended and the minecart led straight across the barren wasteland of the Nether. There were pigmen all around, putting down iron blocks.

Looks like they're still building this part of the corridor, thought Porkins.

Ahead he could see a castle, which looked like it was made of cobblestone. That was where the minecart track was taking him. As he got closer he could see witches in the windows, all wearing the blue robes that witches loyal to Herobrine wore.

THUNK! The Minecart hit a block right outside the castle, coming to a sudden stop. The entrance was a big open archway, with a sign saying 'Headquarters' above it. A horde of pigmen ran over to Porkins, surrounding him and grunting angrily.

"Get back, you fools," said a bored-sounding voice. The pigmen all backed off, and a witch strode up to Porkins.

"What have you got for me?" she asked.

"Rrurk rrurk!" said Porkins, handing her the scrap of paper.

The witch took a look. "No surprise there," she said. "Alright, follow me. The boss might have a message for you to bring back."

The witch walked into the castle, Porkins following behind. Inside, witches were working away, most of them writing things or giving orders to pigmen. On one wall was a huge map of the overworld. As Porkins got closer he saw that it was actually lots of normal sized maps stuck together.

"Any report from Villagertropolis?" a witch yelled across the room.

"The siege is still going on," another witch yelled back. "The last report mentioned something about a robot army turning up."

"Well, send more pigmen," the first witch said. "We need that city."

The witch Porkins was following suddenly stopped.

"Wait here," she told him, and she disappeared into a room, closing the wooden door behind her.

There was so much going on in the castle—witches and pigmen going to and fro, witches shouting orders across the room—but Porkins tried his best to see or hear anything that might be useful.

"Has there been any more word from the boss?" one witch asked.

"What, Isabella? Weren't you there at the meeting this morning?" another witch replied.

"No," said the first witch. "Not Lady Isabella. I'm talking about Lord Herobrine."

As she said *Herobrine* she shivered. It could have been his imagination, but Porkins could have sworn that the room got a bit colder.

"Nothing for days," said the other witch. "And anyway, he calls himself *Emperor* now, so make sure you don't use the wrong title. No, the *Emperor* normally keeps himself to himself, unless he has something to say. I doubt we'll hear much from him until we find a stronghold or that Dave."

The first witch suddenly gave Porkins a funny look.

"Are you listening to us, piggy?" she snapped.

"Don't be a fool," said the other witch. "These pigmen are nothing but brainless husks now. As long as Isabella has that golden staff, they'll do whatever we say."

Golden staff. The words made Porkins think back to Trotter, the evil pigman who had used a magical staff that Herobrine had given him to control the zombie pigmen.

That's how the witches can control zombie pigmen, thought Porkins. *They have Herobrine's staff!*

The witches had mentioned that a witch called Isabella now had the staff, and, sure enough, as Porkins looked around the room he saw a sign that said 'Isabella's Quarters: Restricted Access.'

That staff is here, Porkins thought. *If we can capture it or destroy it, the witches won't have control of the zombie pigmen anymore. We can jolly well stop this invasion!*

"We've found that pigmen village!" a witch yelled as she ran into the castle, waving a scrap of paper. "Shall we prepare an invasion force?"

"Why bother?" said a witch. "We've still got plenty of the Emperor's potion. Let's just turn them into zombies."

Porkins remembered the green liquid that Trotter had had. He'd tried to use it on Porkins and his friends, but instead it had gone over him, and turned him into a zombie.

"Right, you," said a voice. Porkins turned round. It was the bored witch who'd led him inside the castle. She passed him a piece of paper.

"Deliver this back to Dotty," she said. "Come on, what you waiting for? Go!"

"Roink!" said Porkins, and he lurched off, doing his best zombie impression.

He placed a minecart down, climbed into it, and it sped along the track once more. He took a look at the paper, but there was nothing much of interest on it, just orders for Dotty to dig more pits, and dig them faster.

CHAPTER FIVE
Dave Makes a Plan

That evening, Porkins came to see Dave and Carl, to tell them what he'd found out.

"Interesting," said Dave, when Porkins had finished. "So all the control the witches have over the pigmen is because of that staff."

"Exactly," said Porkins. "We destroy that staff and this invasion is finished!"

"You make it sound so easy," said Carl, rolling his eyes.

They were in Sally's home, on the edge of town. Sally lived with Adam, who, Dave had been surprised to find out, was her husband. Even though the two of them argued and disagreed a lot, they seemed to love each other. Or at least tolerate each other.

Dave and Carl had spent the day with Sally and Adam, talking through possible plans of attack. Dave had dug underneath Sally and Adam's house, creating a secret cellar where they could build armor and weapons, and, hopefully, train the villagers to fight.

The only trouble was, all the diamond and iron the villagers had—and everything they dug up in the mines—was always taken back to the Nether by the pigmen. So there wasn't anything to actually build armor and weapons with. Dave had been given a lot of materials when he'd left Cool Island, so he'd used these to make as many weapons as he could, but it wasn't much.

One thing the village did have was trees—plenty of trees. So Dave had decided that tomorrow he and Carl were going to sneak off and get loads of wood, so they could build wooden swords for the villagers. There were herds of cows nearby, so they were going to get as much leather as they could to make armor. It wasn't as good as having iron and diamond, but it would have to do.

"So if this magic staff is as powerful as you say, why don't you just grab it the next time you're sent to the Nether?" asked Adam. He and Sally had joined the conversation too, which was taking place in their kitchen.

"Don't be stupid, Adam" said Sally. "You really think the witches would just leave the staff unguarded?"

"There were a lot of zombie pigmen chaps at that castle," said Porkins sadly. "And we don't know how easy it is to destroy the staff. It might just take a blow from a sword, or it might be more difficult."

"We could always throw it in lava," said Carl. "Lava normally destroys most things. Well, apart from Herobrine, of course. We all saw what happened when *he* fell in lava."

Dave stood up from his chair, walking over and looking out of the window at the night sky.

"I think I'm starting to come up with a plan," he said. "To defeat the witches and end Herobrine's invasion, we need to break their control over the pigmen."

"*Zombie* pigmen," said Porkins.

"Sorry, Porkins," said Dave. "Zombie pigmen."

"Yes, we know all this," said Adam, "but how do you intend to do that?"

"I'm coming to that," said Dave. "One advantage we have over the witches is that they don't know that we know about the magic staff. From what Porkins has told us, it seems that the castle is guarded well, but not *too* well. With a small force we should be able to overwhelm their defenses and get the staff. The trouble we have is that as soon as we attack the castle, they'd send hundreds of zombie pigmen to defend it. They have minecart tracks, so they can easily send more troops from elsewhere."

"Are you going to tell us your plan or not?" said Adam.

"Let the man speak, Adam, for goodness sake!" said Sally. "Carry on, Dave."

"Ok," said Dave, "So what we need to do is make sure the

zombie pigmen are too busy to come to defend the castle. We need to launch as many attacks as we can at the same time—not just at Greenleaf, but in as many of the occupied towns and villages as possible. The witches and zombie pigmen will be so busy fighting rebellions, that they won't be able to send reinforcements to the castle."

"How are we going to do that?" said Adam.

"We need to send envoys to as many settlements as possible," said Dave. "Sally, can you provide me with a list of nearby towns and villages, and maps that say how to get to them?"

"I sure can," she grinned.

"Good," said Dave. "Then we arrange a date, and we all launch rebellions at the same time. Herobrine's forces will be overwhelmed."

"One question," said Carl, "if everything goes to plan and we destroy the magic staff and defeat the witches, what next? What do we do about Herobrine?"

The room went silent.

"Can't we all go and attack him?" said Sally. "I know he's meant to be powerful, but if we defeat the witches and the pigs first, we'll easily be able to beat him."

"I'm not so sure, old bean," said Porkins. "As Carl was saying, we've seen the blighter survive falling into lava. I'm not sure he *can* be killed."

"Herobrine is powerful," said Dave, "but without his army, his invasion will be over. We'll destroy his base in the Nether, we'll destroy his portals, and then there won't be anything he can do."

"Except come and destroy us all," said Carl.

"Yes," said Dave, "except for that."

CHAPTER SIX
The Plan Begins

The next day, they started to put the plan into motion.

Dave, Sally and Adam were forced by the zombie pigmen to go to work in one of the pits, but when they were there they started spreading the word about the rebellion, and recruited some of the villagers to be envoys to go and spread the word to other settlements.

The envoys sneaked out of the village that night to go to other towns and villages nearby. Dave and Sally had decided that the rebellion should take place in two weeks' time, to make sure there was enough time to get things sorted.

Every night, villagers would sneak over to Sally and Adam's house, and in the basement Dave would teach them to sword fight. Dave was reminded of his own time training with Ripley back in Snow Town. It didn't seem that long ago, but now Dave was the trainer. He'd enlarged the basement, digging it out so that it was much bigger than the house above. In fact he'd made it so big that it went underneath other houses in the village, allowing the villagers to sneak back and forth without the pigmen seeing.

Porkins and Carl kept themselves busy too. Carl sneaked out at night in his iron golem suit, guarding a group of villagers as they cut down trees for wood and dug up as much iron as they could find. Then they'd sneak it back to Sally and Adam's basement where it would be smelted and turned into weapons and armor. Then, during the day, Carl would put more pink makeup on and go back to pretending to be a pig.

Porkins kept pretending to be a zombie, living in the barracks with all the other zombie pigmen. It was a bittersweet experience, as he was, finally, surrounded by his own kind again, but they were mindless zombies.

He kept thinking about what he'd heard in the castle in the Nether: about the pigman village that the witches had found, and their plan to turn all the pigmen into zombies. He hoped that Dave's rebellion would defeat the witches before that could happen.

So everyone in the village was doing their part. They'd spread the word to other settlements, and they were training for the fight themselves. Everything was going to plan. But, as with many plans, there was something that hadn't been considered: that one of their own would betray them.

Adam had disliked Dave and his friends from the start. Since he was a baby villager, Adam had always followed the rules. He'd always done what he'd been told and had never been in trouble, but now he was being asked to be part of a *rebellion!*

To Adam, there was nothing wrong with working in the mines, even if they were being forced to do it by the pigmen. It was good, honest work. In Adam's opinion, many of his fellow villagers were far too lazy anyway, and a bit of hard work would do them good.

So as his wife and his fellow villagers prepared to fight the pigmen, Adam grew increasingly uneasy. In his opinion, rebelling against the pigmen would only lead to trouble. Better that the villagers kept doing what they were told and behaved themselves.

When he said as much to his wife one evening over dinner, she laughed in his face.

"Don't be such a coward, dear," she said. "Why don't you go down to the basement tonight and practice with the others? I don't think I've even ever seen you hold a sword."

"You never *will* see me hold a sword," snapped Adam. "Villagers aren't meant to be warriors. This *Dave* is putting ridiculous ideas into everyone's heads. Villagers are meant to behave themselves. Maybe do the odd bit of trading. Fighting is for Steves!"

"You know, Dave's fought alongside Steve," said Sally, taking a bite of chicken. "He's a villager, and he's fought with Steve. He's proof that we don't have to be who we were born to be. We can be whoever we want."

"Bah," said Adam.

That night, Adam tossed and turned in bed, unable to decide what to do. But by morning he'd made his decision. He got up as quietly as he could, so as to not wake his wife, and left his house. The morning air was crisp and there was no-one around. He walked straight over to the nether brick building, where he was confronted by four zombie pigman guards.

"I need to speak to your boss," he told them. "I need to speak to Dotty."

CHAPTER SEVEN
Porkins's Dilemma

Porkins couldn't stop thinking about the pigman village.

He was lying on the floor in the pigman barracks. The zombie pigmen around him were all snoring and grunting, but that wasn't what was keeping him awake.

What should I do? he wondered, for the thousandth time. Every since Gammon had told him that there was a pigman village, back on Cool Island, Porkins hadn't been able to stop thinking about it. He'd always assumed that he was the last non-zombie pigman left, but now he knew that wasn't true. And now the witches were plotting to turn the pigmen in a village they'd found into zombies. Porkins didn't know if this pigman village was the same as Gammon's one, but he knew that he couldn't just do nothing. He couldn't let more of his people get turned into zombies by Herobrine.

Eventually he made up his mind. He got up, then tiptoed over to a certain block in the corner of the room.

Dave and the other villagers had built secret tunnels underneath the village, so the villagers could sneak around without the pigmen knowing. They'd even built one that went underneath the nether brick building. The passageway was underneath the pigman dormitory where Porkins slept, underneath one of the nether brick floor blocks.

Porkins smashed the block with his fist, jumped inside the passageway, then replaced the block. The pigmen in the dormitory above would be none the wiser.

The passageway was only small—two bricks high, one brick wide—and lit by the occasional torch along its dirt walls. As Porkins traveled he passed entrances to other passageways, with signs such as 'To Mrs Bogg's House' or 'Secret Armory'. It reminded Porkins of the iron tunnels in the Nether.

He followed the signs to 'Sally and Adam's House', which led to a ladder. He climbed the ladder, opened a trap door and found himself in the cellar that Dave had built underneath the house. There were weapons lying about the place, and item frames with apples in them attached to the mud walls, which the villagers had been using for archery practice. Dave was the only person there, swinging his sword and practicing his technique.

"Hey Porkins," Dave said. "Any news? Or have you just come to train?"

"Neither," said Porkins nervously. "Dave, old bean, I need to ask you something. I know you need me here, but... when I was inside that castle in the Nether I heard the witches talking about a village of pigmen. Normal pigmen, not these zombie blighters. The witches are planning to turn the poor chaps into zombies. They might be the last normal pigmen in the world, apart from me, and I need to go and help them. Do I... do I have your blessing?"

"Oh Porkins," said Dave. And to Porkins's' surprise Dave went over and gave him a hug. "Of course you do. I know how much this must mean to you. Go—go and save your people. Do you want me to go with you?"

"I can't ask you that, dear chap," said Porkins, wiping a tear from his eye. "This village needs you. Besides, I'm the only one who can sneak into the Nether. When I'm pretending to be a zombie, they'll be none the wiser."

"Ok," said Dave, "but stay safe."

"I will," said Porkins. "And if I find the pigmen in time I'll rally the chaps to join the revolution as well. Herobrine won't stand a chance!"

"He certainly won't," grinned Dave.

"You really think we stand a chance against Herobrine?"

It was Carl. He'd climbed down the ladder from Sally and Adam's house above.

"Don't get me wrong," continued Carl, "I like these villagers.

And that's me talking—the creeper who hates everyone. But is this revolution idea really going to work?"

"It has to," said Dave. "It sounds like Herobrine isn't going to stop until he conquers the whole world."

"Come on," said Carl. "You know that's not what Herobrine really wants."

Porkins was confused. "What does the blighter want then?" he asked.

"What he's always wanted," said Carl. "He wants to get to the End. That's why he's told everyone to be on the lookout for Dave; that's why he's digging all these pits. He knows that the only way to reach the End is to find an ender portal. He's forcing the villagers to dig, hoping that they'll eventually find a stronghold. But he also knows that Dave found a way to *find* strongholds, so Herobrine wants Dave as well. From what we've seen of his power, he could have conquered the world ages ago, if that's what he wanted, but he doesn't care about that. It's a means to an end. Or, rather, a means to *the* End."

Dave sat down, rubbing his forehead with his hands.

"You're right," he said. "Maybe... maybe I should just hand myself over to him. If I hand myself over to Herobrine and tell him about the eyes of ender, maybe he'll leave everyone alone."

"No," said Porkins. "Remember what your grandmother told you, in your head—Herobrine must *not* find his way to the End, or terrible things will happen!"

"Oh yeah," said Carl. "I forgot about your magic grandma and her crazy talking-in-your-head thing."

"I wish we could talk to her properly," sighed Dave. "Find out what's really going on with Herobrine. I've been trying to speak to her in my head again, but I think it only works when those good witches are nearby."

"Talking to your grandma in your head is the first sign of madness," said Carl. "Everyone knows that."

"You'd better go, Porkins," Dave said. "Find your people in time. Save them."

"I will," said Porkins. "I will."

Porkins said his goodbyes to Dave and Carl, then went back down into the secret passage. He returned to the nether brick building, where the zombie pigmen were still asleep, then made his way to the portal. Thankfully, it was unguarded.

As soon as he walked through into the Nether, two angry pigmen guards rushed up to him.

"Rrurk rrurk!" said Porkins, showing them a scrap of paper he'd taken from Dotty's desk. It was blank, but, as Porkins suspected, the zombie pigmen were too stupid to know any different, and they stood back and let him pass.

Porkins looked up at all the signs on the iron wall, all pointing to different settlements.

Which one is the pigman village? he wondered. Then he saw a sign saying:

'Little Bacon.'

Ah, he thought. *That's probably the one.* He took out a minecart from the treasure chest, then sped off down the powered rail.

CHAPTER EIGHT
The Night Before

It was the night before the rebellion, and Dave was giving the villagers one last training session.

"And swing... and parry... and swing and swing!"

He stood at the front of the room with them all behind him, copying his moves. They were in the huge basement underneath Sally and Adam's house.

From the back of the room, Dave could hear the twanging of arrows as the villagers on archery duty practiced their shots. Carl was training them. Well, at least he was meant to be training them. What he was really doing was yelling things like "shoot straight, you dirt-brained idiot!" and "a sheep could aim better than you!" How useful this 'training' was to the archers Dave wasn't sure.

Dave finished his sword lesson, then let the villagers practice by themselves for a bit. As he watched them practicing their sword techniques with each other, he felt a great sense of pride. A few days ago they hadn't known one end of a sword from the other, but now they were ready for battle. Or at least he hoped they were.

There was almost a full set of iron armor for every villager now, and an iron sword. Some of them would have to make do with leather armor and wooden swords, as Carl and his diggers hadn't managed to find quite as much material as they may have hoped, but Dave made sure to give the worst weapons and armor to the best fighters, as the worst fighters would need all the protection they could get: Dave had even given some of them diamond armor, using up the last of his diamonds.

For himself he took leather armor and a wooden sword, to lead by example. He would have much preferred diamond, but he knew that if he went out in diamond armor with a diamond sword, it wouldn't be very inspiring for his troops.

Carl had sneaked his iron golem suit into the basement the night before. It was currently propped up in a corner, and Dave knew that Carl was itching to get inside it again and fight.

That morning two of the envoys had returned from their quest to stir up the nearby towns and villages against the pigmen. The envoys were pleased to report that between them they'd convinced six settlements to join the fight. Disappointingly they hadn't managed to get Villagertropolis on side, which was a shame as it had by far the biggest population. According to the envoys, the city had closed its gates, and no-one was coming in or out. Whether it was still under the control of the pigmen, they didn't know.

So Greenleaf and at least six other settlements were ready to launch their attack tomorrow. *This is going to work,* thought Dave happily.

As Dave was lost in his thoughts, Sally and Adam came down the ladder from their house.

"This is so exciting!" said Sally, giving Dave a hug. "We're really going to teach those pigmen a lesson!"

"*Zombie* pigman," said Dave with a smile. "Porkins would never forgive me if he heard we'd just been calling them *pigmen.*"

"Hmmph," said Adam. "Whatever they are, we don't stand a chance. You should just give up this silly plan. Villagers aren't meant to be warriors, how many times do I have to tell you all?"

"Oh do be quiet, Adam," said Sally. "You'll be eating your words tomorrow, when we win."

"We'll see," said Adam. "Somehow I don't think tomorrow is going to go exactly as you've planned."

And he stormed off, climbing back up the ladder.

"Sorry about him, Dave," said Sally. "He's a good man really, it's just... like all of us in the village, he was raised to believe that villagers aren't meant to be heroes."

"I was raised that way too," said Dave. "Let's prove to him that he's wrong."

Dave turned to the other villagers, who were still practicing their archery and swordplay.

"Ok everyone, let's stop now," he said. "We've got a big day ahead of us tomorrow. Remember, we attack at first light—so be ready. Get some sleep, you're going to want to be well rested."

The villagers all trundled off, back through the secret tunnels to their own homes. They were in good spirits, Dave was pleased to see, all of them eager for the fight.

Dave went over the battle plans in his head a few more times, then lay down in bed. He and Carl were staying in separate beds in Sally and Adam's spare room.

We're going to win, was his last thought before drifting off. But that night his dreams were full of doubt. He dreamed of Herobrine's empty white eyes. *You can't defeat me,* those eyes seemed to be saying. *No-one can defeat me...*

CHAPTER NINE
Little Bacon

Porkins walked out of the portal and found himself in an unfamiliar biome. It was night, but he could make out tall trees all around him. He could barely see the sky; it was blocked from view by a canopy of leaves.

In the darkness he saw a couple of small creatures staring back at him, their eyes reflecting the moonlight.

"*Mew!*" one of them said.

"MEW!"

"Hello, little chaps," said Porkins, walking towards them. The creatures immediately scampered off.

Which way is the village? wondered Porkins. The nether portal behind him was in the middle of nowhere. Back in the Nether the sign above the portal had said "Little Bacon", but there was no sign of anyone on the other side.

Porkins thought back to what he'd heard in the witches' castle. From the sounds of it, the witches had found the pigman village but hadn't conquered it yet.

He started walking through the trees, looking for any sign of life. Occasionally he'd catch sight of one of the little mew-ing creatures, but as soon as they saw him looking at them they'd run away.

Eventually he saw some faint lights up ahead. He kept walking and eventually realized that the lights were coming from up in the trees. As he got closer he started to hear voices as well, and eventually he saw, to his shock, that there were *buildings* in the trees.

That's the village! he realized. He could just make out a few faint figures moving about, but it was so dark and they were so high up that he couldn't see them properly.

At the bottom of one of the trees was a ladder. Next to the ladder was a sign:

'Little Bacon'

Porkins began to climb the ladder. It was a long climb, and when he got nearer the top he noticed something strange: all the voices he'd heard earlier had stopped.

Maybe they all go to bed at the same time? he thought.

When he reached the top he found himself on a wooden platform. The village was a series of wooden platforms attached to trees, connected to each other by wooden bridges. The houses were all small and made of wood too. There were torches burning, but no sign of life.

"Hello?" Porkins called out. "Hello chaps, is there anyone here?"

"Put your hands in the air and drop your weapon."

Porkins turned towards the sound of the voice. A pigman was aiming a bow and arrow at him from the roof of one of the houses. Then he noticed another pigman. And another. There were at least ten pigmen, all aiming at him.

"Hello chaps!" said Porkins. "It's so good to finally meet you!"

"He's one of those zombies," said one of the pigmen. "We should just kill him."

"The zombies can't talk though," said another.

"Oh no," said Porkins, realizing the misunderstanding. "This is just makeup!"

He wiped off some of the zombie makeup with his hand.

"I TOLD YOU TO DROP YOUR WEAPON!" the first pigman shouted.

Porkins quickly dropped his golden sword.

"My... my name's Porkins," said Porkins nervously. This wasn't quite the positive reception he'd been hoping for. "I've come to warn you, you're all in grave danger."

"What kind of danger?" asked one of the pigman.

"The fiend Herobrine has started taking over the world," said Porkins. "He has witches and zombie pigmen working for him, and they know you're here. They want to turn all of you into zombies too!"

"Ok," said the pigman. "We'll take you to see the village elder. But if we find out you're lying to us, we're throwing you off the top of this tree."

"Oh crumbs," said Porkins.

CHAPTER TEN
Elder Crispy

Before Porkins knew what was happening, a big pigman grabbed him and roughly pushed him along, guiding him across a bridge towards the biggest house in the tree village. It was the only house with two stories, and it had two guards outside.

"Wake Elder Crispy," said the big pigman to one of the guards.

Porkins was guided inside, into a small chamber with a wooden throne at one end. On the wall were paintings, many of them of events that Porkins recognized: famous events in pigman history.

A tall pigman with a huge barrel chest walked down the stairs, into the chamber.

"So," said the barrel-chested pigman. "Who might you be? And why shouldn't I throw you out of my tree?"

"He says the village is in danger, Elder," said the big pigman who'd brought Porkins inside.

"Silence, Ricco," said the Elder. "I want the stranger to tell me the story in his own words. I will determine whether or not he speaks true. And if he is false, he'll—"

"—be thrown out of the tree, yes, yes, I know," said Porkins. "Listen old bean, time really is of the essence here, so I'll make this quick."

The chamber had got busy now, Porkins saw. The other pigmen had all squeezed their way inside, eager to hear what he had to say. There were even baby pigman. That made Porkins smile: he had thought he might never see a baby pigman again.

"Ok," said Porkins, "here goes..."

He took a deep breath.

"Herobrine is taking over the world invading all the villages and towns and cities he can find with his army of zombie pigmen and witches and now he's found your village so he's sending his army here and he's going to turn you all into zombies to be his slaves so we need to act fast and tomorrow there's going to be a revolution and we're going to rise up against Herobrine and the witches so we could do with your help as we want to create a distraction so we can sneak into the castle in the Nether that the witches use for their base so we can destroy the magic staff that lets them control the zombie pigman as without it they'll have no army anymore."

"Sorry, old chap," said an elderly pigman, "I didn't have my hearing aid turned on. Could you repeat that?"

"Ah, ok..." said Porkins, struggling to get his breath back. "Herobrine is taking over the world invading all the villages and towns and cities he can find with his army of zombie pigmen and witches and now he's found your village so he's sending his army here and he's going to turn you all into zombies to be his slaves so we need to act fast and tomorrow there's going to be a revolution and we're going to rise up against Herobrine and the witches so we could do with your help as we want to create a distraction so we can sneak into the castle in the Nether that the witches use for their base so we can destroy the magic staff that lets them control the zombie pigman as without it they'll have no army anymore."

"That was better, thank you kindly," said the elderly pigman.

"Herobrine," said Elder Crispy, his voice gruff. "We have heard stories of him. It is a long time since we left the Nether, but we know what happened to the pigman who remained there. We thought they were all turned to zombies, but here you are."

"Yes, here I am," said Porkins. "By the way I met a chap who came from your village, I think. Went by the name of Gammon."

Elder Crispy spat on the floor. "Gammon was a criminal," he growled. "He and two others from our village were exiled months ago for their crimes."

"Ah, that makes a lot of sense," said Porkins. "He seemed like a good egg... but then he tried to kill me and my friends, which wasn't very nice."

"Stop babbling," said Elder Crispy. "You tell us that we're in danger, but as you can tell we are fierce warriors. We've defended our village from villains in the past, and we can defend it again."

"I can see that," said Porkins. "It's clear to me that you're all pretty robust chaps. I'm sure if the witches and zombie blighters came here you'd give them a darn good hiding. Which is why I'd like you to join the revolution. My friends will need all the help they can get to win their battle tomorrow. Most of the villager chaps have never fought before, so having some seasoned warriors like you and your people on side would be just the ticket."

"*Just the ticket*," said Elder Crispy, with a smile. "You sound just like one of the old folk, the ones who first left the Nether all those years ago."

"Yes, you jolly well do," said the elderly pigman with a smile.

"As you can tell," said Elder Crispy, "the way we speak has changed. When we left the Nether, our people traveled for many years. The way was hard and we had to become hard too."

"I'm sorry to hear that," said Porkins. "But please do come and join the villager chaps in the battle tomorrow. Together we can give Herobrine a thrashing!"

Elder Crispy sighed.

"What is your name, stranger?"

"Porkins," said Porkins.

"Porkins," said Elder Crispy, "you seem like a good pig, but this is not our fight. If the villagers want to go to war, that is their business. My people keep to ourselves. That is how we've survived so long. That is why we chose to live in this jungle, far away from civilization."

"But the villagers need your help!" insisted Porkins.

"And did the villagers come to your aid when your people were turned to zombies?" asked Elder Crispy.

Porkins tried to think of a response, but he couldn't.

"I thought not," said Elder Crispy. "Porkins, I wish you well, but the pigmen of Little Bacon will not be joining your fight. Ricco, Nathan, please escort Porkins out of the village.

The big pigman Ricco and a normal-sized one grabbed Porkins, and gently led him out of the chamber, pushing past the crowd of pigmen.

"Please help," Porkins begged, looking round at the faces of his fellow pigmen. "If we don't all stick together, villains like Herobrine will keep on winning!"

They led Porkins out of the Elder's house and back to the ladder that led down the tree.

"Sorry," said the normal-sized pigman, who Porkins assumed must be Nathan. "If it was up to me I'd help you, but I can't go against the wishes of Elder Crispy. He's been a good leader for our people."

"Good luck," added Ricco.

Porkins made his way sadly down the ladder.

That could have gone better, he thought miserably.

CHAPTER ELEVEN
Attack!

Dave couldn't sleep. There was still hours to go until sunrise, but he had too much on his mind. He suspected that many of the other villagers must be feeling the same way: too excited and scared to sleep.

He went over the plan again in his head. As soon as the sun began to rise the archers would sneak onto the rooftops of houses all round the village. Then the swordsmen would charge into the nether brick building, taking out the zombie pigmen and capturing Dotty before she could escape to the Nether and raise the alarm.

From the intel that Porkins had given them, Dave knew exactly where the zombie pigmen all slept, so it would be easy to take them by surprise. Dotty was a different matter, as she'd surely try to use the nether portal as soon as she realized the villagers were rising up. So Dave had arranged a surprise for her: some of the villagers had dug a tunnel directly underneath the nether portal (they knew where it was thanks to Porkins), and once the attack began they would dig up into the room above and surround the portal, making sure she couldn't use it.

The other villages and towns that had agreed to join the revolution would be launching their attacks at sunrise too, Dave knew. Then once they had defeated the pigmen in their settlements they would march into the Nether, fighting the zombie pigmen on their home turf. Meanwhile Dave, Carl and a select group would make their way to the witches' castle, storm it, take the magical staff and then destroy it.

It was a solid plan, but Dave couldn't help but worry. He knew from experience that even the best-laid plans could go wrong.

"Having trouble sleeping?" muttered Carl from his bed on the other side of the room.

Dave sat up in his own bed. "Yeah," he said. "Just worrying about the morning."

"It'll be fine," said Carl. "You'll have me there to protect you. You've seen how awesome I am in my iron golem suit. Those pigmen won't know what's hit them."

Suddenly Dave heard a sound. A *snorting* sound outside of the window.

"What was that?" he whispered.

"What was what?" said Carl.

Dave reached over and slowly, quietly grabbed his wooden sword.

"I think there's a pigman outside," he said. "Maybe more than one."

"So what?" whispered Carl. "They own the village, for now, they can go wherever they like."

Carl was right, Dave knew, but normally at night the pigmen stayed near the nether brick building, or around the edge of the town to stop anyone from escaping. They never wandered near the houses.

"Prepare yourself," said Dave.

"For what?" said Carl.

SMASH!!! A zombie pigman smashed through the glass pane of the window, leaning through and swinging his golden sword about. Behind it, Dave could see a whole hoard of zombie pigmen, all trying to get in.

"Waaaa!" said Carl.

"Come on, to the basement," said Dave. "Let's get some weapons and your iron suit."

Dave and Carl jumped out of bed and ran through the house. They ran into Sally and Adam's room and shook them awake.

"The pigmen are attacking!" Dave yelled. Then SMASH!!! a zombie pigman smashed his way through their bedroom window.

"They must have found out about our attack!" wailed Sally. "But how?"

"We can work that out later," said Dave. "They won't know about the basement and the underground passages, so we can get some weapons and regroup there. Come on!"

The four of them ran to the kitchen, then opened the secret trapdoor under the rug, climbing down the ladder that led to the basement. Once they got down there though, it was full of zombie pigmen too.

"Hey, get off that!" yelled Carl. Some of the pigmen were hitting his iron suit with their swords, obviously thinking it was a real golem. "You idiot pigs!"

The pigmen charged at them. From the secret passageways Dave could hear villagers shouting and fighting taking place.

The pigmen knew, he thought desperately. *Someone must have told them!*

"Come on!" said Dave. He ran back towards the ladder that led up to the house, the other three following behind him, but when they got there they saw more pigmen coming down the ladder. Dave drew his sword, ready to fight, but soon the pigmen had surrounded them, snorting angrily.

"Put your sword down, fool," Adam snapped at Dave. "You really think you can take them all on with a wooden blade? We need to surrender."

For once, Dave had to agree with Adam. He dropped his sword and put his hands up.

"We surrender," he said.

The zombie pigmen marched Dave, Carl, Sally and Adam back up the ladder, then into the town square. All the other villagers were there too, with their hands in the air. The sun was beginning to rise, orange light spreading across the village. It was a beautiful sight, but no-one was in the mood to appreciate it.

"What happened, Dave?" one of the villagers asked him, tears in her eyes. "This was meant to be the day we fought back."

"Well, well, well," said a voice. Dave turned and saw Dotty looking down at them from the balcony of the nether brick building. "So your name isn't *Dean* after all? I thought I recognized you, *Dave*."

Dave touched his face. He hadn't drawn on his fake beard.

"So now you know," he said to Dotty.

"Oh, I knew already," grinned Dotty. "The same way I knew about the little invasion you had planned today. You really should be more careful with who you trust."

Adam stepped forward.

"You promised that my wife and I would be allowed to leave unharmed," he said to Dotty. "That was the deal."

"*You?*" gasped Sally, looking at her husband in horror. "You're the one who betrayed us?"

"It was for your own good," said Adam. "This was a stupid plan. I'm *saving* us, Sally! Lady Dotty has promised that you and I can leave. We can start a new life together somewhere new."

"I'm not going anywhere with you," said Sally. "You disgust me."

"Aww," said Dotty, "that's not very nice. Your husband did a very nice thing for you. Adam, you and your wife are free to go."

Adam held out his hand. "Come on, Sally," he said, "let's go."

"No," said Sally.

"Sally, please," begged Adam. "I want to save you!"

"You could have saved me by fighting," said Sally. "You could have helped save us all. But instead you betrayed us, and I never want to see you again."

Adam's mouth fell open in shock. He looked like he wanted to cry.

"Well, are you leaving or not?" said Dotty. "Either leave now, or you can share the same fate as the rest of your pathetic villagers."

Adam looked like he was about to say something, then he sadly walked away.

"Coward," said Sally. She was crying.

"Right," said Dotty, once Adam was gone, "it goes without saying that your revolution is over. Now, my pigmen are going to escort you all into the Nether, and you're all going to be good little villagers and do what you're told. Oh, and you," she said to Dave, "I'll be bringing you to Lord Herobrine myself."

"I thought he was Emperor Herobrine now?" said Carl.

"Of course," said Dotty, with a grin. "Although calling him by the correct title won't save you, little creeper."

Dotty looked down at the zombie pigmen.

"Take our prisoners into the Nether," she told them.

"Not so fast, you dastardly cad!"

Suddenly a golden sword appeared at Dotty's throat. Holding it was a zombie pigman who Dave recognized.

"Porkins!" he said happily.

"The very fellow," grinned Porkins. "Right, you rotter," he said to Dotty, "I'm guessing that these zombie chaps will do whatever you say, so tell them to ruddy well back off!"

"You really think you can stop Lord Herobrine?" laughed Dotty. "We know about your revolution. As we speak my witch sisters will be shutting down all the other rebellions. You're finished."

"You're the one who's finished," said Dave. "You were going to bring us all into the Nether. Why?"

Dotty grinned. "Once Lord Herobrine learned of the rebellion, he decided that villagers were too much trouble. So he's got bigger plans for all of you."

"And are you going to tell us what those plans are?" said Dave.

"He's going to turn you into zombies," said Dotty. "It's probably happening to all the other villagers right now."

Dave had heard enough. "Right," he said to Dotty, "tell the zombie pigmen to leave the village and get as far away from here as possible. If you don't, Porkins will chop your head off."

"It would be my ruddy pleasure," said Porkins.

Dotty rolled her eyes. "Why does everything with you have to be so dramatic? Ok, piggies, leave the village and get as far away as possible. Go on, go!"

With lots of grunting and snorting the pigmen shuffled off,

filing out of the village, into the plains and trees that lay beyond.

"Your army's gone now," said Dave to Dotty, once the zombie pigmen were out of sight.

"The good thing about zombie pigmen is that there's always plenty more," said Dotty. She gave Porkins a nasty grin. "In fact, I've heard of a whole village of normal pigmen living in a jungle biome. Once they're zombies, they can be my new army."

"You shut up!" said Porkins.

Suddenly a lot of things happened at once. Dotty shoved an elbow into Porkins's face. "Ow!" he yelled, and dropped his sword. Dotty grabbed the sword and ran back inside the nether brick building.

"Stop her!" Dave yelled. They all charged into the nether brick building, just in time to see Dotty disappear into the nether portal.

"Now what?" asked Sally.

"We've lost the element of surprise," said Dave, "but if Dotty was telling the truth, all the other villagers who joined our rebellion will be being taken to the Nether to be turned into zombies. So I'm going to go to the Nether, free the villagers and then storm that castle. I can't promise it'll work, but anyone who wants to is welcome to come with me. Anyone who doesn't want to come, I understand. Just make sure you get as far away from the village as possible, before Herobrine's forces come back."

"We're with you, Dave," said Sally. "All of us."

The villagers all cheered.

"Right," said Dave, grinning, "let's get our armor on."

CHAPTER TWELVE
Once More Into the Nether

The villagers gathered in the village square outside of the nether brick building. As Dave stood in front of them, he felt proud. A few days ago they'd been ordinary villagers, but now they were warriors, wearing armor and ready to fight. Carl was there too, in his iron golem suit. Not long ago Carl had tried to avoid fighting whenever he could, but now the creeper was rearing to join the battle.

As Dave stepped forward, the villagers all stopped talking and looked at him.

Oh dear, thought Dave, *do they want me to give a speech?*

His mind went blank. He didn't know what to say.

"Give us a speech, you idiot!" yelled Carl.

"Er, right," said Dave, trying to sound braver than he felt, "we know why we're doing this. We're not fighting just for this village, but for all the other villagers who Herobrine has enslaved. We're fighting for the pigmen, who Herobrine turned into zombies without a care in the world. We're doing this to save the other brave villagers of the rebellion, who right now may be being taken to be turned into zombies as well. So we're going to fight, and we're going to defeat the witches, destroy their base, and kick Herobrine's back side! Who's with me?"

A mighty cheer went up, all the villagers waving their swords or bows in the air. Even Carl was caught up in the excitement, punching the air with his huge iron arms. Porkins was there too, his zombie makeup all washed off and his leather armor back on. He was smiling.

Dave turned towards the nether brick building. "Onwards!" he yelled, marching through the building, the army of villagers marching behind him.

He opened the iron door and led them down the corridor to the room with the nether portal. He stepped up into the portal and...

... found himself in an iron corridor. Dave had been in the Nether plenty of times now, but had never seen it like this. The villagers were all coming out of the portal behind him now, so he stepped out of the way.

"Those pigmen have been busy," Dave said to Porkins.

"Oh yes, old bean," said Porkins. "And this stretches on for miles—corridors going in every direction."

Once all the villagers were through, Dave, Porkins, Carl and Sally led the way down the corridor, following the signs that led to the 'Headquarters'. It would have been quicker to travel by minecart, but there were far too many of them, and Dave wanted them to stick together.

"Keep your eye out for an attack," Dave said. "Remember, Dotty will have told them we're coming."

Suddenly Dave spotted something up ahead: minecarts were speeding towards them down the tracks, but they appeared to be empty.

"Porkins," said Dave. "You've got good eyes... what's going on with those minecarts?"

Porkins squinted. Then his mouth dropped open.

"Good gravy!" he gasped. "TNT! The minecarts are all full of TNT!"

Dave could see now that Porkins was right: each cart had a TNT block inside of it.

Panic broke out, all the villagers pushing and shoving. They tried digging at the iron blocks of the walls, but they had no pickaxes and would never get through before the TNT reached them.

What are we going to do? thought Dave. And then he had an idea.

"Archers, get in formation!" Dave yelled.

The archers pushed forward, preparing their bows. Porkins was with them.

"Ok," said Dave, "aim... fire!"

The arrows flew, whizzing through the air and smacking into the TNT blocks, but they didn't explode.

"We need fire!" said Sally. "Flaming arrows destroy TNT!"

"Of course!" said Porkins. "Dave, old bean, give me your flint and iron... and a block of netherrack!"

Dave pulled his flint and iron and the block from his backpack and threw it to Porkins.

"Hurry," Dave said. The minecarts were almost upon them now; in a few seconds they'd be blown to bits.

Porkins placed the netherrack block down and struck the flint and iron across it, setting it alight. Then he strung his bow, dipped the arrow in the fire and let it fly. The arrow's path was true; it flew through the air and hit one of TNT blocks.

KAAAABOOOOOM!!!!!!!

There was a gigantic explosion, the force of it sending Dave and the others flying backwards. But they were alive: Porkins had saved them.

They walked forward to inspect the damage. The corridor had been completely destroyed, leaving a huge chasm with only lava below.

"Well done, Porkins," said Dave. "Everyone, we'll have to take another route."

Then he heard a sound coming from behind them: the sound of hundreds of snorting and grunting pigmen.

"The pigmen are coming!" Dave heard a villager yell.

They were trapped: pigman coming from one end of the corridor, a fall into lava on the other end.

There was only one thing they could do.

"Fight them!" Dave yelled. "Fight them back!"

The villagers charged forward against the zombie pigmen, sword clashing against sword as they fought. Dave, Carl, Porkins, Sally and the archers were at the back, next to the broken section of the corridor, so they couldn't join the battle; the corridor was too narrow to get through, and it was jam packed with villagers.

"We have to keep moving onwards," Dave said. "They'll keep sending more and more troops at us if we stay still."

He rummaged around in his backpack and pulled out some blocks, any blocks he could find, and threw them to Porkins, Carl and Sally.

"Come on," said Dave, "let's get this corridor rebuilt."

They got to work putting blocks down, rebuilding the broken section of corridor. When they finished it was a mish mash of different blocks, but it was enough; the floor was complete and the walls were two blocks high so no-one would fall over the edge.

"Oh no," Porkins said, the color draining from his face, "more zombies!"

Porkins was right, Dave saw. Coming from up ahead, from the direction the minecarts had come, was another army of zombie pigmen.

"Pigmen behind us, pigmen in front," said Carl. "That's just great."

"*Zombie* pigmen," said Porkins.

"Archers, get in front!" Dave yelled. The archers ran forward, aiming their bows at the zombie pigmen.

"On my mark..." said Dave. He was waiting for the zombie pigmen to get close enough to hit. "Wait for it... FIRE!"

The archers loosed their arrows, and they flew through the air, *poof*ing some of the zombie pigmen.

"Prepare your bows again!" Dave yelled. "And fire!"

More arrows hit more zombie pigmen, taking a lot of them out, but there were still plenty more, charging towards them.

"Archers step back," said Dave, "swordsmen forward."

He could still hear the clatter of battle down the corridor behind him. He hoped the villagers back there were doing ok.

Dave, Carl and the other swordsmen down this end of the corridor stepped forward and drew their blades. The zombie pigmen were almost upon them now.

"For Greenleaf!" Sally yelled.

"For Greenleaf!" The other villagers repeated.

And then the zombie pigmen were upon them. It was chaos: Carl swinging his huge iron arms, swords clashing, archers firing shots. The villagers were trapped in the iron corridor with zombie pigmen coming from either side, fighting for their lives.

All around Dave could hear the familiar *POOF* sound as either a villager or a zombie pigman was slain; he hoped there were more pigmen being slain than villagers, but it was so chaotic that it was hard to keep track.

Dave was fighting as hard as he could, but his wooden sword wasn't doing much good. He spotted a diamond sword on the floor, and for a second he didn't want to pick it up, as he knew it must have been dropped by a slain villager, but then a zombie pigman charged at him and he had no choice. He dropped his wooden blade, grabbed the diamond one and thrust it through the pigman's chest.

Dave had been in battles before, but never one as ferocious as this. It was every man for himself; there was no time to use tactics or clever moves, they just had to fight. And there was nowhere to retreat to either, so they had no choice but to keep fighting.

"We've won!" Dave heard someone yell. He looked around: they were right. All the zombie pigmen were gone. The battle had been so crazy that he hadn't even noticed.

"Grab... grab the best weapons and armor you can," Dave said, struggling to get his breath back. As he looked round he realized how few of them were left. It seemed like less than half the villagers had made it through the battle.

"I know these weapons and armor belonged to your friends, but we need to make sure we're well armed," said Dave. "So kit yourself out."

Dave picked up some diamond armor for himself.

To Dave's relief, Porkins, Carl and Sally had all survived the battle.

"This is all Adam's fault," said Sally angrily. "If he hadn't told the witch our plans, we would have taken them unawares. All these deaths are on his hands."

"Sometimes even the best plans can go wrong," said Dave. "There's no point thinking over what might have been. Even if Adam hadn't told, it probably wouldn't have gone smoothly."

Once the remaining villagers had kitted themselves out with the best weapons and armor that they could find, Dave addresses them once more.

"I'll understand if anyone doesn't want to go on," he said. "This will be probably be the last chance you'll get to turn back, so if anyone wants to leave, now's the time."

None of the villagers wanted to leave. Dave was pleased, but also worried.

Am I just leading them to their doom? he couldn't help but wonder.

"Come on then," he said, "let's go and pay these witches a visit."

CHAPTER THIRTEEN
The Pit

So they marched down the long iron corridor, Dave, Porkins and Carl in the lead. They crossed the open-air bridge that Porkins had crossed before, and the villagers got their first real look at the Nether.

"It's so red!" said one.

"It's a bit of a dump," said another. "Too much lava for my taste."

As they followed the signs to the 'Headquarters' the route was eerily quiet. No more zombie pigmen came to attack them, no more minecarts full of TNT were sent their way.

"Be on edge," Dave told everyone, "we're probably walking into a trap."

Eventually the iron corridor ended, just as Porkins had said it would, and they found themselves walking across the Nether. In the distance they could see the cobblestone castle, but still they saw no pigmen or witches.

"Wait," said Carl, "can you hear that?"

Dave could just about make it out too. It sounded like a lot of people. A lot of people yelling and screaming.

They cautiously made their way forward. The voices got louder as they got nearer.

"I think those are villagers," said Sally.

As they got nearer Dave could hear that she was right. It sounded like hundreds of villagers, all yelling for help, but he couldn't see where the voices were coming from.

Then they came over a ridge, and Dave realized why he hadn't been able to see the villagers until then. A huge pit had been dug in the ground; its walls lined with iron blocks, and inside it were hundreds of villagers.

"Help!" they yelled, as Dave and the others cautiously looked over the edge, "let us out!"

It was hard to understand what the villagers were saying, with so many of them talking at once, but Dave eventually got the gist of it: they were the villagers from the other towns and villages who were going to revolt against Herobrine. Just like in Greenleaf, the zombie pigmen had launched a surprise attack in the night. They'd all been marched into the Nether and left in this pit.

"We have to get them out," said Sally.

Dave was scanning the rocky landscape for signs of zombie pigmen or witches.

They must be nearby, he thought. *They must know we're here.*

Then he heard a voice from one of the rocky cliff tops above them.

"Hello, Dave!" it said.

Dave looked up. One moment there was no-one there, but then Dotty appeared. And then another witch, then another, then another, until there were around twenty witches, all looking down at them.

"So good to see you again, Dave," grinned Dotty. "Potion of invisibility. You've got to love it."

Dave noticed she was standing next to some sort of iron device. Then he noticed other iron devices, all manned by witches.

"You recognize these, I'm sure," said Dotty, tapping one of the iron devices. "A TNT cannon. I think some of my sisters tried to blow you up with one before."

"We did," said another voice. It came from a tall witch, who Dave vaguely recognized. "But he played a clever trick on us, making the zombie piggies attack us. But that won't be happening this time, because we have this."

The tall witch pulled out a golden staff with an emerald on top.

"Trotter's staff!" gasped Porkins.

"It never really belonged to Trotter," said Dotty. "Lord Herobrine just lent it to him, and that fat pig betrayed Lord Herobrine's trust by being an idiot. Now Lady Isabella has it, and we have complete control over all the pigmen."

"That's right," said the tall witch, Isabella.

"*Zombie* pigmen," said Porkins angrily.

Dotty laughed.

"Aww, are you offended, piggy?" she laughed. "What a precious little snowflake you are."

"Look," said Dave, "I'll hand myself over to Herobrine if you just let the villagers go. You still need them to work in your mines, don't you?"

"We did," said Isabella, "but now we have you, I think Lord Herobrine may have no use for them anymore. All he wants is to get the End. If you'd told him how to get there before, none of this would have happened."

"Besides," said Dotty, "Lord Herobrine has decided that villagers are too much trouble. So he's working on a new magic staff—one that will let him control *all* zombies. It's not quite ready yet, but he's decided that he wants to turn all of you into zombies anyway: so you're ready when the time comes."

There were terrified shouts and pleas from the villagers inside the pit, all of them begging to be let out, begging not to be turned into zombies.

"Right," said Isabella, "Dave, piggy, creeper, and all your friends, it's time to get in the pit. Either you get in of your own free will or we blow you to bits. There are five TNT cannons aimed at you; there's no escape."

Dave looked at Carl and Porkins, but they looked as clueless as he was. What were they going to do?

"Come on piggy," Dotty said, grinning down at Porkins. "Don't you want to join all your pigmen friends?"

Suddenly an arrow struck Dotty in the head. She toppled down from the cliff and landed with a *smack* next to the pit. Then *poof*, she was gone.

"*Zombie* pigmen," said a voice from above. "Those freaks aren't pigmen anymore. You witches need to know the difference."

Dave looked up and saw an army of pigmen—not zombie pigmen, but actual pigmen—standing on the cliffs above the witches. The one who'd spoke was a huge pigman with a barrel chest, holding a bow and arrow.

"You came!" Porkins said happily.

"We did," said Elder Crispy. "We came to fight."

CHAPTER FOURTEEN
Zombie Potion

"Get them!" Isabella screamed. "Kill them all!"

Porkins watched as a huge battle broke out on the cliffs above, between the pigmen and the witches. Suddenly zombie pigmen were appearing everywhere as well, coming out from wherever they'd been hiding.

Zombie pigmen charged at Porkins, Dave, Carl, Sally and the Greenleaf soldiers, who charged back at them. It was another chaotic battle, with swords clashing and arrows flying. At one point Porkins almost fell into the pit, but a pig-girl saved him, grabbing his hand just in time.

"Watch your step," she grinned at him.

"Thanks," said Porkins.

"Pat, watch out!" another pigman yelled. The pig-girl pushed Porkins out of the way just before a potion thrown by a witch could hit them. It shattered on the ground, the liquid inside it exploding into a blue fireball.

*

Carl was having the time of his life, battering zombie pigmen with his iron arms, sending them flying.

"Come on then!" he yelled. "I'll take you all on!"

A witch tried to throw a potion at him, but Carl quickly grabbed a zombie pigman and threw it at her.

"Who would have thought that fighting could be so much fun?" said Carl to himself.

417

He was just about to charge into another group of pigmen when he spotted some zombie pigmen in the distance carrying something along. It looked like a giant bucket, and he could make out a green liquid sloshing about inside it.

Oh no, thought Carl. *That's all we need.*

He knew what that green liquid was, he'd seen it once before, back in the Nether; it was the liquid that King Trotter had tried to use to turn them into zombies. It hadn't ended well for Trotter, he'd turned himself into a zombie instead.

The bucket was far too big for one zombie pigman to carry, so they were carrying it as a group, bringing it towards the pit.

So that was their plan, thought Carl. *They were going to get us all in that pit, then pour the liquid onto us, turning us all into zombies.*

Carl ran towards the bucket-carrying zombie pigmen as fast as his iron legs could carry him. He had almost reached them when something smashed into his chest, exploding in a burst of blue fire. He looked up and saw two witches above him with potion bottles. They threw bottle after bottle, sending him staggering backwards.

"Argh, stop!" yelled Carl. He stepped backwards and, to his horror, accidentally bashed into the giant bucket. It tipped over, the green liquid flowing down towards the pit.

"No!" Carl yelled.

*

Dave looked up when he heard Carl yell. The battle was raging all around him, but on the other side of the pit he could clearly see a green liquid flowing down a rocky slope towards the pit. Villagers, pigmen and witches alike were jumping out of the way of the liquid, but the villagers in the pit had nowhere to go.

That's the zombie-making liquid! Dave realized, to his horror.

Dave knew he could never get there in time, but he saw Porkins nearby, fighting back-to-back with a female pigman.

"Porkins!" Dave yelled. "Stop that liquid!"

*

Porkins turned and saw the green liquid.

"Cover me," he said to Pat the pig-girl. "Make sure to keep those zombie blighters away from me!"

Porkins took off his rucksack, reaching in and grabbing any blocks he could find. Then he quickly placed the blocks down—*thunk thunk thunk thunk thunk*—to block the pit.

SPLOSH! The liquid hit the wall and stopped, now just a big puddle of green on the ground. Porkins breathed a big sigh of relief, but then he felt something wet on his hand. He looked down and saw a drop of the green liquid had landed on his skin.

"Oh," he said.

*

The battle was practically over. The last of the witches were running away and there were very few zombie pigmen left. Dave breathed a sigh of relief, but then he looked over and saw Porkins on the ground, looking ill.

"What's wrong with him?" Dave said, rushing over.

Sally had Porkins's head resting on her lap. The female pigman was there too, as was Carl, leaning down in his iron golem suit.

"It's all my fault," said Carl. Dave had never heard the creeper sound so upset.

Then Dave saw what was wrong: an infection was creeping up Porkins's arm, the flesh turning green and rotten.

"He's turning into a... a zombie," said Sally, wiping tears from her eyes.

"No," said Dave. "No no!"

"Looks like... this is the end for me, old chap..." said Porkins weakly, giving Dave a smile. "But don't feel sad... I had a great adventure... with you and Carl... my two best friends."

"There must be something we can do!" said Dave. He was crying now too.

"You know... that there's no cure for zombie pigmen," said Porkins. "Just promise me that you'll continue your quest... find the ender dragon. Prove to the world that you're a... a hero."

Dave had never felt so helpless. He could see the zombie infection rising up Porkins's arm; it was almost at his shoulder now. Soon Porkins would be a zombie pigman, a mindless creature, all of his memories lost forever.

Dave pulled out his diamond sword.

"Get back," he said to Sally.

"Dave, what are you doing?" she said.

"Please, get back," said Dave.

Porkins's eyes were closed now. It wouldn't be long before the infection would spread to his brain, Dave knew. He'd seen the same happen to Trotter.

Sally placed Porkins's head down on the ground and then stood back.

"What are you doing?" said Carl to Dave.

"Saving our friend," said Dave. And he swung his sword down...

CHAPTER FIFTEEN
Goodbyes

Elder Crispy brought Isabella before Dave and threw her on the ground.

"My men Nathan and Ricco found this one trying to escape," he said gruffly. "And she had this on her." He pulled out the gold and emerald staff and threw it at Dave. Dave caught it.

"Thank you," Dave said. "What made you guys come and join us? Porkins said you refused to fight when he came to see you."

"We did," said Elder Crispy, "but something he said stuck with me. He said that if we don't stick together, people like Herobrine will keep on winning."

"Pah," said Isabella. "Lord Herobrine will get his revenge. You just wait and see."

Elder Crispy looked around.

"Where is Porkins? I want to thank him."

Dave sighed. "He..."

"Hello old bean!"

Porkins walked towards them, his torso wrapped in bandages.

"Do you really think you should be up and about?" said Dave. "You need rest."

"I can rest later," smiled Porkins.

"What happened to you?" Elder Crispy said, looking at Porkins's bandages.

"Oh this?" said Porkins. "Dave cut my arm off."

"He what?!" snarled Crispy, drawing his bow.

"No, no, it's a good thing!" laughed Porkins. "If he hadn't cut off the infection, I would have turned into one of those zombie chaps. He saved me."

"I must say," said Carl, coming over to them in his iron suit, "you look awfully happy for someone who's just lost an arm."

"Well, I guess there's no arm in that," said Porkins. And then he started laughing hysterically.

"Carl," said Dave, "I think that potion Sally gave him to stop the pain has made him go a bit light-headed. Do you mind carrying him?"

For once the creeper didn't complain, and he reached down and picked Porkins up in his arms. Dave could see from the look on Carl's face that he still felt guilty.

They built a staircase down to the pit so the villagers could get out. There was much hugging and laughter and promises from the different settlements to help each other if there were any more attacks in the future. Carl, Porkins and some of the injured villagers from Greenleaf made their way back home, and the other villagers began making their way back to their settlements as well.

Next Dave threw the gold staff in the lava. For a moment it just sunk down, and then they was a KRAKOOM and it exploded.

"You know, Herobrine could just build another one," said Elder Crispy.

"I know," said Dave. "But from what that witch was saying, they seem to be quite hard to make. We might slow him down a bit at least."

Dave had been worried that Herobrine might appear during the battle, but he never had. Dave suspected that Herobrine knew that his invasion was finished, so hadn't bothered to get involved. Dave led a group of villagers and pigmen down the iron corridors, following the signs that led to 'Herobrine'. He knew in his heart that Herobrine would probably be long gone, but they needed to check.

Eventually they reached a nether portal with the word 'Herobrine' above it. Dave stepped through first, and found himself in the bedrock castle, where Herobrine had kept him, Porkins and Carl prisoner. It was empty now, but Dave and the others searched the castle anyway. There was nothing there; all of Herobrine's things had been removed.

Afterwards, everyone said their goodbyes, ready to go back to their own homes.

"Make sure you keep in touch," Sally said to Elder Crispy. "We all need to stick together. Herobrine is still out there somewhere."

"Aye," said Elder Crispy. "You too."

Dave went back with Sally and the remaining Greenleaf villagers, taking Isabella with them as a prisoner. When they got there, Carl had tucked Porkins up in bed in Sally's house. Porkins was fast asleep.

"Will he be alright?" Carl asked Sally.

"He'll be fine," said Sally. "He's healing well. I... I'm sorry again about Adam."

"That's not your fault," said Dave. "You fought well. Everyone in Greenleaf did. You should all be proud."

Sally smiled, then went off to her bedroom and left Dave, Carl and Porkins alone.

"It's my fault anyway," said Carl miserably. "I messed up."

"No you didn't," said Dave. "And anyway, Porkins is going to be fine."

Suddenly there was a flash of purple light and a villager appeared in the room next to them, his face hidden in shadow.

"No he's not," said the villager in a gruff voice. "None of you are, unless you do exactly as I say."

Dave stood up and drew his sword.

"Who are you?" he demanded.

The villager stepped forward into the light. His face was scarred and he had an eyepatch on one eye, but Dave knew that face.

"I'm you, Dave," the villager said. "I'm you from the future."

"Oh dear," said Carl. "Something tells me that things are about to get awfully complicated..."

EPILOGUE

Adam was colder than he'd ever been. Until last week he'd never even left Greenleaf, and now he was wandering through a snow biome, exiled from the place he called home.

This is all Dave's fault, he thought bitterly. *If it weren't for him, I'd still be at home, and I'd still be with my wife!*

Suddenly he tripped over in the snow. He tried to push himself to his feet but he was too weak.

Maybe I'll just stay here, he thought miserably. *What's the point in going on?*

"Get up, Adam."

Adam looked up. Standing over him was a man in blue jeans and a t-shirt. The snowstorm was so thick that he couldn't see his face.

"Who... are you?" said Adam.

"Do you hate Dave with all your heart?" said the man. "Do you want to get vengeance on him and revenge for all the wrongs that he has done to you?"

"Yes!" said Adam. "Yes, more than anything!"

"Then take my hand," said the man, reaching down. "And join me."

Adam reached up and took Herobrine's hand.

TO BE CONTINUED...

Printed in Great Britain
by Amazon

64291772R00244